Knowing Educational Administration

Knowing Educational Administration

Contemporary Methodological Controversies in Educational Administration Research

by

COLIN W. EVERS
Monash University, Australia

and

GABRIELE LAKOMSKI
University of Melbourne, Australia

PERGAMON PRESS

Member of Maxwell Macmillan Pergamon Publishing Corporation

OXFORD · NEW YORK · BEIJING · FRANKFURT
SÃO PAULO · SYDNEY · TOKYO · TORONTO

U.K.	Pergamon Press plc, Headington Hill Hall, Oxford OX3 0BW, England
U.S.A.	Pergamon Press, Inc., Maxwell House, Fairview Park, Elmsford, New York 10523, U.S.A.
PEOPLE'S REPUBLIC OF CHINA	Pergamon Press, Room 4037, Qianmen Hotel, Beijing, People's Republic of China
FEDERAL REPUBLIC OF GERMANY	Pergamon Press GmbH, Hammerweg 6, D-6242 Kronberg, Federal Republic of Germany
BRAZIL	Pergamon Editora Ltda, Rua Eça de Queiros, 346, CEP 04011, Paraiso, São Paulo, Brazil
AUSTRALIA	Pergamon Press (Australia) Pty Ltd, PO Box 544, Potts Point, NSW 2011, Australia
JAPAN	Pergamon Press, 5th Floor, Matsuoka Central Building, 1-7-1 Nishishinjuku, Shinjuku-ku, Tokyo 160, Japan
CANADA	Pergamon Press Canada Ltd, Suite No 271, 253 College Street, Toronto, Ontario, Canada M5T 1R5

First edition 1991

Library of Congress Cataloging-in-Publication Data
Evers, C. W.
Knowing educational administration: contemporary methodological controversies in educational administration research/by Colin Evers and Gabriele Lakomski. — 1st ed.
p. cm.
Includes bibliographical references.
1. School management and organization.
2. School management and organization—Research.
I. Lakomski, Gabriele. II. Title.
LB2805.E92 1990 371.2'0072—dc20 90-44398

British Library Cataloguing in Publication Data
Evers, Colin
Knowing educational administration: contemporary methodological controversies in educational administration research.
1. Education. Administration
I. Title II. Lakomski, Gabriele
379.15

ISBN 0-08-036765-8

Printed in Great Britain by BPCC Wheatons Ltd, Exeter

Contents

PREFACE   vii

ACKNOWLEDGEMENTS   x

Chapter One
Educational Administration and the Theory of Knowledge   1

Chapter Two
Knowledge and Justification   19

Chapter Three
The Theory Movement: Past and Present   46

Chapter Four
The Greenfield Revolution   76

Chapter Five
Hodgkinson on Humanism in Administration   98

Chapter Six
The Cultural Perspective   112

Chapter Seven
Administration for Emancipation   137

Chapter Eight
Ethical Theory and Educational Administration   166

Chapter Nine

Policy Analysis: Values and Complexity   192

Chapter Ten

Research in Educational Administration: Against Paradigms   213

AUTHOR INDEX   237

SUBJECT INDEX   241

Preface

RECENT debates in educational administration have often focused on purported limits to scientific views of administration and on the provision of alternatives. For example, scientific approaches are said to be incapable of dealing with ethical issues; yet the practice of administrators, managers, and policy analysts is irreducibly value-laden, being routinely concerned with questions of what *ought* to be done or what is the *right* course of action to advise or follow. Or, since organizational behaviour involves vast networks of intentional human activity, no adequate understanding of organizations seems possible without some appeal to human subjectivity, to the interpretations people place on their own actions and those of others. Yet scientific models of administrative behaviour in the name of objectivity seek to eschew interpretations, intentions and the inner life of agents in general. In the realm of research too, case studies, cultural studies and ethnographic methods seem able to deliver important detailed knowledge about administrative processes. But again, these are methodologies that are hard to place within a scientific tradition of controlled experiment or statistically significant reproducible results.

Such major differences between the orientation of traditional scientific approaches to educational administration on the one hand and the focus and direction of often quite systematic rivals or alternatives on the other, clearly lie behind much of the perceived intellectual turmoil in the field. Educational administration, in common with most of the applied social sciences, has experienced a growing appreciation of the methodological weaknesses inherent in positivistic construals of science and its methods. Ironically, however, the natural sciences go from strength to strength and, certainly over the last four hundred years, have been delivering knowledge hand over fist. Hardly any part of modern life remains untouched by the application or use of some aspect of natural science: for example, medicine, transport, and communications. So at a time when natural science has never been more successful in explaining and predicting phenomena and in enhancing our understanding of the world, paradoxically its methods and content are increasingly being questioned or even denied in the social sciences.

This book offers a resolution of this paradox as it arises in educational administration (although we expect our proposals will have some bearing on the social sciences in general). In our view the paradox is generated principally by the still widespread but mistaken belief that positivism, in its many varieties, can be equated with science. However, in the academic field of philosophy, all the main forms of positivism are now regarded as false, their key tenets clearly refutable. The most plausible current developments in philosophy of science and theory of knowledge reflect post-positivist views. Our point therefore, is that while many of the criticisms of administrative science in educational administration are sound, they are directed at a narrow target. They discredit only positivistic versions of administrative science.

Our main aim is to show how an alternative post-positivist science of educational administration is not only possible but theoretically and practically desirable. The argument we employ for this conclusion has the following broad structure. First, we acknowledge the importance theoretical writers have attached to epistemology or theory of knowledge, by arguing that the weaknesses critics have identified in traditional administrative science flow from *foundationalist* epistemological assumptions embedded in traditional views. We believe the whole quest for some antecedently certain or reliable foundation for knowledge, such as sensation, observation, intuition, or introspection, upon which all knowledge may be based, inferred, or deduced, is a mistake. Instead, we claim that the proper justification of knowledge is structured by *coherentist* considerations such as theoretical simplicity, consistency, comprehensiveness, conservativeness, and fecundity. If the justification of scientific claims, including administrative claims, proceeds according to the coherentist canons of our holistic epistemology, then the scope of science is very much broader than is usually conceived and will fail to sustain significant distinctions between fact and value, the subjective and the objective, and the alleged 'paradigms' of educational research.

Second, we note that major recent criticisms of traditional administrative theory assume theories that in turn share foundationalist epistemological structures. Critics tend to argue for more or different foundations for knowledge to supplement the deficiencies of positivistic science. We advance our case for a new science of educational administration by offering coherentist epistemological critiques of these rival theories.

Finally, in addition to these critiques, we elaborate the application of our epistemology to educational administration by considering a number of specific topics; for example, the nature of values, research methodology, and the conduct of policy analysis.

Despite our ambitions, this work is not a systematic treatise on the science of educational administration. Neither the critiques nor the topics covered offer a comprehensive coverage of the rich and detailed work being done in the field today. Rather, what we have tried to do, by considering a range of quite different theoretical approaches in at least some historical framework of intellectual development, is to indicate the main features of our own perspective on a number of key issues of importance, debate, and controversy. The topics we have selected are therefore those most amenable to philosophical discussion. That they enjoy some prominence in discussions of educational administration is testimony to the importance of philosophy for the field.

Although readers with a background in educational theory will recognize some themes from Dewey in our writing, an identification of more specifically philosophical influences may be helpful in understanding the orientation of this work. Our position is a species of scientific realism that is thoroughly naturalistic, favouring reduction (in principle) to the physical as a methodological constraint on good explanation. Some scientific realisms sustain a dichotomy between the mental and the physical by maintaining that mental properties cannot reduce to (in some suitable sense of 'reduce'), or be eliminated by, physical properties. And since social phenomena involve the mental, the dichotomy underwrites a distinction between the social and the natural sciences. Our scientific realism, on the other hand, is uncompromisingly naturalistic or physicalistic, even for properties. More specifically, from the writings of W. V. Quine we have been persuaded of the merits of coherentism over foundationalism, physicalism over mentalism, desert landscapes over lush domains of being and, in methodology, of eschewing meaning as an explanatory category. On the details of coherence epistemologies and their workings we have learned much from the work of Michael Williams and Lawrence BonJour. And last, on all the big questions of realism, physicalism, reductionism, philosophy of mind, epistemology, and philosophy of science we have had constantly before us the writings of Paul and Patricia Churchland.

The chapters that follow are relatively self-contained, although the way in which the debate has developed historically in educational administration might best be seen by reading in order. However, Chapter Two, which deals with the somewhat technical subject matter of epistemology, will repay rereading, following a more familiar treatment of its applications in later chapters.

Acknowledgements

MANY colleagues have contributed to our thinking on the topics in this book. Our principal debt is to Jim Walker who helped develop the main position on epistemology and social science. Portions of the book were presented to meetings at Deakin University, University of Melbourne, Monash University, University of New England, Pennsylvania State University, and the University of Tasmania. We are grateful for the many helpful suggestions that were offered. In this regard we would particularly like to thank Lawrie Angus, Richard Bates, Jill Blackmore, Judith Chapman, Pat Duignan, Peter Gronn, 'Mac' Macpherson, Valina Rainer, Fazal Rizvi, and Robin Small. Work in progress was also presented to meetings of the Philosophy of Education Society of Australasia, the Australian Association for Research in Education, the American Educational Research Association, and the British Educational Management and Administration Society, where critical scrutiny by specialist audiences was a source of further improvements to the text.

Some of the published papers on which this book is based have attracted replies, and in reworking and developing the ideas in these papers we have tried to respond, either strengthening earlier arguments or conceding errors. We expect we have conceded rather too little to satisfy everyone, but it may be useful to view this work as one more contribution to an ongoing debate.

Although there is much here with which they would disagree, we would like to acknowledge our gratitude to Thomas Greenfield, Christopher Hodgkinson, Denis Phillips, and Donald Willower for the support they have given this project.

In preparing the present work we have made use of the following previously published material:

EVERS C. W. (1985). Hodgkinson on ethics and the philosophy of administration. *Educational Administration Quarterly,* **21** (4), pp. 27–50.

EVERS C. W. (1987). Philosophical research in educational administration, in R. J. S. Macpherson (ed.) *Ways and Meanings of Research in Educational Administration.* (Armidale: University of New England).

EVERS C. W. (1987). Ethics and ethical theory in educative leadership, in

C. W. Evers (ed.) *Moral Theory for Educative Leadership*. (Melbourne: Victorian Ministry of Education).

EVERS C. W. (1987). Naturalism and philosophy of education, *Educational Philosophy and Theory*, 19 (2), pp. 11–21.

EVERS C. W. (1988). Educational administration and the new philosophy of science, *Journal of Educational Administration*, 26 (1), pp. 3-22.

EVERS C. W. (1988). Policy analysis, values and complexity, *Journal of Educational Policy*, 3 (3), pp. 223–233.

EVERS C. W. (1990). Ethics and educational administration, in T. Husen and T. N. Postlethwaite (eds.) *The International Encyclopedia of Education*, Supplementary Vol. 2. (Oxford: Pergamon Press).

EVERS C. W. (1990). Schooling, organisational learning and efficiency in the growth of knowledge, in J. D. Chapman (ed.) *School Based Decision-Making and Management*. (London: Falmer Press).

LAKOMSKI G. (1986). Greenfield and the problem with values, *Educational Administration Review*, 4 (1), pp. 3–13.

LAKOMSKI G. (1987). Critical theory and educational administration, *Journal of Educational Administration*, 25 (1), pp. 85–100.

LAKOMSKI G. (1987). Case study methodology and the rational management of interaction, *Journal of Educational Management and Administration*, 15 (2), pp. 147–157.

LAKOMSKI G. (1987). Values and decision-making in educational administration, *Educational Administration Quarterly*, 23 (3), pp. 70–82.

LAKOMSKI G. (1987). The cultural perspective in educational administration, in R. J. S. Macpherson (ed.) *Ways and Meanings of Research in Educational Administration*. (Armidale: University of New England).

LAKOMSKI G. (1988). Critical theory, in J. P. Keeves (ed.) *Educational Research, Methodology, and Measurement: An International Handbook*. (Oxford: Pergamon Press).

LAKOMSKI G. (1989). The journal of educational administration: mainstream, tributary or billabong? in G. Harman (ed.) *Review of Australian Research in Education: No. 1*. (Armidale: Australian Association for Research in Education).

LAKOMSKI G. (1990). What price democracy? An examination of Arrow's impossibility theorem in educational decision-making, in J. Chapman (ed.) *School Based Decision-Making and Management*. (London: Falmer Press).

WALKER J. C. and EVERS C. W. (1982). Epistemology and justifying the curriculum of educational studies, *British Journal of Educational Studies*, 30 (2), pp. 213–229.

WALKER J. C. and EVERS C. W. (1988). The epistemological unity of educational research, in J. P. Keeves (ed.) *Educational Research, Methodology and Measurement: An International Handbook*. (Oxford: Pergamon Press).

We thank all of the publishers and editors in question for permission to make use of this material.

Finally, we would like to thank Michelle Ryan, who managed to maintain her speed, efficiency, and kindness in typing the final version and numerous earlier drafts.

1

Educational Administration and the Theory of Knowledge

Since the mid 1970s, educational administration, as an area of study, has undergone a fundamental transformation. From following mainly models of theory and research associated with more traditional views of science, the field has moved to a position of much greater diversity. It is true that traditional views of science still dominate understandings of theory, research, and administrative practice, but there are now systematic alternatives to this approach. As a result, educational administration is now theoretically much richer, more diverse, and complex than at any other time in its short history.

These developments have not occurred without controversy. For example, following a relatively brief period of intense, indeed unprecedented, academic debate in journals, books, and conferences, Daniel Griffiths remarked that:

> if educational administration is not in a state of intellectual turmoil,
> it should be, because its parent, the field of organizational theory,
> certainly is (Griffiths 1979, p. 43).

Griffiths could well have added a number of related areas of applied social science to make his point. Policy analysis, educational studies and educational research methodology, and social theory in general were all in turmoil and undergoing transformation during this period, and for much the same reason (see Garson 1986, Phillips 1987, and Giddens 1982). The traditional scientific view of knowledge was increasingly perceived to be inadequate as a basis for social science. Critics claimed that it ignored values, that it ignored human subjectivity, and that it ignored the social and political context in which organizations exist and in which administrative practices occur.

It is unlikely that objections such as these would have been so effective in reshaping the agenda of educational administration were it not for the existence of alternative philosophical perspectives on the nature of knowledge which could function as frameworks for rival systematic conceptions of administration. And in our view, what has made the alternatives seem credible is the work done in the 1960s by Thomas Kuhn, Paul Feyerabend,

1

and other philosophers of science which showed, successfully, that traditional views of scientific knowledge are inadequate even for the physical sciences. (For a review of the evidence as applied to educational theory see Phillips 1987.)

The importance for administrative theory of philosophy in general and theories of knowledge, or epistemologies, in particular has been widely acknowledged. For example, in defending a particular perspective on organizations, Thomas Greenfield argues that:

> the implications of the phenomenological view are of critical importance in shaping our views both of the social sciences and of a study of organizations founded on them (Greenfield 1975, p. 71).

Partly in response to the sort of issues Greenfield raises, Griffiths observes that:

> the most important first step to be taken in the evaluation of current organizational theory is to clarify and come to some agreement on the *epistemological* question: Can there be a science of organization comparable to the sciences of physics and chemistry? (Griffiths 1979, p. 59).

And Willower (1981), in a reply to a series of objections to mainstream administrative theory, begins by noting that, 'Clearly, the big philosophical questions bear heavily on current concerns in educational administration' (p. 115).

These judgments concerning philosophy and administration should not be seen as applicable only to some particular period of intellectual development in the field. In a recent analysis of the state of educational administration conducted as part of a review of contributions to the *Handbook of Research on Educational Administration*, Willower (1988, p. 730) identifies six trends representing ' . . . directions in which educational administration as field of inquiry appears to be moving'. He completes the list by remarking: 'The sixth trend is a turn towards philosophy, and especially towards epistemological questions' (p. 731).

In our view, Willower is perfectly correct. The only caveat we would want to enter — and one with which we expect he would entirely agree — is that philosophy, especially epistemology, has *always* been significant, though perhaps not widely recognized as such until lately.

Epistemology and Administrative Knowledge

It is a key claim of this book that *all* major developments in educational administration, from the rise of the Theory Movement (see Culbertson 1981) in the late 1940s onward, have been driven by philosophical considerations.

Although the reasons for this are complex and vary with the particular developments in question, the general pattern is clear enough. Any set of organized interrelated claims that purports to be knowledge, such as a theory of administration, is subject to constraints that apply to all knowledge claims. However, within philosophy it is epistemology that deals with questions concerning the nature of knowledge, what makes claims knowable, and how they may be justified. Our central argument is that what epistemology counts as a satisfactory justification imposes powerful constraints on the content and structure of administrative theory. Or, in other words, the structure of justification, as specified by epistemology, determines much of the overall framework in which theorizing in administration is conducted.

Three major developments in epistemology may be cited to illustrate this point. Two of these have already had a significant impact on educational administration. The third, and most recent, provides the basis for our own critique and suggestions for new directions in the field. *Logical empiricism*, which developed out of, and partly in opposition to, the logical positivism of the Vienna Circle, provided the first systematic philosophical influence (see Achinstein and Barker 1969). In particular, it is Herbert Feigl's version of logical empiricism which has been critical in the development of the Theory Movement which in turn has shaped much of mainstream educational administration throughout the 1960s, 1970s, and the 1980s (see Feigl 1974). In it may be found the bases for separating fact from value and observation from theory, for employing the methodological constraint of operational definitions, and for seeing administration theory as a classical hypothetico-deductive structure with laws at the top and facts at the bottom (Feigl 1953).

The second development is the *paradigms approach* associated with the work of Kuhn and Feyerabend. Originally formulated as a systematic critique of logical empiricist views of scientific knowledge, their work — and especially Kuhn's since it is written in nontechnical language — has functioned increasingly to underwrite attacks on objectivity in the social sciences, and to promote varieties of relativism and subjectivism. It has been able to do this because, crucially, a paradigm is supposed to contain within itself the standards for its own assessment (Kuhn 1962, pp. 109–110). In this intellectual climate, if alternative views of administration are construed as either different paradigms, or as developing within different paradigms, then they are presumed to enjoy some methodological immunity from objections arising from one particular paradigm, say a systems scientific view. At the extreme, different paradigms are said to be incommensurable, or unable to be compared or adjudicated (Kuhn 1962, p. 150).

Two important results of the Kuhn–Feyerabend critique of logical empiricism are alleged to support this extreme view as well as a number of other familiar subjectivist conclusions. The first result is that empirical adequacy is not a sufficient criterion for deciding the merits of competing theories, for the same empirical foundation may adequately confirm any number of different theories. This is analogous to the fact that we can construct an arbitrary number of curves to fit the same set of data points. The second is that what counts as empirical evidence is partly determined by theory. Observations are said to be theory laden, mainly because the vocabulary used to describe observations is also part of a wider theoretical vocabulary. It is as though the very positions of data points depend in some way on the mathematical structure of curves of fit rather than vice versa (Hanson 1971).

Consistent with the paradigms approach, a further conclusion drawn from these results is that science is significantly nonempirical, that considerations of empirical adequacy place no essential constraints on the construction of scientific theories. Thomas Greenfield, whose writings have been largely responsible for the subjectivist turn in educational administration, needs to presume something as strong as this in order to say:

> The process of truth making in the academic world . . . does not differ materially from what goes into truth making in the world at large. Truth is what scientists agree on or what the right scientists agree on. It is also what they can get others to believe in (Greenfield 1978, p. 8).

And this, in turn, yields talk of reality being mind-dependent, of us inhabiting different worlds, or their being multiple realities all of which outrun any empirical evidence for distinguishing them. It also suggests a certain methodological infirmity when it comes to the question of evidence for adjudicating the merits of different interpretations of human behaviour, the stuff of hermeneutics, ethnographies, and cultural studies of organizational life (Evers 1988).

The third, and most recent, approach acknowledges the soundness of certain key results arising out of the 1960s critiques of logical empiricism; notably the underdetermination of theory by observation and the theory ladenness of observation. However, the correct conclusion to be drawn from these results is not a flight from objectivity and realism. Rather, it is the admission that there is more to evidence than observation or the establishing of mere empirical adequacy (Churchland 1985). After all, any theory can be made to square with empirical findings if we are prepared just to go on adding statements to it. What is more, a contradictory theory will square with any finding whatsoever. On this third approach, which we endorse, theory choice needs to be guided by a consideration of the extra-empirical virtues possessed by theories. These virtues of system include simplicity, consistency, coherence, comprehensiveness, conservativeness, and fecundity, though they are often referred to collectively as coherence considerations or as the elements in a coherentist account of epistemic justification (see Churchland 1985, Quine and Ullian 1978, Williams 1977).

The principal aim of this work is to show how the constraints on justification imposed by our preferred coherentist or holistic epistemology can be used to reshape and redefine the substantive content of educational administration in the direction of a new science of administration. In the chapters that follow we attempt this by way of epistemological critique and commentary on some influential past and current approaches to educational administration and some particular theoretical and practical issues. In the remainder of this chapter we offer a brief introduction and orientation to the book's characteristic pattern of argument, beginning with some remarks on epistemological issues followed by three short examples of coherentist epistemological critique.

Foundational Epistemologies and Coherence Justification

Since coherentist epistemologies are best seen as responses to the problems of foundational theories of justification, it will be useful to begin by sketching a classical solution to the problem of knowledge. How do we know anything at all? What is knowledge and what makes it possible? The kind of answer Plato gave and one offered countless times since, runs as follows:

Person x knows that p, where p is some particular claim to knowledge, if and only if

(i) p is true
(ii) x believes that p, and
(iii) x is justified in believing that p for the reason q.

This is known as the Justified True Belief (JTB) account of knowledge (Armstrong 1973). As it stands it contains a number of difficulties which need to be resolved. For example, q itself needs to be an item of knowledge if it is to supply a justifying reason for believing p. But if q is assumed to be known, the JTB formula, as a definition, is circular as it contains an appeal to 'knowledge' implicitly in the definiens. More seriously, if we assume q is known, then an infinite regress threatens, as it can only be known by virtue of knowing something else. The usual way of resolving both the circularity problem and the regress problem is to distinguish between *derived* knowledge and *immediate* or underived knowledge. The above account of knowledge then is an account of derived knowledge, of claims known in virtue of being implied by further knowledge. The chain of implications is not infinite however, as it stops at knowledge that is immediate or underived. On this view, all our (derived) knowledge must rest on or be derivable from some foundation of immediate knowledge.

Within the classical empiricist tradition the candidates for immediate knowledge — the foundations — have been, in decreasing order of strictness, sense data, first person sensory reports, and observation statements (Hooker 1975). However, as the history of philosophy readily attests, the hope of justifying all knowledge in this way is fraught with difficulty, especially in view of some of its consequences for science. For example, many of the objects posited by physics — such things as time, curved space, electrons and quanta — are unobservable, at least directly and are known only through economical theorizing about more gross observable consequences. Worse still, the lawlike universal generalizations characteristic of our best theories seem to require as evidence an infinite number of observations. Yet only a finite range of observations is ever available for justifying claims of the form 'all X are Y'. It would be nice if we had some sound principle of induction that would enable us reliably to infer from a finite set of observations to an infinite set of past, present, and future events of the sort that scientific laws can delimit; but no such principle has ever been forthcoming (see Popper 1963, especially ch. 1). Because so little of what ordinarily passes for reliable knowledge can be deduced, according to the JTB formula, from empirical foundations, classical empiricism functioned more as an attack on knowledge, with scepticism the end result, rather than a rational reconstruction.

The crucial methodological worry here is that the knowledge claims ruled out appear more reliable than the epistemology that rules them out. This is because an epistemology, in specifying conditions for claims to count as knowledge, also embodies a theory of the powers of the mind (see Churchland 1987). For what we can know will depend, to some extent, on our cognitive capacities, our skills for learning and, in general, what sort of creature we are. One weakness of classical empiricism is that it embodies a singularly implausible empirical pyschology of learning. For example, the process of learning from perception is not one in which a passive mind more or less faithfully records copies of sensory images, permuting them (or their decomposable components) according only to the laws of logic. Our current most sophisticated neurological theories of sensory information processing tell a vastly more complex story of human knowledge acquisition (Churchland 1986).

A further methodological worry with the classical view is that it appears to be unknowable on its own account of itself. The epistemology makes general or universal claims concerning all (human) knowing which, on its own terms, are known either directly or indirectly. But classical empiricist epistemology in all its generality cannot itself be a sensory experience, that is, part of the foundations, if for no other reason than that only a limited number of relevant observations are ever possible. Nor can it count as derived knowledge because of the problem of induction, the problem of using finite observational evidence to infer a general claim. On our view, these methodological problems suggest that the epistemology is *incoherent*.

In response, principally to the difficulties over induction and the non-observability of theoretical entities like electrons or quanta, logical empiricism, in common with twentieth century varieties of positivism, reversed the earlier classical relationship between theory and foundational evidence.

For logical empiricists like Hempel (1965) or Feigl (1974), observation statements are deduced from theories rather than the other way around. That is, logically, theories imply observations. The relationship between theory and observation is therefore one of *testability*. According to Hempel, saying an empirical statement is

> . . . testable in principle means that it is possible to state just what experiential findings, if they were actually obtained, would constitute favourable evidence for it, and what findings . . . would constitute unfavourable evidence; in other words, a statement is called testable in principle if it is possible to describe the kind of data which would confirm or disconfirm it (Hempel 1965, pp. 3–4).

Roughly speaking, theories, as networks of general and particular empirical statements, are supported by evidence to the degree that the observation statements they imply are confirmed, or the tests are successful. As a method for testing hypotheses by matching deduced observation statements against actual observations, logical empiricism is sometimes identified with the hypothetico-deductive method. (We think this identification leads to an unnecessary narrowing of the scope and possible context of such methods, however.)

Although we shall canvass many of the epistemological issues associated with logical empiricism in more detail in Chapter Two, two clear difficulties which lead to revisions along coherentist lines may be briefly noted. The first, mentioned earlier, is that the same finite observational base may equally confirm different theories. As Karl Popper has remarked in this context,

> . . . nothing is easier than to construct any number of theoretical systems which are compatible with any given system of accepted basic statements (Popper 1959, p. 266).

Popper's point is that piling up more and more confirming instances is of little value when it takes only one disconfirming observation to falsify a theory. (For example, Newtonian mechanics, which is false, has an infinite number of confirmations.) It is falsification that is crucial for promoting the growth of knowledge, for improving our theories, not confirmation. Theory change is driven by counter-examples, unexpected observations and predictions that are shown to be false. And our best theories are those that have been subject to the most severe testing but have not been falsified.

However, more is required for excellence of theory than just passing severe tests, for it is never individual hypotheses that are tested but, rather, whole networks of statements (Hesse 1970). And if networks or conjunctions of statements are needed to deduce observation statements for testing, a counter-example, or unexpected observation, shows at most only that one or more statements in the network are faulty. It does not, by itself, show which particular statements are in need of revision. As Quine has argued, methodologically there is vast scope for manoeuvring:

> Any statement can be held true come what may, if we make drastic enough adjustments elsewhere in the system (Quine 1951, p. 43).

We can even adjust the troublesome observation statement if we feel that those parts of our theory under threat are more reliable than the theory implicit in making the observation. (This means that observation statements are part of the total network or global theory, which is another argument for their theory ladenness.) To rephrase Popper's remark on confirmation, nothing is easier than to construct any number of revised theoretical systems which are compatible with any given potential falsifier.

How then are we to choose the best theory from among an infinite number of empirically adequate alternatives, all equally supported by whatever they deem to be a foundation for knowledge? Our suggestion, defended in detail in Chapter Two, is to choose the most *coherent* theory, that is, the one that enjoys more than any other the extra-empirical virtues of system (see Lycan 1988 and BonJour 1985). To see how a coherence approach can work over the question of choosing theories of knowledge, consider again the two methodological weaknesses we noted in classical empiricism. One was that the epistemology could not explain how it could ever be known. It failed to be comprehensive over the matter of self-reference. In seeking to adjudicate on the status of all knowledge claims it assumed an external vantage point which it could never know to be true. Other things being equal, therefore, we would prefer an epistemology that was truly comprehensive; one whose embodied psychology of knowledge acquisition renders it knowable.

Once we see an epistemology as itself a set of knowledge claims, we can ask whether the claims it rules out as knowledge are more reasonable or plausible than the epistemology that rules them out. For classical empiricism this is an acute methodological issue since it attempts to disqualify all of the most characteristic features of good science on the strength of a very modest empirical psychology used to select foundations for knowledge. It renders this particular programme of foundational justification incoherent by robbing it of its point. The way to avoid the problem is to require an epistemology to embody our most powerful and sophisticated theories of knowledge acquisition. But if we are appealing to our best natural science of human learning to justify knowledge there is no need to bother with foundations. We just appeal to science outright to justify and explain how scientific knowledge is possible. In our view, there is no knowable epistemically secure and privileged vantage point from which the whole of knowledge can be adjudicated. There is just our most coherent scientific practice. Epistemology becomes naturalized, as Quine (1969) suggests, and falls into place as part of psychology.

How then can we apply coherence criteria to theories of educational administration? In general we require consistency; we would aim for more comprehensive theories: those able to explain more phenomena rather than less, and with fewer anomalies, counter-examples, and falsifying instances rather than more. We would prefer simplicity to complexity in the sense of using the least amount of explanatory apparatus to account for the largest range of phenomena. We prefer theories that do not outrun their own explanatory resources, that do not posit distinctions for which there is, on their own terms, no evidence. Finally, we require that administrative theories be *learnable* in the sense that they meet the following two demands that were applied specifically to epistemologies: first, that they cohere with the broad demands of our best naturalistic accounts of human learning; and second, that they are not inconsistent with more reliable bodies of knowledge elsewhere in our total or global world view. The net effect of these demands is to require administrative theory to be a part of the most coherent global theory we can construct. We end up with a science of administration to the extent that this global theory also includes our most reliable scientific knowledge (Evers 1988).

Applying these general considerations is always a matter of detailed critique of particular issues. Coherence justification, because of its global character, is just a more intricate and difficult business than foundational justification. However, since foundationalism is mistaken, there is really no serious alternative. The following applications, because of their brevity, are only methodological guides to later more detailed treatments. Nevertheless, they do go some way towards illustrating the use of a coherentist methodology.

Justifying Educational Administration

(a) The Theory Movement

In the late 1940s, and especially from the period of the Kellogg Foundation's support of the Cooperative Program in Educational Administration begun in 1950, an increasing number of research scholars sought to develop a more systematic and rigorous basis for their work and findings. (For a good history of this period see Moore 1964.) As an antidote to the so-called 'naked empiricism' (Halpin 1958, p. 1) of fact finding and anecdote collection assumed typical of the field, a number of attempts were made to establish a theoretical structure for administrative theory as it was then being applied in educational studies. The notion of theory that found favour, as we noted earlier, was Herbert Feigl's logical empiricist account of scientific theory, and so what became characteristic of the Theory Movement was the attempt to structure administrative theory and research according to the strictures of Feigl's vision of science and its methods (see Feigl 1953, for the paper that probably had the most influence). The results, always energetically pursued, met with varying degrees of success (as we shall see in Chapter Three). We here consider one.

Of the many ways in which the epistemological doctrines of logical empiricism shaped the early development of the movement, none is perhaps so counter-intuitive and unrepresentative of ordinary administrative thought and practice as the removal of values from the scope of administrative theory. Andrew Halpin put the case as follows:

> No one will deny that we need normative standards — in the ethical meaning of the term — for how administrators *ought* to behave, but these prescriptions do not constitute a theory. These standards cannot be secured through the methods that we must use for constructing a theoretical model in science. In this model we must confine our attention to how administrators *do* behave. In short, the description of events and their evaluation must be kept distinct. To state the issue in other terms: the immediate purpose of research is to enable us to make more accurate predictions of events, not to prescribe preferential courses of human action (Halpin 1958, pp. 6–7).

(Daniel Griffiths in his 1964 *NSSE Yearbook* contribution also uses this argument, citing part of the above passage approvingly.) Now there is no denying that administrators with limited knowledge of the consequences of alternative courses of action would find immensely useful any theory that delivered more accurate predictions of events. But in many cases people know what the options are even if they don't know the detail. What they really want guidance on is the right course of action. Administrative theories that disqualify themselves from addressing the value question have a theory/practice problem: theory fails to be relevant for a large part of administrative practice.

This methodological infirmity arises if it is believed that every empirically significant term in a theory is meaningful because it corresponds to some specific range of sensory experience. Terms like 'chair' and 'table' readily satisfy this condition; terms like 'good' or 'just' appear problematic. Similarly, we have a fair idea of what counts as favourable or unfavourable evidence for testing the claim 'there is a chair in my office'; for a claim like 'that person was treated unjustly' there is a difficulty. Essentially the difficulty is this. All the sensory evidence we may ever gather for the claim will merely describe how the person was in fact treated, the facts of the matter, as it were. But the injustice is not a fact there to be observed. It is not some kind of object that produces sensations of injustice. Rather, so the story goes, the basis for our judgment of injustice resides in our subjective response to the observational evidence. So if cognitive significance resides in term by term correspondence with specific sensory experiences, or even in testability then, as Hooker remarks in his critique of empiricism's theory of language, '. . .

empiricists, like positivists, offer no cognitive content to ethics, aesthetics, religion, metaphysics, or indeed to philosophy . . .' (Hooker 1975, p. 191). Stripped of its cognitive content, moral deliberation and judgment collapse down into mere affective preference.

We will outline here just one line of response to this argument. We can begin by noting that if the argument is sound our knowledge of scientific concepts like electron or quantum is as problematic as our knowledge of moral concepts, since many of the theoretical terms of science and the sentences in which they figure do not correspond to any definite range of observations. The demand that all concepts be operationally defined — that is, defined as the operations to be performed in some test — is the traditional way of meeting this difficulty (Hempel 1966, pp. 88–97). Hence the common practice of attempting to give operational definitions in traditional science of administration. (See Griffiths 1959, pp. 75–91 for examples. But Griffiths 1964, p. 106 notes some difficulties.) However, strictly speaking, every purported definition admits of an infinite number of alternative possible operations, which would make a scientific vocabulary potentially limitless, and hence unlearnable. To be sure, many of the differences would seem trivial; for example distinguishing 'length$_1$' as measurement with a wood rule from 'length$_2$' as measurement with a plastic rule. But the distinction between trivial and nontrivial differences is a theoretical distinction, drawn with the aid of an antecedent grasp of the concept to be operationally defined. This is an instance of a logical empiricist epistemological procedure outrunning its posited resources.

The source of this difficulty, as Hempel ends up acknowledging after a discussion of the woes of operational definition, is the belief that a specific range of sensory experience exhausts the meaning of a term. Once we need to use theory (as turns out to be the case in foundational justification) to *select* the relevant sensory experiences, we end up blurring the distinction between observation and theory. Since the portions of theory being used are assumed to be cognitively significant, in our view it is more reasonable to suppose that the significance of more theoretical terms like 'electron' or 'quantum' resides in their conceptual role within the theory rather than in any immediate connections with experience, a point, incidentally, that Hempel concedes (Hempel 1966, pp. 93–94).

The view we wish to defend is that moral terms like 'good' or 'right' are significant in the same way that the most theoretical terms of science are. In realist fashion, we assume the unobservables of science exist because they are posited by the most coherent global account we can give of our interpreted experience (Quine 1976). Similarly, we suppose a moral theory and its associated judgments to be warranted to the extent that they are also part of the same global theory. On a coherentist approach to scientific knowledge there is therefore no sharp epistemological boundary to be drawn between administrative theory on the one hand and a large class of naturalistic moral theories and their normative claims on the other. In Chapter Eight we offer such a theory and suggest how it might work in administrative decision making in educational contexts.

(b) Critical Theory and Administration

Among the many critics of traditional science of administration are those who have been influenced by the writing of Jürgen Habermas. There is now a considerable body of literature in educational administration that might be regarded as falling within the critical theory perspective. (For a recent systematic presentation see Foster 1986.) Although critical theory approaches to administration are complex and multifaceted, covering ethical, political, social, linguistic, and personal dimensions, at least one strand of Habermas's thought that has been developed and applied to administrative contexts is uncompromisingly epistemological and lends itself readily to some brief coherentist remarks here. A more systematic treatment may be found in Chapter Seven.

We have in mind Richard Bates's thesis that a science of administration is essentially manipulative and concerned with social control (see, e.g., Bates 1980a, 1983). In developing this claim Bates draws on a reading of the early work of Habermas for an understanding of science; particularly the epistemological theses of *Knowledge and Human Interests* and the 'General Perspective' lecture published as the appendix to the English translation (Habermas 1972, pp. 301–387). In this work, Habermas identifies

> . . . three categories of processes of inquiry for which a specific connec-
> tion between logical-methodological rules and knowledge-constitutive
> interests can be demonstrated. . . . The approach of the empirical-
> analytic sciences incorporates a *technical* cognitive interest; that of the
> historical-hermeneutic sciences incorporates a *practical* one; and the
> approach of critically orientated sciences incorporates [an] *emancipatory*
> cognitive interest . . . (Habermas 1972, p. 308).

Traditional (so called positivistic) science which Bates, following Habermas, identifies with empirical-analytic science, is seen as hypothetico-deductive after the Nagel/Hempel empiricist model, with predictive success a measure of technical exploitability. For Habermas

> . . . theories of the empirical sciences disclose reality subject to the
> constitutive interest in the possible securing and expansion, through
> information, of feedback-monitored action. This is the cognitive interest
> in technical control over objectified processes (Habermas 1972, p. 309).

In Bates's view, the technical scientific definitions of knowledge and rationality are far too narrow for social science and need to be supplemented by critical discourse. A suitable broadening, he suggests,

. . . is argued at length by Habermas, who contends that the annexation of rationality by dominant scientific, technical, manipulative interests has prevented the continuation of an historical discourse directed towards a rational administration of the world . . . (Bates 1980b, p. 68).

He goes further, asserting that 'as currently conceived by professor and professional alike, educational administration is a technology of control' (Bates 1983, p. 46). And finally, in summarizing a robust and systematic indictment of poor philosophy for this state of affairs, he declares:

> The inadequacies of the hypothetico-deductive model of positivist science and the positivist, apolitical model of society were argued to be intellectual products that provided the illusions necessary for the continued employment of techniques of hierarchical administrative control that perpetuate the injustices of an unequal society (Bates 1983, p. 30).

There are a number of things that are puzzling about this account of science and administration, especially in view of the fact that Bates thinks traditional empiricist accounts of the practice and conduct of science are mistaken. For if the traditional view of science is wrong, and we know that it is thanks to the work of Quine, Kuhn, Feyerabend, Hesse and others, then the story Habermas tells of empirical science being constituted by technical interests of control and manipulation is also wrong. This is because Habermas's account of empirical-analytic science is as much dependent on traditional empiricist theories of science as the traditional science of administration that Bates is using Habermas's machinery to criticize. In more recent work Habermas recognizes some of these difficulties. Responding to Hesse's (1982) citing of new coherentist views of science in an evaluation of his work, he remarks:

> During the past decade I have been only cursorily occupied with questions in the theory of science and have lost the feeling for the relevant discussions. . . . In the light of the debate set off by Kuhn and Feyerabend, I see that I did place too much confidence in the empiricist theory of science in *Knowledge and Human Interests* (Habermas 1982).

Habermas is right to be concerned about his earlier prominent use of this model. The powerful coherentist-realist theories of scientific knowledge, inspired by Quine's writings and developing out of research conducted in the 1970s by philosophers like Churchland, Hesse, and Hooker, weakens the case for science as constituted by instrumentalistic technical control and manipulation of its required premises.

One attempt at avoiding the major incoherence threatening knowledge constitutive interests is worth briefly noting. The key move would involve distinguishing between traditional accounts of science being wrong on the one hand, and people acting as though these wrong accounts are true on the other. A revised Habermasian argument might then run as follows: If traditional views of science (positivism, logical empiricism, and the like) were true then technical control and manipulation would occur. Therefore, if everyone (professor and practitioner alike) acted as though they were true then technical control and manipulation would occur. The missing premise in this argument is a subjectivist claim to the effect that my having a particular theory of the world somehow makes the world that way, or brings it into line with my theory. This is perhaps an extravagant extension of the reasonable epistemological thesis that all observation is theory laden. To see the limits of the thesis, however, consider another example. Suppose, for the moment, that the dominant orthodoxy concerning water says that it flows uphill. We know that the orthodoxy is wrong but we also know that if water did flow uphill it would require a special form of technical handling. It does not follow that if everyone acted as though water flowed uphill, water would then require a special form of technical handling. Presumably, water would continue to defy orthodoxy in a range of ways.

Critical theorists may be sympathetic to certain subjectivist theses since bad theory may influence humans more than it influences water. But they cannot be too sympathetic to this one without undermining the reality of human suffering and injustice, or the objectivity of the class and political analyses that underwrite their approaches to human emancipation.

Administrative Decision Making

The last two examples of epistemological critique were directed mainly at views of the content and structure of administrative theorizing. Our final example will draw attention to the importance of epistemological views for organizational design.

The classical work in the field of administration is undoubtedly Herbert Simon's *Administrative Behavior*, first published in 1945. In that work Simon identifies rational decision making as the locus of administrative theory. He observes, however, that

> . . . if there were no limits to human rationality, administrative theory would be barren. It would consist of the single precept: always select that alternative, among those available, which will lead to the most complete achievement of your goals. The need for an administrative theory resides in the fact that there *are* practical limits to human rationality, and that these limits are not static, but depend upon the organizational environment in which the individual's decision takes place. The task of administration is so to design this environment that the individual will approach as close as practicable to rationality . . . in his decisions (Simon 1945, pp. 240–241).

As against the prescription to make *optimal* decisions, the cornerstone of Simon's theory of decision making is the *bounded* or limited nature of human rationality. We satisfice rather than optimize. He identifies three sources of limitation that organizational structures would need to address to enhance decision making. First, an individual is limited in skills: dexterity, reaction times, powers of computation, thought, and understanding. A second limitation concerns individual values and the understanding of organizational values and goals. Finally, there are limits to relevant knowledge, both knowledge of theory and knowledge of all the conditions that must obtain for a sound application of theory (Simon 1945, pp. 34–41).

Simon is reluctant to endorse any 'principles of administration' for enhancing administrative efficiency in advance of specific analyses of case-by-case administrative arrangements for reducing these limitations. Nevertheless, a particular approach to administrative reform is suggested by his theory. For example, if the growth of knowledge is a matter of accumulating more and more information, as the empiricism behind *Administrative Behavior* implies, a satisficing strategy will have a characteristic emphasis. For if optimal decision making requires optimal initial information inputs to best theory, a less than optimal or second-best approach will involve not a difference in kind but a difference in degree of ambition. Resulting administrative arrangements will place a premium on ensuring the highest practicable quality of initial input into the actual point of decision making. Depending on cases, reforms may focus on ensuring suitable concentrations of expertise, communications structures aimed at enhancing the availability of that expertise, and so on.

But on a coherentist epistemology, very large changes in knowledge are seen to occur through the promotion of a systematic virtue like simplicity in a theory network that includes among its statements a number of theory laden contrary observations. For the big gains in knowledge appear to flow more from the theoretical resolution of error than the incremental accumulation of data. Now given that the existence of limitations to our knowledge is likely to promote the occurrence of error, a case-by-case analysis of decision making may show greater gains to be had by the promotion of error correction at the expense — given only finite resources — of extensive attention to error prevention. Of course, in any administrative design for sound long-term decision making there is always some trade-off, in the allocation of resources, between error prevention and error correction. But a theory of learning, the core of which conceives knowledge as growing through a process of conjecture and refutation, is more sensitive to the possibility of learning through mistakes. The option of securing efficiencies in decision making through the rapid correction of error becomes, on this approach, a more explicit methodological guide to defining a suitable prevention/correction trade-off. Empirical studies by Chris Argyris and associates show some of the conditions under which error correction by administrative feedback loop structures is more valuable (see e.g. Argyris 1982, Argyris and Schön

1978). Not surprisingly, these are where the organizational environment is unstable or undergoing rapid change, where organizational knowledge and expectations are most likely to be falsified, and where there is a greater premium on more rapid acquisition or growth of knowledge.

This epistemological consideration suggests that theories of organizational learning can impose important constraints on the administrative structures of decision making. Simon's position in *Administrative Behavior* does not deny this. However, in noting the relevance of epistemology for administrative theory it is sufficient to observe, for our purposes, that significant differences in organizational consequences can flow from adopting divergent theories of human knowledge acquisition.

Summary

Philsophy, and in particular epistemology, has always been important for educational administration. Logical empiricism was a major influence on the development of the Theory Movement and derivatively, on much current administrative theory. The view that knowledge clusters into paradigms — a view arising out of Kuhnian and other critiques of logical empiricism — has underwritten much of the recent attack on traditional science of administration, and has more explicitly sanctioned a range of theories of educational administration, especially subjectivist theories. Epistemology influences administrative theory because, to lay claim to a right to influence action and policy, theory needs to be warranted or justifiable.

Standards of justification, including the issues of whether justification is even possible, are thus able to shape the content of such theory. On our view, however, theories shaped by both logical empiricism and the paradigm's alternatives are broadly foundational in structure. That is, they claim to be justified (or not) according to whether their characteristic theses follow, in some way, from some epistemically privileged body of experience, say, observations, or sensations, or feelings, or intuitions, or acts of introspection.

On our view, foundational epistemologies are mistaken. There is more to evidence for the adjudication and choosing of theory than experience. The coherentist, holistic approach to justification that we urge, includes such additional criteria of excellence of theory as simplicity, consistency, comprehensiveness, conservativeness, and fecundity. We also require that any theory be learnable. This particular requirement implies that accounts of learning be used to provide a link between empirical evidence (or experience) and theory.

In applying coherentist considerations very briefly to some issues concerning the Theory Movement, critical theory, and a view of decision making, we suggested a number of conclusions. Since our holistic epistemology places severe limits on attempts to partition knowledge into different compartments, we challenged both the fact/value distinction posited by logical empiricism and the three-fold division in knowledge posited by Bates's use of the earlier work of Habermas. Both challenges have extensive consequences for the administrative theories that employ these partitions in knowledge. Finally, we explored some organizational consequences of different views of the growth of knowledge on the question of enhancing structures for decision making.

References

Achinstein P. and Barker F. (1969) (eds.). *The Legacy of Logical Positivism*. (Baltimore: Johns Hopkins Press).

Argyris C. (1982). *Reasoning, Learning and Action*. (San Francisco: Jossey-Bass).

Argyris C. and Schon D. (1978). *Organizational Learning: A Theory of Action Perspective*. (Menlo Park: Addison-Wesley).

Armstrong D.M. (1973). *Belief, Truth and Knowledge*. (London: Cambridge University Press).

Bates R.J. (1980a). Educational administration, sociology of knowledge and the management of knowledge, *Educational Administration Quarterly*, 16 (2), pp. 1–20.

Bates R.J. (1980b). New developments in the new sociology of education, *British Journal of Sociology of Education*, 1 (1), pp. 67–79.

Bates R.J. (1983). *Educational Administration and the Management of Knowledge*. (Geelong: Deakin University Press).

BonJour L. (1985). *The Structure of Empirical Knowledge*. (Cambridge, Mass.: Harvard University Press).

Churchland P.M. (1985). The ontological status of observables: in praise of the superempirical virtues, in P.M. Churchland and C.A. Hooker (eds.) *Images of Science*. (Chicago: University of Chicago Press).

Churchland P.S. (1986). *Neurophilosophy: Towards a Unified Science of the Mind-Brain*. (Cambridge, Mass: M.I.T. Press).

Churchland P.S. (1987). Epistemology in the age of neuroscience, *Journal of Philosophy*, 84 (10), pp. 544–553.

Culbertson J.A. (1981). Antecedents of the Theory Movement, *Educational Administration Quarterly*, 17 (1), pp. 25–47.

Evers C.W. (1988). Educational administration and the new philosophy of science, *Journal of Educational Administration*, 26 (1), pp. 3–22.

Feigl H. (1953). The scientific outlook: naturalism and humanism, in H. Feigl and M. Brodbeck (eds.) *Readings in the Philosophy of Science*. (New York: Appleton-Century-Crofts). Also reprinted in Feigl 1974.

Feigl H. (1974). *Inquiries and Provocations: Selected Writings 1929–1974*. (Boston: Reidel).

Feyerabend P.K. (1981). *Philosophical Papers*, Vols. 1 and 2. (Cambridge: Cambridge University Press).

Foster W. (1986). *Paradigms and Promises*. (New York: Prometheus Books).

Garson G.D. (1986). From policy science to policy analyses: a quarter century of progress, in W.N. Dunn (ed.) *Policy Analysis: Perspectives, Concepts and Methods*. (London: JAI Press Inc.).

Giddens A. (1982). *Sociology: A Brief but Critical Introduction*. (London: Macmillan).

Greenfield T.B. (1975). Theory about organization: a new perspective for schools, in M.G. Hughes (ed.) *Administering Education: International Challenge*. (London: Athlone Press).

Greenfield T.B. (1978). Reflections on organization theory and the truths of irreconcilable realities, *Educational Administration Quarterly*, 14 (2), pp. 1–23.

Griffiths D.E. (1959). *Administrative Theory*. (New York: Appleton-Century-Crofts).

Griffiths D.E. (1964). The nature and meaning of theory, in D.E. Griffiths (ed.) *Behavioral Science and Educational Administration*. (Chicago: University of Chicago Press).

Griffiths D.E. (1979). Intellectual turmoil in educational administration, *Educational Administration Quarterly*, 15 (3), pp. 43–65.

Habermas J. (1972). *Knowledge and Human Interests.* (London: Heinemann).
Habermas J. (1982). A reply to my critics In J.B. Thompson and D. Held (eds.) *Habermas: Critical Debates.* (London: Macmillan).
Halpin A.W. (1958). The development of theory in educational administration, in A.W. Halpin (ed.) *Administrative Theory in Education.* (Chicago: Midwest Administration Centre).
Hanson N.R. (1971). *Observation and Explanation: A Guide to Philosophy of Science.* (London: Allen and Unwin).
Hempel C.G. (1965). *Aspects of Scientific Explanation.* (New York: The Free Press).
Hempel C.G. (1966). *Philosophy of Natural Science.* (Englewood Cliffs: Prentice-Hall).
Hesse M. (1970). Duhem, Quine and a new empiricism, in G.N.A. Vesey (ed.) *Knowledge and Necessity.* (London: Macmillan).
Hesse M. (1982). Science and objectivity, in J.B. Thompson and D. Held (eds.) *Habermas: Critical Debates.* (London: Macmillan).
Hooker C.A. (1975). Philosophy and meta-philosophy of science: empiricism, Popperianism and realism, *Synthese*, **32**, pp. 177–231.
Kuhn T. (1962). *The Structure of Scientific Revolutions.* (Chicago: University of Chicago Press).
Lycan W.G. (1988). *Judgement and Justification.* (Cambridge: Cambridge University Press).
Moore H.A. (1964). The ferment in school administration, in D.E. Griffiths (ed.) *Behavioral Science and Educational Administration.* (Chicago: University of Chicago Press).
Phillips D.C. (1987). *Philosophy, Science and Social Inquiry.* (Oxford: Pergamon Press).
Popper K.R. (1959). *The Logic of Scientific Discovery.* (London: Hutchinson).
Popper K.R. (1963). *Conjectures and Refutations.* (London: Routledge and Kegan Paul).
Quine W.V. (1951). Two dogmas of empiricism, *Philosophical Review*, **60**, pp. 20–43. Cited as reprinted in W.V. Quine (1961) *From a Logical Point of View.* (Cambridge, Mass.: Harvard University Press).
Quine W.V. (1969). Epistemology naturalized, in W.V. Quine *Ontological relativity and other Essays.* (New York: Columbia University Press).
Quine W.V. (1976). Posits and reality, in W.V. Quine *The Ways of Paradox and Other Essays.* (Cambridge, Mass.: Harvard University Press, revised and enlarged edition).
Quine W.V. and Ullian J.S. (1978). *The Web of Belief.* (New York: Random House, second edition).
Simon H.A. (1945). *Administrative Behavior.* (New York: The Free Press). All references are to the 1976 third edition.
Williams M. (1977). *Groundless Belief: An Essay on the Possibility of Epistemology.* (Oxford: Blackwell).
Willower D.J. (1981). Educational administration: some philosophical and other considerations, *Journal of Educational Administration*, **19** (2), pp. 115–139.
Willower D.J. (1988). Synthesis and projection, in N.J. Boyan (ed.) *Handbook of Research on Educational Administration.* (New York: Longman).

2

Knowledge and Justification

In the last chapter we introduced the idea of using epistemological considerations to critique administrative theories. In doing so we sketched briefly some reasons for preferring a coherentist epistemology over foundational rivals. As our theory of knowledge plays such an important part in our analysis and critique of administrative theory in education, we offer in this chapter a more detailed account and defence of its main features. Thus, the discussion of epistemology that follows will be explicitly philosophical in character. In view of the fact that hidden philosophical considerations have influenced recent theoretical debate in educational administration, there are some advantages in being more explicit about philosophy. Clarity is one obvious gain. Another is the opportunity for a more direct focus on very basic issues, such as the nature and scope of theories of educational administration. These issues are more conspicuously philosophical in character than others. A further gain is the opportunity to *practice* philosophy, for in educational administration philosophy is mostly something talked about rather than actually done. This does not prevent philosophical theories from exerting a powerful influence in administration but it does hinder the process of their evaluation. The lingering influence of positivistic empiricisms — long after their demise in philosophy — is a case in point. In setting out in some detail our reasons for preferring a coherentist approach to epistemological critique we acknowledge, in our methodology, the importance of this process of evaluation.

Our discussion of epistemology is not exhaustive. We deal instead with the main features of views that figure in subsequent argument. Furthermore, on some epistemological issues, for example ethics, we have elected to develop our views within the particular chapters where they most apply. Nevertheless, we try here to give enough detail to cover what for us are the central reasons for adopting a particular coherentist theory of justification over a range of foundationalist alternatives.

Scepticism and Foundational Epistemology

There is a long tradition in philosophy that sees the epistemological enterprise in terms of assuaging sceptical doubts. David Hamlyn, in a discussion of this tradition, summarizes matters thus:

> In a certain sense, however, all the problems of the theory of knowledge, even the more general ones, arise against and by contrast with a quite different point of view. That is that knowledge is impossible, or at least that we can never be sure that we have attained it (Hamlyn 1970, p. 7).

On this approach to knowledge, the question of whether we are justified in believing anything, whether we know anything, turns on the extent to which our beliefs can be defended against rational doubts. We can be said to have knowledge only inasmuch as doubt can be defeated or scepticism is unreasonable. The plausibility of this approach is further reinforced if we apply the method of doubt to the corpus of our beliefs, one belief at a time. Thus, consider someone's claim to know that there is a chair in their office. When pressed how may they defend this claim? One way is to gain the testimony of others who have seen a chair suitably located, and to defend their reliability as witnesses. Another way is for the person to recall seeing it there and to defend the reliability of their powers of recollection. Yet a third way is for all concerned to intrude upon the office scene to witness and corroborate each others' testimony. In this case once all and sundry actually get down to sensing or experiencing the chair located as required, we evidently run out of reasons. Yet, philosophers have asked, how do we know that sensory evidence, yours, ours, or anyone else's, is reliable, especially given the possibility of such deception as is occasioned by illusion, hallucination, or outright dreaming? How do we know that anything at all corresponds to the chair-like sensations people may experience? Putting the matter more dramatically, what could possibly count as evidence for the existence of an external world beyond our various perceivings?

Questions like these are what prompt the familiar *regress of reasons* pattern of justification. They express doubts that call for justifying reasons to be given in support of purported knowledge claims, reasons which in turn must survive the scrutiny of doubt. Since doubt can be applied to each preceding reason, we generate a sequence of justifying reasons for our beliefs, the kind of regress seen earlier in the classical Justified True Belief theory of knowledge. A regress unchecked is an infinite regress, and on any theory of learning that implies humans have finite capacities, it makes knowledge impossible. This is because to know anything at all we would have to know an infinite number of things, namely all the preceding reasons. Not surprisingly, all knowledge justified by the linear ordering imposed by a regress of reasons is supposed to be derivable from some foundation of underived knowledge, some place where the regress stops. In Anthony Quinton's words:

It is natural to suppose that such an order will have a beginning, a kind of belief that while supporting others does not owe its justification to any other kind of belief. Such beliefs, as the possessors of absolute epistemological priority, will be the foundations of knowledge (Quinton 1973, p. 115).

Quinton's assertion that knowledge has foundations aptly sums up the idea that the task of justifying knowledge halts at some sort of underived, or noninferential, knowledge.

Radical Strict Foundationalism

Following Pappas and Swain's formulation, we may express this notion more precisely by calling an epistemology *strictly foundational* if:

(1) some statements are noninferentially justified, and
(2) every item of derived, or inferential, knowledge is such that there is at least one regress of reasons leading from it to a statement which is not inferentially justified (Pappas and Swain 1978, p. 32).

In the face of sceptical doubts, attention now shifts to the class of non-inferentially justified knowledge claims, the possessors of so-called absolute epistemological priority. What justifies the foundations? Here opinions differ as to what is to count as an acceptable standard of justification. Radical foundationalists, in the spirit of Descartes, require of foundational knowledge that it be incorrigible, or infallible, or absolutely certain. Modest foundationalists, on the other hand, are less demanding of foundations, accepting a number of options that fall short of certainty.

From the time of Descartes until fairly recently most strictly foundational epistemology has been radically foundational, looking to certainty as a hedge against error. Thus Descartes' strictures on knowledge are shaped by his quest for a mode of justification sufficient to overcome the logical possibility of doubt. To get some feel for what is at issue and also the style of argument, let us follow Descartes' reasoning. His argument begins with the observation that the senses

. . . may sometimes deceive us about some minute or remote objects, yet there are many other facts as to which doubt is plainly impossible, although these are gathered from the same source (Descartes 1954, p. 62).

But when these other facts purporting to be from the senses are examined, he speculates that they may have originated in a dream. He thus retreats to arithmetic for certainty: 'whether I am awake or asleep, two and three add up to five' (Descartes 1954, p. 63). But now, he maintains, rational doubt is possible here too. This is because one can speculate that if there is 'an evil spirit, who is supremely powerful and intelligent and does his upmost to deceive me' (p. 65) then not only may the senses deceive about everything, but reasoning itself may be made to go systematically wrong. It is the logical possibility of a deceitful demon that appears to inflict the possibility of error on all belief. To avoid the very possibility of error Descartes went looking for logically indubitable truths, that is, beliefs such that their being believed entails that they are true (see Armstrong 1973, pp. 156–157). Moreover, in examining the presuppositions of doubt, he thought he found one. For to be deceived there must be an 'I' which is the object of deception. So, he reasoned, it is not logically possible to be deceived about one's own existence: 'If [some deceiver] deceives me, then again I undoubtedly exist' (Descartes 1954, p. 67). This is because '. . . this proposition "I am", "I exist", whenever I utter it or conceive it in my mind is necessarily true'. To doubt is to think and to think is to exist.

As an answer to the sceptic it is generally believed that this reply is unsuccessful. There are a number of reasons for this but one will suffice to indicate the main difficulty. If it is supposed that we can be deceived about arithmetic and arithmetical reasoning, then it is not clear why the logic of presupposition is any more secure. We may simply be mistaken in identifying our existence as something logically presupposed by our being deceived. For the Cartesian method of doubt also applies to the apparatus used to select or identify suitable foundations for knowledge.

Ordinary language philosophy, which prospered during the 1950s and 1960s, has provided some more recent resources for countering the Cartesian sceptic. Perhaps the most important of these has been the move to deny the coherence of universal doubt, the notion that everything can be doubted. Consider, for example, J.L. Austin's remark that 'it is important to remember that talk of deception only *makes sense* against a background of general non-deception' (Austin 1962, p. 38). Gilbert Ryle makes a similar claim when he says 'there can be false coins only where there are coins made of the proper materials by the proper authorities' (Ryle 1954, p. 95). The argument here is that it is incoherent to raise the possibility of doubting everything; that since illusion and misperception are understood only relative to veridical experience it makes no sense to talk of illusions without presuming some contrasting veridical experience. Is this argument decisive?

In our view, the flaw in it has been noted by A.J. Ayer, who draws attention to an ambiguity in the scope of the word 'everything'. Ayer concedes that we cannot coherently doubt everything at once, but that this is different from doubting all things taken, say, one at a time. He argues:

From the fact that our rejection of some of [our judgments] is grounded on our acceptance of others it does not follow that those we accept are true (Ayer 1956, p. 38).

In other words, our describing some experiences as illusions may be parasitic on us presuming some experiences to be veridical, but presumption is no guarantee of truth. So universal doubt, provided it is applied one belief or more (but not all) at a time, is coherent. It is therefore possible that every one of our beliefs is false. If the standards of justification imposed by radical strict foundationalism are to be met at all, it will not be by this challenge to the coherence of its method of doubt.

Another strategy issuing from the ordinary language approach to philosophy, involves challenging the demand for radical foundations, the demand for claims that are infallible or absolutely certain. The basic idea is to argue that a correct understanding of the meaning of the term 'knowledge' shows that these demands are unreasonable, that we can settle for more modest foundations to justify what we ordinarily claim to know. We quote Hamlyn, who begins his argument with a statement on meaning:

> If a concept is to exist at all, as is in effect maintained by Ludwig Wittgenstein, there must be some general agreement about its understanding, and that includes the understanding of how it is applied (Hamlyn 1970, p. 21).

From this it follows, according to Hamlyn, that

> . . . if the sceptic allows that the term 'knowledge' has meaning, he must also be prepared to say what he understands by the term, what would count as knowledge. If, as is likely, he also deviates from the normal conceptions of what counts as knowledge, the onus is upon him to justify that deviation (Hamlyn 1970, pp. 21–22).

He concludes that there is a '. . . presumption that normal conceptions of what is to count as knowledge are correct . . . (p. 22). Or as Austin once said about the possibility of doubting a first person report of seeing, in broad daylight, a nearby chair: "Well, if that's not seeing a real chair then *I don't know what is*" (Austin 1962, p. 10).

What this argument tries to show is that we learn to use the word 'knowledge' under conditions that make no demands for certain or incorrigible foundations. Therefore, we may be reasonably said to know something without having to meet radical strict foundationalist requirements for justification. Peter Unger (1971) took the widespread acceptance of this argument to be the principal reason why 'contemporary sophisticated philosophers do not take scepticism seriously' (p. 198). Such a comfortable result leaves intact as knowledge just about everything we ordinarily thought we knew and leaves out what we thought we did not know. As Austin's example illustrates, it makes the justification of knowledge easy.

The main trouble with the argument lies in what is now recognized to be the central difficulty with ordinary language philosophy. Understanding how a word functions in everyday language, knowing the correct use of a term, does not settle the question of truth. At most, ordinary language expresses particular theories. (The classic attack on epistemic privilege in ordinary language, notably on analytic truth, is contained in Quine 1951.) So if our everyday use of the term 'knowledge' implies that it means we can know claims without a regress to radical foundations, that modest fallible foundations like observations are sufficient for justification, then at best language presents us with a particular theory of knowledge. But language, which usually embodies commonsense or 'folk' theories about things, can be wrong. It can be wrong because there may be better theories available, perhaps those produced by science, or by systematic reflection, or by scholarship. Consider, for example, a word like 'witch', once embedded in the commonsense world views of past language users. Since the word was used meaningfully — people communicated with each other about witches, their magical powers, and their associations with the devil — there must have been (to use Hamlyn's formulation) some general agreement about its understanding, including an understanding of its application. There were also sceptics, perhaps people who believed in neither magic nor the devil. But on Hamlyn's argument, if sceptics allow that the term 'witch' has meaning they must also be prepared to say what they understand by the term, what would count as a witch. Deviations from the normal conception of what is a witch require justification. So analogously Hamlyn must conclude that there is a presumption that normal conceptions of what is to count as a witch are correct.

The reason why this conclusion sounds silly is because the commonsense theory of another era is nowadays widely recognized as false. But if witches do not exist, why presume that knowledge exists, at least as currently ordinarily conceived? Alternatively, if we want to say witches exist in some modern sense such as 'persecuted women mistakenly believed to possess magical powers', we might likewise say that knowledge exists but in some sense provided by a theory superior to that embedded in ordinary language. So when it comes to criticizing radical strict foundationalism, we need to do more than just show that it conflicts with ordinary commonsense epistemology. We need to go and justify our preference for the latter, if that is possible, or some other theory of knowledge.

Given strict foundationalism's terms of justification, appeals to both radical and modest foundations will fail to blunt the sceptical challenge. Consider radical foundations first, and in particular, the radical foundations of phenomenalism, that most influential strand of classical empiricism. Let us suppose for argument that this set of foundations, namely a body of sense data or raw unarticulated sensory experience, is known incorrigibly. We still have the problem of justifying the move from experience to claims about experience and the world. This is because experiences are neither true nor false. Rather, it is their expression in sentences (or perhaps propositions) that is true or false. Experiences need to be expressed sententially, or in some other way, in order to figure in the inferences required by a regress of reasons. But the process of expressing experience requires an act of cognition, some considerable learning, and a fair bit of theorizing. Even to bring experiences of red patches, pains, and tickles to a form of expression suitable for this logic of justification requires the mediation of cognitive machinery. Unfortunately, the required machinery is not known non-inferentially; it is not part of the foundations. So if only appropriately cognized experiences can be used in justification, and if cognition is fallible, nothing can be justified from the radical foundations posited by phenomenalism. In fact it does not seem possible even to identify sense data without some cognitively laden, or theoretical, scheme of individuation.

Here we have a *reductio* argument against the existence of a particular radical foundation for knowledge. Inasmuch as sense data are incorrigible they cannot involve fallible cognition. And inasmuch as they do not involve cognition they cannot function in a regress of reasons. To this line of thought, and its implications for the role of science in justification, the radical strict foundationalist H.H. Price goes so far as to argue that the study of our apparatus of sense-perception 'lies outside the sphere of science altogether'. (Price 1964, p. 2). It is easy to see how this argument can be generalized to apply to other purported radical foundations for knowledge that rely on fallible cognition for the demarcation and identification of foundations. Our conclusion is that this view of knowledge is incoherent because its theory of justification makes incompatible demands on evidence.

Modest Strict Foundationalism

Retreating to modest, or fallible, foundations also has its difficulties. (A survey of these difficulties can be found in Churchland 1979, especially ch. 2; for a short history of epistemology and philosophy of science see Churchland 1986, ch. 6. A comprehensive analysis of foundationalism from a coherentist perspective is to be found in Williams 1977.) It is true that if we relax our standards of justification we can let in Austin's example of seeing a chair. Reports of observations of familiar middle-sized dry physical objects, made under normal viewing conditions by persons of normal viewing capacities can indeed be used as a basis for justifying knowledge. And we can simply stipulate that the sceptical regress halts at this kind of evidence. However, if we are trying to overcome scepticism, there is much that we would wish to count as knowledge that fails to be justified according to modest strict foundationalism. Two areas of difficulty should illustrate the kinds of limits this theory places on knowledge, and also, when further explored, what is wrong with the theory.

The first concerns our knowledge of unobservables, things that are perhaps too tiny to be seen, even in principle, or are too far away, or are of such disposition as not to trigger our sensory apparatus. How do we know these objects exist, or more precisely that our sentences asserting their existence are true, given that they can correspond to no item of foundational knowledge? It is tempting to say that these objects do not matter, that we can be indifferent to the truth or otherwise of the sentences that may presuppose them. After all, everything we may expect to have dealings with in our ordinary commerce with the world can be traced back to suitably chosen modest foundations. What more could we want? A quick glance into our best science shows that we evidently need much more. One does not have to press modern scientific explanation back very far to reach talk of molecules, atoms and quanta, radio waves and gravitational waves, or any number of other unobservables. The behaviour of gross observable objects seems to be determined very much by the behaviour of a multitude of hidden things. What is more, given the immense utility of science in predicting and controlling gross observables, there is considerable practical value in attending to the laws that are purported to govern the behaviour of these underlying micro-objects. The paradox is that the modest foundationalist's theory of evidence rules out knowledge of unobservables while at the same time acknowledging their value in predicting and controlling the course of experience.

The standard empiricist resolution of this paradox is, in a word, instrumentalism. (The most sophisticated recent defence of empiricism is Van Fraassen 1980.) The observable is real while the rest is no more than a useful fiction, an instrument, or an aid to calculation. Chairs and tables are real, atoms and electrons unreal or nonexistent. Sentences dealing with the former can be known to be true or false; sentences concerning the latter are unknowable. So although science purports to deal in a world of unobservables, such posits really outrun all the possible foundational evidence. As a reply to the sceptic concerned about unobservable theoretical entities and the truth of vast stretches of modern science this resolution has, in the words Bertrand Russell used in another context, all the advantages of theft over honest toil. We think this reply is open to objections that lead ultimately to an undermining of the strategy of appeals to modest, fallible foundations for knowledge.

Earlier, we argued that the relevance of fallible cognition for demarcating a class of radical foundations robbed radical strict foundational justification of its point. We will now show that a similar problem invests the task of demarcating a class of modest foundations. The key difficulty emerges when we try to specify precisely some principled epistemological distinction between the observable and the unobservable. Consider an example. You collect stamps which you view under normal conditions with normal eyesight. One stamp, however, is of a special kind which you suspect may have an important watermark. But you suspect rather than are sure because normal conditions of viewing do not settle the matter. The watermark is not normally observable. Yet a glance through a weak magnifying glass would show a watermark. Is the watermark observable?

If the answer is no, then we appear to be holding out against the manifest reliability of very modest apparatus for enhancing our perception (see Hacking 1985). To give other examples, a telescope's accuracy can be checked by simply approaching distant objects under scrutiny and confirming the presence of detail with the naked eye. Glasses can restore one's eyesight to the norm that obtained prior to the onset of the familiar longsightedness that comes with age. The theory of optics, even instrumentally construed, draws no epistemological boundary between the operation of glass lenses and those that come naturally with each eye. The discrimination of sounds is enhanced by turning one's head to a more favourable orientation, by cupping a hand to one's ear, or by using a piece of curved cardboard instead of a hand to the same effect. Acoustic theory points to no epistemologically principled distinction among these manners of hearing, only a continuum of increasing discriminability. Now the crucial methodological point is this. Once we begin to use instrumentally interpreted macroscopically verified theory to justify the reliability of perception-enhancing apparatus, we admit an epistemological basis for legitimately expanding the notion of observation, at least where very simple, low technology apparatus is involved. Indeed, theory may be used to suggest improvements to a set of modest foundations comprising reports of observations made by normal perceivers under normal conditions; improvements resulting from the wearing of glasses or the viewing of objects under more favourable lighting conditions. Needless to say, the epistemological possibility of improving foundations begins to undermine the structure of modest strict foundationalism.

A further undermining occurs when we acknowledge that the normal operation of sensory apparatus in nature is a highly parochial and variable affair. Some species make observations above and below the frequency range of light visible to humans. Others distinguish objects by electric fields, special sound frequencies, smells, and variable pressures in the environment. Do the objects observed in these ways exist? To say no is to attempt to draw a fundamental ontological distinction between reality and fiction on the basis of the particular evolutionary history of our species' current sensory systems (Churchland 1985, pp. 44–45). Given that the accuracy and reliability of such different sensory systems in performing a common or shared epistemological task like demarcating the boundary of some object is not in question, even on our own admissible evidence of success, there appears to be no sound reason for adopting a narrow, species-specific criterion of observation.

If we agree that watermarks, distant and microscopic objects are counted as observable by virtue of the contribution of apparatus, and if we admit as evidence the perceptions associated with other sensory systems, then it is arguable that the distinction between foundational and derived knowledge collapses altogether. We can begin by noting that a considerable extension of the idea of observability must be countenanced, for our sensory apparatus can be enhanced by technology in arbitrarily complex, subtle, and sophisticated ways, from electron microscopes through to radio telescopes and spectroscopes. Whether equipment is designed (like sonar) to imitate the behaviour of other sensory systems, or whether the constraint is whatever technology can devise to convert information-laden patterns into interpretable sensory stimuli — for example, in the control of electromagnetic radiation — the possibilities are enormous. Moreover, some devices may work in ways that are not even remotely analogous to the operation of organic sensory systems. The appeal to modest foundations, as an epistemological strategy for justification, becomes problematic when we admit that a blip on a radar screen can provide more reliable knowledge than a scan of the skies with the naked eye.

To see why this is so it is important to gain a general perspective on the problem. In the case of the radar screen as a source of observational evidence, we are clearly relying more heavily on the theoretical integrity of the machine than we are on natural, unmediated observation. That is, the network of epistemologically significant influences sustained by talk of blips is heavily circumscribed by assumptions as to the correctness of radar theory. Let us call this network of inferences an interpretation. So our interpreted observation of a blip will perhaps figure in attempts to justify claims from 'that machine over there is switched on' to 'there is a green patch moving on that screen' to 'there is a light aircraft coming in to land'. Because of their obvious dependence on at least some radar theory, as evidenced by the use of some theory-specific vocabulary, it is customary to call these observation statements *theory laden* (see Hanson 1968, 1972). From our other examples it is clear that, in each case, apparatus-mediated observations are also theory laden, dependent for their veracity on the soundness of optics, materials science, acoustics, electronics, and any number of other assorted bodies of theory. But if so it is difficult to see how such observations can play the part of foundations in the justification of knowledge. The whole point of foundational epistemology is to justify high-level bodies of knowledge claims. The above argument puts matters around the other way; namely, our theory laden observations are firmly established to the extent that they draw on firmly established theory.

It is tempting to think that the problem arises as a consequence of failing to distinguish sharply enough between natural perception and perception assisted by apparatus; that it represents a *reductio* argument against conceding a continuity here. Tempting but wrong. The real culprit is the intrusion of theory, not the intrusion of apparatus. For our purposes, talk of apparatus is really just a way of demonstrating, in unequivocal terms, the importance of theory in determining the truth of a large class of observation reports; namely, reports of observations made with the use of equipment. But theory continues to intrude in the absence of apparatus. Some ordinary and arcane examples will illustrate this. Consider someone taking a quick glance at the sun. Do they see it as it really is, or as it was a bit over eight minutes ago? Complex theory specifying a finite velocity for light counsels the latter inference. A stick placed half-way in water appears to bend in the middle. Theory, corroborated by other sensory modalities, overrides the obvious inference. You study an X-ray photograph and notice an outline of bones. A specialist, looking with unaided vision at the same photograph, draws many more quite detailed conclusions. Yet the photograph produces the same ocular irridation patterns in the eyes of both observers. The difference in what is seen can be explained in terms of the very powerful theory the specialist uses to interpret the photograph. A sequence of learning experiences can train the ear to discriminate among different musical notes. Prior to learning, the notes sound the same.

Another example, used by Kevin Harris (1979, pp. 10–17) to illustrate the same point, implies quite extensive theoreticity in ordinary perception. Suppose you are asked to count the number of people, at some particular time, on the university oval. Do you count the very pregnant woman crossing the oval as one or two people; the body of someone who has just died as one or none; or the debilitated stroke patients wheeled out from the nearby teaching hospital as some or none? These cases are sufficiently controversial to produce a different count among observers. However, any differences are not likely to be eliminated by further or closer observations, or by the use of some special apparatus. For the task of counting persons draws on theories of what persons are; their properties and characteristics. That is, a theory of persons is being used in advance to tell an observer what to look for. So quite independently of the issue of normal observers performing under normal viewing conditions, in this case, theory comes before observation. And once again, if our set of foundational statements includes or presupposes statements about the nature of persons, their standing as evidence depends on the prior acceptability of some theory of persons, thus undermining their role in foundational justification.

When radical strict foundationalism failed for want of infallible foundations, we began to explore the possibilities of a more modest variety of foundationalism, one where the regress halted at our best fallible experiences. We noted, however, that we must be prepared to entertain scepticism with regard to unobservables, a seemingly major concession in view of their prominence in much scientific explanation. We then examined the standard empiricist response of instrumentalism; namely, no great scepticism of scientific theory is involved because observable reality is the only reality there is. All the unobservables posited by science are merely useful fictions. Unfortunately for the instrumentalist, a sharp epistemological distinction between the observable and the unobservable proved difficult to draw. For example, the use of apparatus seemed to permit legitimate but extravagant extensions to the class of foundational observation reports. We noted that this creates problems for the logic of foundational justification since it implies that the soundness of purported foundations depends on the soundness of the high-level theory underpinning the workings of apparatus rather than the other way around. When we reconsidered the move to exclude the use of apparatus in observation, however, we discovered that the real source of difficulty was the theory ladenness of observations, not the use of apparatus. Experiences seem to be interpreted, their credibility as foundational evidence thus being dependent on the credibility of the interpretative framework, or theory. This again puts matters around the wrong way for the foundationalist.

Are there any experiences that can be said to be theory-free, occurring without interpretation? In our view, the answer is no, and an argument to this effect will be offered presently when we consider some other issues. However, as we saw in the discussion of radical foundationalism, even if there were theory-free experiences, it is unlikely that they could figure in foundational justification in the required way. For justificatory inference demands a prior cognizing of experience, a framework for the classification and individuation of the objects of perception, in short, a theory. There is an obvious corollary here for the matter of instrumentalism. If all experience is interpreted, and the observable/unobservable distinction is not epistemologically basic, then the place where it marks a corresponding reality/fiction distinction becomes questionable. Furthermore, just as we need to rely on theory in our judgments concerning observations, so we have no choice but to rely on theory to determine what exists. In our view, what exists, what is real, is given by the posits of what epistemology judges to be our best theory. As Quine has argued, this is as much the case with atoms and molecules as it is with such so-called observables as chairs and desks:

> What are given in sensation are variformed and varicoloured visual patches, varitextured and varitemperatured tactual feels, and an assortment of tones, tastes, smells, and other odds and ends; desks are no more to be found among these data than molecules. If we have evidence for the existence of the bodies of common sense, we have it only in the way in which we may be said to have evidence for the existence of molecules (Quine 1976, p. 250).

So if chairs and desks exist so too do atoms and molecules, both sets of objects being posited by our current best science. Since the determination of what counts as 'best' still lives on as an epistemological problem, there is clearly more to evidence than foundational evidence.

A second area of difficulty, in addition to the problem of unobservables, also poses severe sceptical limits to what can be justified by modest foundationalism. This difficulty is usually known as the problem of induction, the classic formulation of which is due to the eighteenth century philosopher David Hume. We use an example to illustrate Hume's argument (Hume 1888, pp. 131–142). Suppose on one occasion you observe a raven and notice that it is black. Suppose further that on all subsequent occasions all ravens you observe are black. On the strength of this evidence you may be tempted to conclude that all ravens are black. But the conclusion is unwarranted. It does not follow from 'all *observed* ravens are black' that 'all ravens are black'. To sustain the inference we need a premise to the effect that nature is uniform, or perhaps that the future is like the past; we need a principle of induction. But now what would count as evidence for such a principle? All we are entitled to say, at most, is that in the past, or up until now, or on all occasions where nature has been observed, it has been uniform, or the principle of induction has held true. What about on other occasions? How can we know that it will always hold? To sustain the inference that some principle of induction will continue to hold on other occasions we need to assume that nature is uniform, or the future is like the past. That is, to justify belief in some principle of induction beyond what is provided by past and current observations of the principle at work, we need to assume just such a principle. This, of course, makes for a circular, invalid justification. Since all the observations that can ever be used in a set of foundations for knowledge are bounded in terms of place and time — we can only ever observe up until now — no principle of induction can justifiably follow from these foundations.

Hume draws the implied sceptical conclusion:

> That even after the observation of the frequent or constant conjunction of objects, we have no reason to draw any inference concerning any object beyond those of which we have had experience (Hume 1888, p. 139).

By this he means we have no sound reason for supposing that the sun will rise tomorrow, that bread will continue to nourish, that the floor will continue to support us, or that our familiar furniture will not blink out of existence in the next instant. We have no reason to believe the universal generalizations of physics, usually taken to be the hallmark of successful inquiry and systematic theory. In short, the attack on induction threatens to warrant an extensive scepticism towards both science and commonsense.

We regard this sceptical consequence as basic to the strict foundational enterprise for justifying knowledge; that is, within the framework of justifying knowledge via a regress of reasons back to some noninferentially known set of claims, the problem of induction is unavoidable. One conclusion is to accept the problem as setting severe limits to what can be known. Another conclusion, and one we shall now pursue, is that since scepticism also applies to the theory used to select and identify foundations, there are further grounds for suspecting a major incoherence in strict foundationalism.

Broad Foundationalism

From the 1920s through to the end of the 1950s philosophers concerned with the logical force of these sorts of criticisms and their effect on the prospects for scientific knowledge, developed a characteristic line of response that came to be known as the 'received view' (see Suppe 1974). Although there are important variations associated with logical positivism, logical empiricism, and falsificationism, and further variations within each of these, in general the received view of scientific knowledge is thought to contain at least the following elements.

It is agreed, for example, that there is a distinct empirical foundation for knowledge that represents a special class of epistemically privileged knowledge claims. However, it is also agreed that logically, the generalizations of science and a great many other scientific claims cannot be deduced from these foundations. Rather, the correct deductive relation between a theory and its empirical foundation is the other way around. Observation statements, for example, are deduced from the statements of a theory (including the theory's statement of required initial conditions). If the observations we actually make, namely the ones expressed as foundational statements, match up with the observation statements that can be deduced from a theory, then the theory is said to be *confirmed* by those observations (see Hempel 1965). Thus the foundations support a theory — give us evidence for believing it — by way of confirmation. The more a theory is confirmed, the greater reason we have for believing it. We refer to this relation between theory and evidence as *broad* foundational support, to distinguish it from strict foundationalism.

Using the logical machinery developed by Russell and Whitehead, theories could be axiomatized (in the first order predicate calculus with identity), their deductive relations displayed, and the logic of confirmation made precise. Or such, at least, was the aim. Under these conditions, discussions about the nature of scientific theory, evidence, and justification, became rather technical. Technical discussions are less accessible to the general reader than those conducted in ordinary language, but corresponding gains in precision and clarity of inference have their compensations. As these are the same kind of gains that accrue for quantitative empirical researchers who commonly master and employ the equally arcane apparatus of modern statistical theory, a brief excursion will not be out of place. It should give something of the intellectual flavour of the methodological issues that writers in the early Theory Movement had to consider.

So, technically speaking, a theory comes out as a deductively related set of sentences whose domain of interpretation is the set of admissible values of bound variables. The values of bound variables are the objects that sentences talk about, and variables, like m for mass or f for force, are just convenient devices for referring to objects without naming them.

A theory's axioms include scientific laws which specify relations holding among objects referred to by theoretical terms. Theoretical terms in general are defined by statements in the theory called correspondence rules which (at least in the earliest versions of the received view) specify equivalences between theoretical terms and observational terms (Suppe 1974, pp. 17–56). Since the background theory of evidence is doing double duty as a theory of meaning, correspondence rules also give the empirical meaning of theoretical terms. Expressed in logical notation, if T is a theoretical term, O one or more observation terms (joined together purely by logical particles), then the correspondence rule giving an explicit definition of T in terms of O is written as:

$$(x)(Tx \equiv Ox).$$

The quantifier (x) placed at the beginning of the sentence is said to bind the variable x. The biconditional $\equiv$ (read as 'if and only if') is the sign of logical equivalence, so that $p \equiv q$ means that either p and q are true or p and q are false. Theoretical terms like 'mass' or 'force' might thus be defined as the observable measurements performed on observable objects. For the logical positivists of the Vienna Circle, observable objects were sense data, the domain of interpretation for sensory evidence being limited to a phenomenalistic ontology. For logical empiricists like Herbert Feigl (1950) on the other hand, observables could be middle-sized physical objects.

Since unobservables caused such difficulties for strict foundationalism, we should note that this way of dealing with theoretical terms has also been thought to work for unobservables. For example, terms for unobservables could be equated with the network of descriptions associated with observable behaviour of apparatus, or the conjunctions of phenomena that suggest such posits. The practice of giving operational definitions, which has been especially influential in educational administration (and social science in general) would thus be a special instance of this type of correspondence rule. So in giving operational definitions of, for example, 'leadership', 'intelligence', 'decision making', or 'organization', theoretical terms are said to be synonymous with the set of corresponding operations performed in measurement or application.

However, we have already canvassed one problem with this kind of explicit definition in the last chapter. Namely, an arbitrary number of definitions of any term is possible because an arbitrary number of distinct operations can be performed. A further technical problem arises for dispositional terms like 'leadership'. Consider the following:

x possesses leadership $\equiv$ if x were placed in circumstances C at time t then x would perform in manner M at time t.

In symbols we have:

$$Lx \equiv (t)(Cxt \supset Mxt),$$

where L, of course, stands for 'leadership'. Now the problem with this formulation is that because of the logic of 'if . . . then . . . ' and 'if and only if', the statement is always true if a person is never placed in circumstances C. That is, the statement contains a *counterfactual*. Similarly, everything is soluble provided it is not put to the test. Everything is brittle provided it is not struck, and so on for all operational definitions as well, where the operations are never actually performed.

The principal response to this difficulty by writers in the received view was to abandon the demand for explicit definition. Instead, the use of partial definitions was proposed. So a partial definition of 'leadership' has the form:

$$(x)(t)[Cxt \supset (Mxt \equiv Lx)].$$

This correspondence rule is called a reduction sentence and it defines a test condition sufficient for the showing of leadership. It says that for all objects, x, and for all times, t, if x is placed in circumstances C at time t then x possesses leadership if and only if x performs in manner M at time t. On this formulation, leadership is not guaranteed simply by the absence of circumstances C. There is no requirement that the test actually be carried out. It is sufficient for defining leadership that performance M would occur if circumstances C obtained. Technical problems also crowd in with this refinement and these have led to yet further developments within the received view. We do not propose to explore the relevant twists and turns any further, however (Suppe 1974). Instead, we make the general point that, as with strict foundationalism, the received view's theories of evidence and meaning depend on the possibility of maintaining a sharp distinction between theoretical terms and observational terms. If this distinction cannot be maintained then again foundational observation reports used to confirm or disconfirm theories will depend on the correctness of the theory with which they are laden for their epistemic force. This is clearly the case with theoretical terms for unobservables where theory intrudes in the interpretation of readings or perceptions mediated by apparatus. And, as we have seen, it can also be the case for unmediated perception. So even for broad foundationalism, where justification is construed in terms of foundational evidence confirming theories, the relations of epistemic support are compromised by the interpenetration of theory and evidence.

A further difficulty concerns induction and the limits of confirmation. Consider a consistent theory that includes the hypothesis H: 'all ravens are black'. If all the ravens so far observed have been black, does that increase the probability of H being true? In general, the answer is no for such infinite probability spaces. The result may be defeated by one future counter-example. Early European evidence for the claim 'all swans are white' did not include Western Australia's black swans. Or consider another consistent theory that includes the hypothesis H^1: 'all ravens are blite'. A blite raven is one which enjoys the Goodman (1979) property of being black if examined up until now and white if examined thereafter. It appears that all known observations support equally both theories, or hypotheses H and H^1. Yet the theories have quite different observational consequences (from now onwards). As we noted in the last chapter, any number of different theories can be constructed to square with all known foundational evidence. This still leaves the problem of induction, the problem of justified extrapolation from known foundations of knowledge, unresolved.

In our view, the most important attempt to solve, or dissolve, the problem of induction from within the broad foundational tradition of justification, is that made by the philosopher of science Karl Popper. Popper begins his *Logic of Scientific Discovery* by restating Hume's argument against inductive inference, and conceding its conclusion:

> For the principle of induction must be a universal statement in its turn. Thus if we try to regard its truth as known from experience, then the very same problems which occasioned its introduction will arise all over again. To justify it, we should have to employ inductive inferences; and to justify these we should have to assume an inductive principle of a higher order; and so on. Thus the attempt to base the principle of induction on experience breaks down, since it must lead to an infinite regress. . . . My own view is that the various difficulties of inductive logic . . . are insurmountable (Popper 1959, p. 29).

As an alternative, he goes on:

> The theory to be developed in the following pages stands directly opposed to all attempts to operate with the ideas of inductive logic. It might be described as theory of *the deductive method of testing*, or as the view that a hypothesis can only be empirically *tested* – and only *after* it has been advanced (Popper 1959, p. 30).

By testing a theory, what Popper is really talking about is attempts to refute it, or disconfirm it. In essence, the best theories are those which make bold empirical claims, that is, claims which have extensive empirical consequences and can be extensively tested, and yet have survived those tests or have not been falsified. Correspondingly, the growth of scientific knowledge proceeds not by piling up more and more confirming evidence for theories but by a process of conjecture and refutation, by theories being proposed, tested, and found wanting, and then new ones being proposed that overcome these objections but must face new tests. And so on. The foundations of knowledge for this epistemology — the empirical claims or basic statements that are used in attempts to falsify theories — thus function to justify knowledge in a more indirect way. Popper (1969) summarizes his theory of knowledge in the following schema:

$$P_1 \rightarrow TT \rightarrow EE \rightarrow P_2$$

All scientific discussions start with a (theory laden) problem, P_1, to which we respond with a tentative theory, TT, which is our attempt at a solution. Our tentative theory is in turn criticized to eliminate errors, EE, and the new or revised theory gives rise to new problems, P_2. Such is the broad outline. Some interesting detail emerges when we examine perhaps Popper's most important argument for his epistemology.

One way of arguing the merits of this epistemology over other broad foundational rivals is by claiming that it bypasses the problem of induction. However, if we view an epistemology as a general theory of learning, a much stronger argument can be given. In effect, Popper tries to show that his epistemology, or something very much like it, cannot be avoided if learning is to be possible. Consider again Hume's attack on induction: logically we are not entitled to believe that the sun will rise tomorrow, but psychologically we expect it will. How do we acquire, or learn to have, this expectation? Hume's answer is that it is a matter of habit or custom arising out of seeing past regularities in nature. It is repetition of similar episodes, of suns rising in the past, that gives rise to expectation. But now Popper points out that logically this account cannot be right. Repetition based on similarity must be construed as repetition-for-us based on similarity-for-us:

> we must respond to situations as if they were equivalent; *take* them as similar; *interpret* them as repetitions (Popper 1963, p. 44).

Similarity is always from a point of view, a prior system of classification. For Popper:

> this means that, for logical reasons, there must always be a point of view — such as a system of expectations, anticipations, assumptions, or interests — *before* there can be any repetition; which point of view, consequently, cannot be merely the result of repetition (Popper 1963, pp. 44–45).

Expectation cannot always arise out of repetition; rather we need some prior expectations in order to identify or classify episodes as repetitions.

Popper thus concludes 'that there is an infinite regress involved in Hume's psychological theory (1963, p. 45). A regress which prevents us from having any expectations. On the other hand, for Popper, the regress stops at *inborn* expectations:

> The theory of inborn *ideas* is absurd, I think; but every organism has inborn *reactions* or *responses*; and among them, responses adapted to impending events. These responses we may describe as 'expectations' without implying that these expectations are conscious (Popper 1963, p. 47).

It is these reactions or responses which provide our first hypotheses, or conjectures, about the world, and which the course of experience from time to time refutes.

Coherentism

We think that Popper's strictures on learning theory are correct and that it is refutation, or *falsification*, that drives the growth of scientific knowledge (and indeed *all* knowledge, since the argument he offers is so general). However, there are important limits to this kind of falsificationism; it cannot be the whole story if we are adequately to explain the very powerful learning strategies of human 'epistemic engines' (Churchland and Churchland 1983, Churchland 1987). In our view, considerations of *coherence* play a major part in directing the process of conjecture and refutation towards the *growth* of knowledge. We propose now to indicate more explicitly what these considerations are, why we need to invoke them and how they may work in the business of justifying knowledge claims.

We have already indicated in general terms what we think are the major extra-empirical virtues of coherent theories: consistency, comprehensiveness, simplicity, conservativeness, fecundity, and explanatory unity. However, like measuring the overall goodness of a state of affairs on even the modest criterion of utility, determining the overall coherence of a theory involves great difficulties. The principal difficulty is with the concept of coherence. Laurence BonJour remarks that:

> Intuitively, coherence is a matter of how well a body of beliefs 'hangs together': how well its component beliefs fit together, agree or dovetail with each other, so as to produce an organized tightly structured system of beliefs . . . (BonJour 1985, p. 93).

But in looking beyond this intuition to detailed philosophical investigations, he adds that work 'has scarcely been begun, despite the long history of the concept' (p. 94). Now in the case of measuring goodness, it is much easier to make relative judgments or comparisons, to say that one state of affairs is better than another, than to give an absolute measure. (As Peter Singer often argues, e.g. 1979, if two systems are equal in all relevant respects, save for the fact that the first inflicts pain and death on animals to provide a bigger variety of foods for humans, then the second is better.) Similarly, in the case of coherence, it is a little easier to make relative judgments, to say that one theory is more, or perhaps less, coherent than another.

While acknowledging oversimplification where there is great complexity and ambiguity, William Lycan suggests five rules for guiding the comparison of two theories, T1 and T2. If the theories are equal in other respects:

1. Prefer T1 to T2 if T1 is simpler than T2.
2. Prefer T1 to T2 if T1 explains more than T2.
3. Prefer T1 to T2 if T1 is more readily testable than T2.
4. Prefer T1 to T2 if T1 leaves fewer messy unanswered questions behind (especially if T2 itself *raises* messy unanswered questions).
5. Prefer T1 to T2 if T1 squares better with what you already have reason to believe (Lycan 1988, p. 130).

Of course, terms like 'simpler' and 'explains' await more detailed elaboration, but at least we have a framework for moving towards the making of particular judgments.

To see why we need such a coherentist framework to augment falsificationist resources, let us begin by following a further suggestion of Lycan's (1988, pp. 117–118) and consider a very simple deductive argument from premises P and Q to some knowledge claim R, expressed as follows:

$$P \, \& \, Q \supset R,$$

or, using more words, if P and Q, then R.

This argument can be expressed in another, equivalent way. Representing the denial, or negation, of R by not-R, the argument is equivalent to the claim that the set

$$\{P, Q, \text{not-R}\} \text{ is inconsistent,}$$

which amounts only to the claim that we must deny one of P, Q, or not-R. The claim that we should deny not-R and conclude R is based on the assumption that P and Q are true. But how is this assumption justified? If a deductive justification is attempted, a regress threatens. To avoid a regress we must end up with nondeductive arguments for our initial premises. We need a basis for declaring some claims in a set to be more plausible than others. How, for example, do we justify asserting P and Q to be more plausible than not-R?

The simplest hypothetico-deductive arguments of traditional empiricism settle the matter by appeals to foundations. Thus, if a theory, T, implies, or predicts, an observation, O, and we observe not-O, then using *modus tollens* (i.e. the argument schema: if p then q, not-q, therefore not-p)

$$((T \supset O) \text{ \& not-O}) \supset \text{not-T}$$

we conclude that the theory has been falsified because the observation is epistemically privileged. That is, we conclude 'not-T' given premises 'not-O' and 'if T then O'. Or, from the inconsistent set

$$(T, \text{ not-O})$$

we deny T. In view of our earlier criticisms of foundationalism, however, this move is not open. In fact two important complications invest the whole business of falsifying theories.

The first concerns the complexity of all test situations. Theories are actually collections of hypotheses associated in various ways. On the very simplest of associations a theory is a conjunction of hypotheses.

$$T = H1 \text{ \& } H2 \text{ \& } H3 \text{ \& } H4 \text{ \& } H5 \text{ \& } \ldots Hn$$

and it is the conjunction that implies or predicts an observation (see Quine 1951)). But when it comes to applying *modus tollens* the resulting inconsistent set, which captures the elements of the conjecture and refutation process is

$$\{H1, H2, H3, \ldots, Hn, \text{ not-O}\}.$$

Of course, not all hypotheses of a theory are involved in deducing O, but logically, all that are can figure as elements in this set. We can still privilege not-O and take the error to reside somewhere in one of the hypotheses of the theory but, from a logical point of view, the fact of falsification leaves open the matter of what hypothesis to amend.

The second concerns theory ladenness. If refuting observations depend on some prior theory, we can represent this as follows:

$$P1 \text{ \& } P2 \text{ \& } P3 \text{ \& } \ldots Pr \supset \text{not-O}$$

where the various Pr are the hypotheses necessary to generate not-O. (These may overlap with Hn.) If we now feed this result back into the *modus tollens* formula, the resulting inconsistent set, representing the complex test situation, becomes

{H1, H2, H3, . . ., Hn, P1, P2, . . ., Pr}.

Since we presume this set contains *all* the relevant hypotheses, empirical and theoretical, the task of determining both whether a refutation obtains and what hypotheses to change, if it is to be done at all, will have to be a matter of looking to that revised set which enjoys the most extra-empirical virtues. (There is much literature on this issue, especially on the question of whether epistemic holism permits crucial experiments. See, e.g., Harding 1976.) Quine offers some suggestions on this task:

> We want to maximize prediction; that is, we want a theory that will anticipate as many observations as possible, getting none of them wrong. We develop the theory by progressive observation and correction. When we have to modify the theory to accommodate a wayward observation sentence, we have various possible corrections from which to choose; and here the guiding considerations are simplicity and conservatism. We prefer the correction that makes for the simpler theory, by our subjective standards of simplicity, unless the other alternative is more conservative, that is, a less drastic departure from the old theory. But a big simplification can warrant a fairly drastic departure. We arbitrate between these two interests, simplicity and conservatism (Quine 1974, p. 137).

Quine does not specify precisely how this process of arbitration takes place, although from his naturalistic epistemology, one might expect that science would eventually provide some kind of answer. This, incidentally, does not boil down to privileging science among the totality of knowledge claims as some kind of foundation. The point, rather, is that by assuming the greater plausibility of some hypotheses, in this case particular scientific ones, we can produce a revised global set that enjoys more extra-empirical virtues than any other set developing under the pressures of guided trial and error. It is the resulting virtues that constitute the justification of this plausibility assumption.

Given that appeal to coherence is unavoidable in the adjudication of theories, or alternatives for improving theories, we have some further suggestions on applying coherence criteria. In defending a new science of administration, one of the strategies we pursue throughout the book is to note that theories of educational administration which assume the falsehood of science put great pressure on maintaining the coherence of global theory. Of course, this point needs to be argued for specific theories over specific issues, but some of the key difficulties can be indicated in more general terms. An obvious incoherence threatens those theories which both attack science and can be shown to presume those features attacked. The same goes for theories that discount the plausibility of a group of scientific hypotheses, on the strength of another group, when by their own (no doubt implicit) reckoning the first group is more plausible than the second. Scope for enhancing explanatory simplicity occurs when the resolution of an inconsistency is guided by positing more hypotheses. In general, we regard posits whose sole virtue is their role in resolving such inconsistency, as *ad hoc* unless they can be deduced from hypotheses remaining in the more coherent set. Where deduction fails we settle for fewer rather than more *ad hoc* additions. Granted the virtue of comprehensiveness, the effect of this premium on simplicity is to penalize theories which specify tasks that outrun their explanatory resources. A number of our criticisms of foundational epistemologies turned on this point: the task of providing certain, or incorrigible knowledge could not be met since the theory used to select foundations and infer consequences was always less than certain. Following Quine, our suggestion for a best theory to account for human knowledge is one that assumes the plausibility of scientific accounts; that treats humans as natural learning systems (Quine 1969).

If refutation, or more precisely, the theory laden recognition of refutation, is the motivation for improving our theories of the world, why not treat fulfilled prediction, or *empirical adequacy*, as the sole criterion of *epistemological adequacy*? Why not just settle for the virtue of consistency between theory and interpreted experience? On this issue we agree with Paul Churchland's argument:

> Since there is no way of conceiving or representing 'the empirical facts' that is completely independent of speculative assumptions, and since we will occasionally confront theoretical alternatives on a scale so comprehensive that we must also choose between competing modes of conceiving what the empirical facts before us *are*, then the epistemic choice between these global alternatives cannot be made by comparing the extent to which they are adequate to some common touchstone, 'the empirical facts'. In such a case, the choice must be made on the comparative global virtues of the two global alternatives, T1-plus-the-observational-evidence-therein-construed, versus T2-plus-the-observational-evidence-therein-(differently)-construed. That is, it must be made on *superempirical* grounds such as relative coherence, simplicity, and explanatory unity (Churchland 1985, pp. 41–42).

In the last chapter we identified two important epistemological influences on much past and current theorizing in educational administration: logical empiricism, and the paradigms approach associated with the views of Kuhn and Feyerabend. In addition to criticizing the epistemological adequacy of appeals to 'the empirical facts' so much endorsed by logical empiricism, Churchland's argument also contains an important comment on the paradigms approach. For if empirical adequacy is all there is to theory choice, and theory ladenness ensures that what counts as evidence is always theory relative, there is no adjudicating between global theories. These theories simply stand for different paradigms, or ways of looking at the world. The question of what the world is really like cannot be raised. Now Churchland's point is that there is more to justification than empirical adequacy. We need to take into account superempirical virtues (or what we have been calling extra-empirical virtues).

One response to Churchland is to say that irrespective of our desire, or need, to choose among global alternatives, that task cannot be done in any nonarbitrary way. Or if choice criteria must be found, why not use length or size of theory rather than coherence? Certainly one of the lessons that Feyerabend drew from the failure of empirical adequacy as a rational criterion for theory choice was that the process of theory choice is, in fact, irrational. Anything goes (Feyerabend 1975). Our approach in Chapter Ten, where we criticize paradigms epistemology in our discussion of research methodology, is to show that coherence is a *touchstone* theoretical virtue, assumed by competing alternative epistemologies. We then argue the incoherence of paradigms. Another defence of Churchland's point might be to argue that our most coherent theory is true. Churchland, himself, is cautious about this kind of defence since he thinks that 'truth' is one concept among a cluster that may be up for revision. In his view terms like 'knowledge', 'belief', 'desire', 'meaning' and 'truth' derive much of their present significance from the role they play in our ordinary everyday commonsense 'folk' theories. He thinks that just as better scientific theories have led to the elimination of many 'folk' notions, so we can expect that in due course even this cluster will succumb (Churchland 1981). We share this view but temper our methodological suggestions in later chapters by the fact that contrary to Churchland's pessimism, folk theories of everyday human behaviours enjoy considerable predictive success. We therefore think that the correspondence issue is worth exploring, and we note one important consideration in its favour.

Since we are concerned with a coherence theory of evidence, or justification, note that this is to be distinguished from a coherence theory of truth. For us, a true theory is one which corresponds to, or matches up with, the way the world is. How we know what the world is like, what objects exist, is something we rely on our best theory to tell us. Once the theory of evidence has done its work, what exists is given by the posits of our best theory, with the details of the correspondence relations between theory and world also being determined by that same theory. The question, then, is why we should expect theories developed and selected according to coherence criteria, to tell us what the world might really be like. BonJour offers the following considerations.

We suppose that our most coherent theory remains stable in the long run despite the addition of sentences that express the theory's interpretation of experience. That is, the theory satisfies in the long term what BonJour calls the 'observation requirement'; it is and remains, by its own reckoning, empirically adequate. But if this condition obtains, it would seem to require explanation:

> If a system of beliefs remains coherent (and stable) over the long run while continuing to satisfy the Observation Requirement, then it is highly likely that there is some explanation (other than mere chance) for this fact . . . [the best explanation for this fact] . . . is that (a) the . . . beliefs which are claimed, within the system, to be reliable are systematically caused by the sorts of situations which are depicted by their content, and (b) the entire system of beliefs corresponds, within a reasonable degree of approximation, to the independent reality which it purports to describe . . . (BonJour 1985, p. 171).

The core of his long and complex argument is his defence of the claim that the best explanation will include the correspondence hypothesis. We do not propose to go into any detail on this, but offer instead one example to illustrate some of the issues involved. Consider the case of your belief that your cat exists. You may think that several of your experiences conspire to make this belief plausible. For example you experience yourself feeding the cat in the morning before you head off for the day, only to return to experience the cat as hungry and in need of another feed. However, a number of networks of hypotheses, or theories, are available to account for these assorted experiences. Descartes' deceitful demon may be at work arranging the flow of your inner experience without the benefit of cats. Another, realist, theory has it that the cat exists as a material body, and continues to exist and undergo certain complex but hidden metabolic processes although it remains unperceived by you throughout the day. In addition to explaining why the unexperienced cat gets hungry during your absence, belief in a real physical cat coheres well with further realist causal accounts of how you acquired your cat beliefs; namely, they are produced by cats. Other alternative theories are possible too. The point, though, is that the realist theory enjoys more extra-empirical virtues than any of its rivals.

This case can be argued in terms of the five rules for theory comparison given earlier. Thus on rule 4, demon theory leaves unexplained why the demon chooses to create the experiences it does. We can try to repair this deficiency by exploring possible *relations* among the experiences, to hypothesize what criteria the demon might use. But if we are successful, it is the criteria that are doing the explanatory work. Rule 1, on simplicity, would therefore counsel us to drop the demon and rework criterial explanations, perhaps in the direction of properties of existent physical objects. Demon theory offends against Rule 3 in not being testable, since every experience, come what may, is demon caused. The theory trivially satisfies the observation requirement. And further arguments can be mounted in terms of the other rules.

Abstracting from further detail, the key point of the strategy is to argue, on coherentist grounds, that the most coherent theory is one whose epistemic virtues obtain because there is a real world for the theory to match, or fail to match up with. As we have said, the above considerations are based on only one example, and so, of course, are incomplete. In addition, we have considered briefly only a few of the features of coherentist patterns of justification. We really need to get down to the business of applying the epistemology in analysis and critique of administrative theories to appreciate the degree to which it can guide theory development, research, and practice. Nevertheless, we hope we have given some idea of why a coherentist epistemological approach to justification is to be preferred, and some suggestions on defending science, the reality of objects posited by science (observable and unobservable), and ultimately, a scientific realist perspective on administrative theory.

Summary

In this chapter we have argued against a number of historically important and influential foundational theories of knowledge, using what we hope are common or touchstone criteria of theoretical adequacy. We distinguished two varieties of strict foundationalism, radical and modest, and two main varieties of broad foundationalism, notably logical empiricism and Popperian falsificationism. Although we used a range of arguments against key features of each position the main strategy remained the same. Essentially, our arguments were directed at showing the *incoherence* of these foundationalist epistemologies. Inasmuch as these arguments were persuasive they amounted to a defence of the touchstone coherence criteria for theoretical adequacy. We concluded by formulating and defending these criteria more explicitly as a coherentist epistemology. Finally, after distinguishing between a coherence theory of evidence and a correspondence theory of truth we gave some reasons for thinking that a coherence theory of evidence will sanction a best theory that corresponds to reality.

References

Armstrong D.M. (1973). *Belief, Truth and Knowledge*. (London: Cambridge University Press).
Austin J.L. (1962). *Sense and Sensibilia*. (London: Oxford University Press).
Ayer A.J. (1956). *The Problem of Knowledge*. (London: Cambridge University Press).
BonJour L. (1985). *The Structure of Empirical Knowledge*. (Cambridge, Mass.: Harvard University Press).
Churchland P.M. (1979). *Scientific Realism and the Plasticity of Mind*. (Cambridge: Cambridge University Press).
Churchland P.M. (1981). Eliminative materialism and the propositional attitudes, *Journal of Philosophy*, **78**(2), pp. 67–90.
Churchland P.M. (1985). The ontological status of observables: in praise of the superempirical virtues, in P.M. Churchland and C.A. Hooker (eds.) *Images of Science*. (Chicago: University of Chicago Press).

Churchland P.S. (1987). Epistemology in the age of neuroscience, *Journal of Philosophy*, **84**(10), pp. 544–553.

Churchland P.S. and Churchland P.M. (1983). Stalking the wild epistemic engine, *Nous*, **17**, pp. 5–18.

Churchland P.S. (1986). *Neurophilosophy*. (Cambridge, Mass.: M.I.T. Press).

Descartes R. (1954). *Descartes Philosophical Writings*. (Middlesex: Nelson. Translated and edited by G.E.M. Anscombe and P.T. Geach).

Feigl H. (1950). Existential hypotheses, *Philosophy of Science*, **17**(1), pp. 35–62.

Feyerabend P.K. (1975). *Against Method*. (London: Verso).

Goodman N. (1979). The new riddle of induction in N. Goodman *Fact, Fiction, and Forecast*. (Hassocks, East Sussex: Harvester Press).

Hacking I. (1985). Do we see through a microscope? in P.M. Churchland and C.A. Hooker (eds.) *Images of Science*. (Chicago: University of Chicago Press).

Hamlyn D.W. (1970). *Theory of Knowledge*. (London: Macmillan).

Hanson N.R. (1968). *Patterns of Discovery*. (New York: Cambridge University Press).

Hanson N.R. (1972). *Observation and Explanation: A Guide to the Philosophy of Science*. (London: George Allen and Unwin).

Harding S.G. (1976) (ed.). *Can Theories be Refuted?* (Dordrecht: Reidel).

Harris C.K. (1979). *Education and Knowledge*. (London: Routledge and Kegan Paul).

Hempel C.G. (1965). Studies in the logic of confirmation, in C.G. Hempel (1965) *Aspects of Scientific Explanation*. (London: Macmillan).

Hume D. (1888). *A Treatise of Human Nature*. (London: Oxford University Press. Selby-Bigge edition).

Lycan W.G. (1988). *Judgement and Justification*. (Cambridge: Cambridge University Press).

Pappas G.S. and Swain M. (1978) (eds.). *Essays on Knowledge and Justification*. (Ithaca: Cornell University Press).

Popper K.R. (1959). *The Logic of Scientific Discovery*. (London: Hutchinson).

Popper K.R. (1963). Science: conjectures and refutations, in K.R. Popper *Conjectures and Refutations: the Growth of Scientific Knowledge*. (London: Routledge and Kegan Paul).

Popper K.R. (1969). Epistemology without a knowing subject, in J.H. Gill (ed.) *Philosophy Today*. Number 2. (Toronto: Macmillan).

Price H.H. (1964). *Perception*. (London: Methuen).

Quine W.V. (1951). Two dogmas of empiricism, *Philosophical Review*, 60, pp. 20–43.

Quine W.V. (1969). Epistemology naturalized, in W.V. Quine, *Ontological Relativity and Other Essays*. (New York: Columbia University Press).

Quine W.V. (1974). *The Roots of Reference*. (La Salle, IL: Open Court).

Quine W.V. (1976). Posits and reality, in W.V. Quine (1976) *Ways of Paradox and Other Essays*. (Cambridge, Mass.: Harvard University Press, revised and enlarged edition).

Quinton A.M. (1973). *The Nature of Things*. (London: Routledge and Kegan Paul).

Ryle G. (1954). *Dilemmas*. (London: Cambridge University Press).

Singer P. (1979). *Practical Ethics*. (Cambridge: Cambridge University Press).

Suppe F. (1974). The search for philosophic understanding of scientific theories, in F. Suppe (ed.) *The Structure of Scientific Theories*. (Chicago: University of Illinois Press).

Unger P. (1971). A defence of scepticism, *Philosophical Review*, **80**(2), pp. 198–219.

Van Fraassen B. (1980). *The Scientific Image*. (Oxford: Clarendon Press).

Williams M. (1977). *Groundless Belief: An Essay on the Possibility of Epistemology*. (Oxford: Blackwell).

3
The Theory Movement: Past and Present

The main facts concerning the development of educational administration as an area of study are covered well enough in most introductory texts. Hoy and Miskel (1987, pp. 8–30), for example, distinguish three broad phases of development. The first, beginning from about 1900, is classical organizational thought which includes the work of such influential writers as Frederic Taylor (1911, 1947) on scientific management; Henri Fayol of Fayol's Elements: 'to plan, to organize, to command, to co-ordinate, and to control' (Fayol 1949, p. 10); and Luther Gulick and Lyndall Urwick (1937), who extended Fayol's Elements to POSDCORB (planning, organization, staffing, directing, co-ordinating, reporting, and budgeting). Taylor, Fayol, and Urwick had engineering backgrounds and it would be fair also to describe this period as the beginning of what Gross calls the 'gospel of efficiency' (Gross 1964, p. 34).

The second phase, which developed partly as a reaction against scientific management techniques, is characterized by the human relations approach. Its beginnings date from around 1930, or a little earlier, and its most influential pioneers are Mary Parker Follett (Metcalf and Urwick 1940) with her work on human integration and the resolution of conflict, and Elton Mayo and Fritz Roethlisberger of the Hawthorne studies (Mayo 1933, Roethlisberger and Dickson 1939). Although there are major differences between Follett's work and that of Mayo and Roethlisberger — for example, Follett studied managers as well as workers, whereas the Hawthorne studies are concerned with shop floor production and contain findings that might readily be incorporated into the efficiency equations of scientific managers — nevertheless, this phase denotes the rise of a significant concern for human relations in administrative theory and practice.

The third phase which Hoy and Miskel distinguish is the behavioural science approach. Chester Barnard (1938) and Herbert Simon are the important early figures identified. Simon's (1945) book contains an interesting discussion of much of this early history of administrative theory.

Although ideas from all these roughly delineated traditions continue to exert influence on current thinking and research in educational administration, our principal concern in this chapter is with that strand of the behavioural science approach that has been developed most systematically in educational administration and has been the dominant orthodoxy; namely, the body of research committed to the scientific study of educational organizations as complex systems. From this considerable literature we have further selected two areas in which to begin our more detailed philosophical reflections and critiques of administrative theories. The first, which we introduced in Chapter One, is the Theory Movement (Culbertson 1981) which marks the beginnings of a systematic traditional science approach to educational administration. The second, which we refer to as the 'new orthodoxy', reflects current attempts at traditional science of administration. We take Hoy and Miskel's *Educational Administration: Theory, Research and Practice* to be an important representative presentation of this perspective, and discuss it in considerable detail.

Despite a span of over 30 years between these two ends of the behavioural science programme, we believe that similar philosophical views have shaped and influenced key elements of each approach. We have already indicated, and shall elaborate below, that Herbert Feigl's account of scientific theory exerted a powerful influence on the thought and development of educational administration in the 1950s. It may come as a surprise, therefore, that in the late 1980s Hoy and Miskel are able to say:

> Some agreement is apparent in the field of educational administration that the definition of theory produced by Herbert Feigl is an adequate starting point (Hoy and Miskel 1987, p. 2).

Of course, the epistemological difficulties associated with logical empiricism are now more widely known, and this definition and its associated philosophy are not as conspicuous in their operation as they were in the 1950s. Part of the reason may lie in the shift towards pragmatism occasioned by Donald Willower's important theoretical writings. Hoy and Miskel acknowledge as much when they say of their book: 'The perspective of this text is open-ended and pragmatic' (1987, p. 28). See Willower (1975, 1980, 1981, 1983, 1985), for writings which capture his attempt to broaden the notion of science in a more flexible pragmatic direction. Still, Hoy and Miskel continue to champion operational definition as desirable 'from a scientific point of view', concluding: 'the researcher must be able to define the concept in measurable terms' (Hoy and Miskel 1987, p. 4). And there is the usual omission of ethics and the full range of research practices now increasingly commonplace in educational research (see Keeves 1988 for a recent compendium); so it is reasonable to suppose that the Feigl definition and associated philosophical methodology are still doing some work. Just how much work it still does, and what consequences flow from it for modern administrative theory, is the subject of our later discussion.

Perhaps the most noticeable difference is the shift that has taken place in the scope of administrative theory. The Theory Movement's expectation of being able to produce a hypothetico-deductive structure of law-like generalizations for administrative phenomena was sustained in part by an excessively narrow view of the range of relevant admissible causes. Organizations tended to be analysed as *closed systems*. From the 1960s onwards, there has been a growing appreciation in the field of the explanatory relevance of extra-organizational factors. Environment and culture, for example, are believed to be causally significant in shaping administrative outcomes and options, and need to be reflected in theorizing. Theories of culture, class, the economy, ethnicity and gender have thus gained a place within comprehensive administrative theories.

In our view, the full implications of combining foundationalist epistemology with an open systems approach have yet to be fully appreciated. True, researchers in traditional behavioural science have become less ambitious in their expectations of theory. But the lessons of complexity and enlarged theoretical scope which functioned to undermine familiar empiricist assumptions about the relationship between empirical evidence and theory spill over into open system accounts. After our discussion of the Theory Movement and the 'new orthodoxy' we offer some reflections on two issues to demonstrate the consequences of approaching open systems from an epistemologically holistic perspective. The direction of our critique is not so much against a behavioural science context for administrative theorizing as against the use of traditional, epistemologically foundationalist, views of science. Similarly, although we applaud the recognition of causal complexity that talk of open systems brings, we are cautious about the status of the substantive empirical claims — claims about adaption levels and equilibrium conditions — needed to turn the systems metaphor into a constraint on the construction of administrative theories.

The Theory Movement: Some Philosophical Influences

Two theorists warrant special attention as important influences on the development of educational administration as a discipline. The first is H. A. Simon, who through his book *Administrative Behavior*, established a powerful, indeed dazzling exemplar of administrative theory. Although we need not concern ourselves with its details, we should note that by his own admission some of its most important features flow directly from his philosophical assumptions. Consider, for example, his account of a distinction between facts and values. This alleged distinction forms the cornerstone of Simon's main early contribution to administration theory: his account of administration as a process of decision making under conditions of bounded rationality. And how does it depend on philosophy? In Simon's words:

> This distinction proves to be a very fundamental one for administration. It leads first of all to an understanding of what is meant by a 'correct' administrative decision. Secondly, it clarifies the distinction, so often made in the literature of administration, between policy questions and questions of administration . . . To ground an answer to these questions on first principles would require that this volume on administration be prefaced by an even larger philosophical treatise. The necessary ideas are already accessible in the literature of philosophy. Hence, the conclusions reached by a particular school of modern philosophy — logical positivism — will be accepted as a starting point, and their implications for the theory of decisions examined (Simon 1945, p. 45).

The literature of philosophy that Simon refers to in a footnote to this passage includes the works of Charles Morris, Rudolf Carnap, P. W. Bridgman, and A. J. Ayer, and there can be little doubt that his views on ethics are indeed congruent with views expressed by these writers. Moreover, it is easy enough to trace some of the epistemological influences of this kind of approach to ethics purely to Simon's answer to the two questions, 'What is a "correct" administrative decision?' and 'What is the distinction between policy questions and questions of administration?' In evaluating an administrative decision, strictly speaking what is evaluated for Simon is the factual relationship that is purported to hold between the decision and its aims (Simon 1945, p. 49). Inasmuch as aims involve an ethical dimension they are either 'given' or else are 'means' to achieve further 'givens'. Where the regress of 'givens' halts is in subjective human values or preferences; at which point there is no fact of the matter, no further question of correctness. However, at the level of rational decision making in organizations, decisions 'must take as theoretical premises the objectives that have been set for the organisation' (Simon 1945, p. 52). In general, therefore, a correct administrative decision for Simon is one that makes for the realization of certain 'given' values in a given situation (Simon 1945, p. 76).

Now granted that values are being treated as givens in this analysis, the correctness of an administrative decision is a factual matter. There is a fact of the matter concerning whether the deployment of resources in realizing goals or objectives or values is effective or efficient. In externalizing values in this way, the question of their origin and status is left open, to be adjudicated by other means. In Simon's usage — a not uncommon usage, incidentally — the arena in which these further issues are formulated and adjudicated is known as *policy*. Hence, for Simon, although the distinction between policy and administration is not always easy to draw in terms of the kinds of considerations that are relevant, it maps onto the distinction between value and fact.

Although Simon's book was in the field of public administration and made no mention of educational administration, it had considerable theoretical scope, partly because of the very general theoretical vocabulary employed, and partly because it attempted to derive a theory of administration 'from the logic and psychology of choice' (Simon 1945, p. xlvi). It also purported to be scientific. For any field of administration concerned with the development of theory, Simon's work could hardly be ignored; and such a concern had clearly developed in educational administration in the 1950s. Writing in 1957, Andrew Halpin claimed that a number of investigators had noted the need for a 'theory' of administration, including Barnard, Leighton, and Simon a decade or more earlier. However, he went on to remark that the cogency of this need

> . . . for educational administration has been recognized only within the past few years, especially by Coladarci and Getzels, Cornell, Griffiths, and Walton. These men have deplored the fact that educational research has relied too heavily upon naive empiricism and has failed to pay sufficient heed to the role of theory (Halpin 1957, p. 156).

And for Halpin, '"theory" in this context refers to "theory" as defined in science, a hypothetico-deductive type of theory' (1957, p. 156). Because the term 'theory' is used in science in several ways, Halpin recommended, finally, the account given by Herbert Feigl (1951).

In 1959, Dan Griffiths, one of the contributors to theory in educational administration that Halpin referred to, reflected on what had been accomplished and why:

> What are the factors which have caused a revolution in the field of educational administration? Interest in theory . . . is relatively recent in educational administration. The field has always been oriented to the 'practical', to the exclusion of theory in a scientific sense. Since 1946 there have been several events which have been the building blocks upon which the present interest in theory is based. The events have ranged from the writings of a single individual to the formation of a national organization. Taken together, they constitute the ingredients which have revolutionized a whole field of human endeavour (Griffiths 1959, pp. 2–3).

Griffiths went on to comment in detail on some of these events. He mentioned, for example, the formation of the National Conference of Professors of Educational Administration in 1947, the inauguration of the Cooperative Program in Educational Administration in 1950, and the formation of the

University Council for Educational Administration in 1956 (Griffiths 1959, pp. 3–5).

Now, whatever organizational structures might have facilitated research on the contribution of theory to educational administration, the direction of that research certainly depended critically on how theory was understood; and once again the influences of philosophy loomed large. For according to Griffiths:

> the logical positivist position that the data of man's social life lend themselves to scientific study in the same manner as do those of physics or biology, so long as we are careful not to confuse the 'is' and the 'ought', has received strong support in the literature of administration (Griffiths 1959, p. 17).

In a footnote to this passage, Griffiths cites as evidence the work of Halpin, Simon, and J. D. Thompson (who contributes to a volume edited by Halpin). Explicitly on the nature of theory, Griffiths goes on to say:

> Halpin suggests that we accept Feigl's use of 'theory' as the standard and that researchers and theoreticians restrict the use of the word as does Feigl. We agree that this is a needed step (Griffiths 1959, p. 28).

In view of the prominence of both Halpin and Griffiths in the movement to develop a science of educational administration based on a particular scientific model of theory, the influence of Feigl as chief source of that model is surely significant. Indeed, if Simon's views can be said to warrant special attention in understanding the development of the Theory Movement, then it seems entirely appropriate that Feigl's views, especially on the nature of science and theory, should also warrant special attention. We do not propose to go into any detail on this matter, though we think we can clear up a number of misunderstandings that have crept into the literature.

For both theorists within the Theory Movement and historians of it, Feigl is the quintessential positivist. A former member of the Vienna Circle, he is quite rightly regarded as having given the Circle's philosophy its internationally accepted label, 'logical positivism', by the publication (with A.E. Blumberg) of 'Logical positivism: a new movement in European philosophy', in the May 1931 issue of the *Journal of Philosophy*. When he arrived in America in the autumn of 1930 he was, by his own admission, 'deeply imbued with the spirit of the Vienna Circle' (Feigl 1974b, p. 38). He saw himself as 'an *enfant terrible* . . . on the American philosophical scene . . . somewhat like Alfred Ayer in England' (1974b, p. 38). In short, if anyone could claim to be a logical positivist, it would appear that Feigl could. The first misunderstanding to be cleared up therefore, is the belief that the writings of Feigl referred to by the educational administrators of the Theory Movement reflect the doctrines of logical positivism, the beliefs of the Vienna Circle. They do not.

The basis for sorting out this misunderstanding, and the one most easily documented, is the observation that Feigl changed his mind about a number of important Vienna Circle doctrines. Consider, for example, what Feigl in his 1931 paper on logical positivism took to be the central problem of epistemology, namely, how do we know the meaning of a proposition. The answer he gives is: 'To know the meaning of a proposition is to know what must be the case if the proposition is true' (Blumberg and Feigl 1931, p. 287). He gives in short, a version of the verificationist theory of meaning. Complex propositions can be broken down by the apparatus of logic to simple or atomic propositions by showing what experiences verify them, or make them true.

Unfortunately, this formulation obscures at least one ambiguity lurking in the term 'experience'. 'Experience' can be taken to refer to sense data, that is, the subjective content of our perceptions; or it can be taken to refer to physical objects. For a reductive phenomenalism, our claims are true because we have certain kinds of sensations. For an empirical realist they are true because that is the way the physical world happens to be. Feigl inclined to the realist view, while the Vienna Circle positivists tended to support a phenomenalist, antirealist position. With regard to his own contribution to the Circle on this matter, Feigl now says:

> Although I had been in the 'loyal opposition' in regard to the positivism of the Vienna Circle, I had a hard time maintaining against them the sort of critical realism that I had originally learned. . . . Their brilliant and powerful argument overwhelmed me temporarily (Feigl 1974a, p. 9).

When the tide turned in the early 1930s with Carnap's adoption of a more realist perspective, Feigl viewed that change, together with Carnap's subsequent abandonment of reductive phenomenalism and logical behaviourism, 'with a sense of triumphant vindication' (Feigl 1974b, p. 39). As early as 1935 he accordingly abandoned the label first announced in his 'notorious fanfare article' (1974b, p. 38), and adopted the new description 'logical empiricism.'

A further reason for this change in Feigl's view was the influence of Karl Popper. As Popper recalls it in his autobiography, 'in 1929 or 1930 . . . I met another member of the Vienna Circle, Herbert Feigl'. Feigl . . . told me not only that he found my ideas important, almost revolutionary, but also that I should publish them in book form' (Popper 1976, p. 82). The resulting book, *Logik der Forschung* (later expanded, revised, and published in English in 1959 as *The Logic of Scientific Discovery*), was published late in 1934, and was, in part, a criticism of Vienna Circle positivism. Indeed, so successful, apparently, was this criticism and others made in conversation that Popper felt able to answer his question 'Who killed logical positivism?' with, 'I fear that I must admit responsibility' (Popper 1976, p. 88). The essence of Popper's criticism was his attack on the problem of induction. This problem, as we saw in the last chapter, was raised more forcefully by the classical empiricist David Hume, and is, roughly speaking, the problem of justifying the inference from

all observed X are Y

to   all X are Y.

The difficulty is that no finite number of observations can ever confirm, or verify, a universal statement. For the logical positivists, who saw the meaning of a statement as residing in its method of verification, this problem was acute. For the law statements of science, those paradigms of scientific knowledge, cannot even in principle be verified as universal generalizations, and so are meaningless. Or at least their meaning depends on the soundness of some principle of induction. But according to Popper,

> . . . there is no such thing as induction. Thus inference to theories, from singular statements which are 'verified by experience' (whatever that may mean), is logically inadmissible. Theories are, therefore, never empirically verifiable (Popper 1959, p. 40).

For Popper, scientific knowledge consists of networks of hypotheses — both universal and singular — which imply observations that can be tested. However, at best, these tests can merely falsify hypotheses, they cannot confirm them. On this noninductive hypothetico-deductive model, knowledge grows through a series of conjectures and refutations, with good theories being those that have been subject to, and have survived, the most severe testing.

Feigl did not accept all of Popper's criticisms, especially the criticisms of induction, but he did come to see the hypothetico-deductive method as a powerful device for securing empirical realism, for assuming or hypothesizing physical objects. After 'liberation from the narrower logical positivism' Feigl could argue:

> It is of the essence of the hypothetico-deductive method of cognition to make assumptions, to grant oneself the latitude of postulates. It is the typical phobia of positivism and radical empiricism to shy away from such latitude. But the redeeming feature of the hypothetico-deductive method is precisely that its conclusions are permanently open to criticism and refutation (Feigl 1974b, pp. 51–52).

The statements in a network of hypotheses, even the universals, come out as meaningful because, following Carnap, Feigl requires merely that they be indirectly or incompletely testable.

From both an epistemological and a semantic viewpoint, Feigl's logical empiricism is a far more flexible and accommodating doctrine than the logical positivism of the Vienna Circle. Indeed, by the later 1940s, it had mellowed to the point where Feigl could argue for a rapprochement between his philosophically based naturalism and the American humanist tradition. In his much cited paper 'The scientific outlook: naturalism and humanism', Feigl contended that:

> the philosophical foundations of both science and the humanities are widely misconceived; and that the frequently held claim of their basic incompatibilities arises out of philosophical prejudices which, owing to cultural lag, have unfortunately not as yet been completely relegated to oblivion (Feigl 1953, p. 8).

He denied that science could be identified with mechanistic reductionism, maintaining that philosophy, under the impact of science, was abandoning its grandiose claims in favour of the humbler task of exploring the foundations of human knowledge and values, and suggested that human values such as freedom, responsibility, rights, and obligation could be both disengaged from their theological and metaphysical ideologies yet be supported by 'increasingly adequate and nonreductive analyses' (Feigl 1953, p. 9). The account he gives of scientific knowledge, method, and theory, ironically because it is principally concerned with description, explanation, and prediction, is equally benign and reassuring, and will repay more lengthy quotation.

> The quest for scientific knowledge is therefore regulated by certain standards or criteria which may best be formulated in the form of ideals to be approximated, but perhaps never fully attained. The most important of these regulative ideals are:
>
> 1. *Intersubjective Testability.* This is only a more adequate formulation of what is generally meant by the 'objectivity' of science. What is here involved is not only the freedom from personal or cultural bias or partiality, but — even more fundamentally — the requirement that the knowledge claims of science be in principle capable of test . . .
>
> 2. *Reliability, or a Sufficient Degree of Confirmation.* This second criterion of scientific knowledge enables us to distinguish what is generally called 'mere opinion' (or worse still, 'superstition') from knowledge (well-substantiated belief). . . . Modern techniques of experimentation and of statistical analysis are the most powerful tools we have in the

discernment between chance and law and hence the best means of enhancing the reliability of knowledge . . .

3. *Definiteness and Precision.* This obvious standard of scientific method requires that the concepts used in the formulation of scientific knowledge claims be as definitely delimited as possible. . . . On the level of quantitative science the exactitude of the concepts is enormously enhanced through the techniques of measurement . . .

4. *Coherence or Systematic Structure* . . . a well-connected account of the facts is what we seek in science. . . . Explanation in science consists in the hypothetico-deductive procedure. The laws, theories, or hypotheses form the premises from which we derive logically, or logico-mathematically, the observed or observable facts . . .

5. *Comprehensiveness or Scope of Knowledge* . . . Not only through bold and sweeping hypotheses, but especially through the ingenious devices by means of which they are tested, science acquires a reach far beyond the limits of our unaided senses. . . . The resulting increase in the completeness of our knowledge is, of course, popularly the most impressive feature of science . . . (Feigl 1953, pp. 11–12).

In view of the perceived scope and elegance of Simon's model of scientific administrative theory, and given the benign parsimony of Feigl's alleged positivism, it is hardly surprising that the most influential theorists of the Theory Movement saw in Feigl's work an account of science and theory that could readily and plausibly be fashioned to meet the needs of a new science of educational administration. To see how this philosophical work affected the task of theorizing about educational administration, and to explore how some of the objections we raised against foundational empiricisms might apply, we examine a little more closely the early work of the most important theorist of the Theory Movement, Daniel Griffiths.

Logical Empiricism and Griffiths's Administrative Theory

We can begin by noting Griffiths's claim that

> . . . if the study of administration is to become scientific, administration must assume the characteristics of a science. Inquiry in administration must come to be characterized by objectivity, reliability, operational definitions, coherence or systematic structure, and comprehensiveness. The content of administration is capable of being handled in a scientific manner even though it is not now being handled in that manner (Griffiths 1959, p. 45).

Griffiths also thought that administrative theory had the additional functions of guiding action, explaining the nature of administration, and leading to new facts and systematic knowledge about administration. Note that his five requirements for guiding inquiry in administration are based on the five features of science that Feigl expounds in his 'Scientific outlook' article. Similarly, Griffiths's account of administrative theory and its functions is based on Feigl's definition of theory as a set of assumptions from which we may derive a set of empirical laws (Griffiths 1959, p. 28).

As modest and as abstract as these formulations appear, they nevertheless exert powerful constraints on the way Griffiths theorizes, on how he structures his own theory, and on how he represents the theories of others. This assessment may come as a surprise in view of the way Griffiths himself, in 1983, saw matters. Reviewing the connection between philosophy of science and research in administration he remarks:

> A reasonable conclusion to be reached from a review of the prevalent philosophy of science and the four prominent studies of the late 1950s and early 1960s is that they were little related. Although the prevalent scientific philosophy in the rhetoric of the day was logical positivism, no study or line of studies was done completely in the positivist mode (Griffiths 1983, pp. 206–207).

However, we feel it is one thing to say 'they were little related' and another to say that no study 'was done completely in the positivist mode'. If our criticisms of foundational empiricisms are correct nothing can be completely done in the so-called positivist mode because that mode is false. Nothing actually matches up with the mode's descriptions of knowledge, inquiry, and the process of justification. What Griffiths draws attention to, with his focus on empirical studies, is a standard symptom of bad philosophical theory; namely, its failure to imply successful empirical practice. But then philosophical theories can manifest flaws in other ways. For us, the decisive test of logical empiricism's influence is how it figures in the construction, design, and justification of administrative theories; in short, the constraints it imposes on theorizing. We turn then to Griffiths's most systematic presentation of his early position on administration, *Administrative Theory*, and note three ways in which philosophical constraints are manifested.

First, as a consequence of Feigl's hypothetico-deductive framework partitioning statements into hypotheses and testable consequences, Griffiths places great emphasis on identifying and articulating the core assumptions of his theory; for from these will be derived 'a larger set of empirical laws' (Griffiths 1959, pp. 71–74). The empirical laws are not quite forthcoming, but in their place Griffiths does specify a set of testable propositions, some major, some minor, which all taken together represent a serious attempt to create a hypothetico-deductive structure (Griffiths 1959, pp. 89–91). True, there are no purely logico-mathematical derivations as Feigl's framework requires, but then administrative theory, then and now, is not a quantitatively formalized theory. Some of its individual claims, though, do admit of formalization into mathematical expressions. (For an example, see Griffiths 1959, p. 89.) What is in place, however, is the basic logical empiricist epistemological structure for justifying theories. So both the design and the evidential value of administrative theories appear, in Griffiths's examples, to be determined by the structural and testability requirements of logical empiricism.

Second, Griffiths places great store on establishing operational definitions of terms: 'One of the major problems in theory construction is the development of operational concepts' (Griffiths 1959, p. 46). On this matter his authorities are Simon, Bridgman, and Hempel, in addition to Feigl. Of course, as we have seen, for the logical empiricist (and positivist), operational definitions are important because they provide an obvious way in which theoretical terms can be given empirical content. It is a requirement imposed by theory of meaning. In his own account of administration as decision making, Griffiths goes to some trouble to meet this requirement in defining his own key theoretical terms; for example, terms like 'decision making', 'organization', 'power' and 'authority'.

Third, as we indicated earlier in noting Griffiths's support of Halpin on the matter, his account of scientific administrative theory eschews values, essentially for the reason that unlike propositions of fact, they 'cannot be verified empirically' (Griffiths 1959, p. 17). And he follows on by citing Thompson (1958) approvingly:

> The values capable of being attached to education and to administration will not be incorporated into the theoretical system itself; rather the system will treat such values as variables (Griffiths 1959, p. 17).

On this analysis, values as propositional claims cannot be incorporated into a proper theory of administration. The fact that people have certain values, or make value judgments, or assert value claims in ways which affect the practice of administration, is handled by treating values as *variables*. So strictly speaking, administrative theory has no contribution to make to the question of whether organizations should function efficiently, or effectively, or whether managers who make mistakes should be shot, and so on, except perhaps where these values need to be realized as means to meet other (valuable) ends.

We have already seen, from the discussion in the first chapter, that it is possible to raise specific objections to the philosophical doctrines underlying these constraints on theorizing. And we have also seen something of the broad nonfoundational epistemological framework that is the source of these specific objections. We now draw together both sorts of consideration briefly to evaluate their effect on these three points.

The first point to note is that there is no sharp epistemological line to be drawn between the observation reports that figure in the testing of hypotheses, and the hypotheses themselves. We now know that observation reports either employ items of theoretical vocabulary, or, more generally, depend for their warrant on the warrantability of a background network of hypotheses or theories. Because our observational evidence is thus theory laden, coherence considerations can even lead us to use existing theory to correct observations. One of the clearest examples of this in the history of science was when Newton used his theory of optics to correct the Astronomer Royal, Flamsteed's, observational evidence. There is thus no need for administrative theories to meet the narrow and austere standards of structure that were thought necessary by the thinkers of the Theory Movement. There remains, of course, a premium on precision and exactness of formulation, and where there are generalizations to be tested the *modus tollens* logical structure of a simple hypothetico-deductive argument provides a good place to start. But complexity of test situation and theory ladenness together conspire to diminish the value of such arguments as justifications. Justification is rather a matter of theoretical economy and total coherence of global theory. So the value of logical structure in theory does not lie in efficiently mediating the deduction of confirmations or disconfirmations. It lies, instead, in the mediating of evidence for the extra-empirical virtues of theory.

Second, just as the empirical evidence for a hypothesis cannot be associated merely with a particular range of sensory experience as expressed in, say, an observation report, so evidence for meaning must likewise distribute over the whole body of variously linked and interconnected statements, our whole fabric of theory. This means that there is no semantic premium on operational definitions. Theoretical terms derive what meaning they have largely by virtue of their role in a comprehensive network of hypotheses, the whole network being the smallest unit of empirical significance. Since the meanings of most of the terms used in administrative theory derive initially from the causal and inferential roles of those terms in ordinary commonsense folk theories, the chief advantage of operational definitions, where they can be provided, lies in enhancing precision. This is probably a virtue on anyone's reckoning, but terms do not fail to be meaningful for want of it. It is still possible for theorists to stipulate an operational definition for a term, but unless the definition enjoys rich intertheoretical inferential connections, it is difficult to see how it could be very useful. Our example of defining 'length' in terms of the operations performed with a particular kind of ruler is a case in point.

For these reasons it is best to see the quest for operational definitions as really a quest for enhancing the precision of antecedently meaningful terms; especially where measurement is an advantage. Such definitions thus alter existing inferential properties derived from antecedently learned theory, hopefully in the direction of more rigorous, and powerful theory. This accords well with Quine's insight that we build up our most sophisticated theory from infancy onwards, perhaps to the point where, by virtue of altered conceptual role, a term may come to mean something quite different from what it first meant. The big advantage in this approach for those constructing theories is that it accounts for, and sanctions, the gradual and piecemeal nature of much theory construction. It also sanctions a more pragmatic and experimental approach.

Third, a corollary of our epistemological holism is that if ethical statements, or hypotheses, are to be found among the web of our learned beliefs, it is not possible to quarantine ethical statements as somehow meaningless or devoid of empirical content. They are acquired under the same empirical pressures of interpreting experience as all our other beliefs. They may be true or false, like many of our other beliefs but, on any plausible learning theory, they are not massively disconnected from the patterned firings of our sensory apparatus. On the other hand, empirical evidence for ethical claims does not appear to cluster as required for traditional empiricist versions of confirmation and disconfirmation. Since this is also true of high-level theoretical claims, our response is to treat ethical claims as theoretical and conclude 'so much the worse for the demands of traditional empiricisms'. The upshot is that ethical theory can be a part of a comprehensive theory of administration. Precisely what ethical claims in their administrative contexts are justified, is a complex and controversial epistemological question, and we offer some suggestions for a framework for ethics in a later chapter. Our point, however, is that this epistemological complexity and controversy is not an adequate ground for excluding ethical statements from among the propositions of administrative theory.

We have formulated these three responses with an eye not only to providing alternatives to logical empiricist constraints on administrative theorizing, but providing alternatives that can guide theory development. Fortunately, our case for a new science of administration does not depend on us actually developing such a science in detail. Analysis and coherentist epistemological critique provide a sufficient starting point. Still, the further guidelines we provide here, and scattered throughout, should be useful in the larger task of developing a systematic (broadened) science of administration, a task well beyond the scope of this book.

The New Orthodoxy

In addition to its philosophical critics, logical empiricism, particularly as applied in the administrative theories of the Theory Movement, has had its critics over the years from within educational administration. For example, in a review essay published 12 years after his 1957 'A paradigm for research on administrative behaviour' paper, Andrew Halpin suggested that educational administration was then 'between movements', and that 'the "new movement" had not fulfilled its promise' (Halpin 1969). Griffiths himself has since 1966 become more critical of (what he terms) logical positivism noting, for example, that:

> The first thing wrong with logical positivism in educational administration was that developments in theory started and stopped with it (Griffiths 1985, p. 49).

He also points out, amongst other things, that the restricted notion of science held by the logical positivists was inadequate because of the 'theoretical-observational dichotomy' which, following Putnam, he believes to be untenable (1985, p. 51). Nevertheless, Griffiths cannot quite bring himself to break with what he once considered the

> . . . proper antidote for the self-serving testimonials, the pseudo-theories of Mort and Sears, and the plain nonsense that constituted the field of educational administration (Griffiths 1985, p. 49).

He continues to give qualified support to operationalism and the value-freedom of science. While the field of educational administration acknowledges the problems and weaknesses of positivism, it is nevertheless true, according to Griffiths, that prominent present researchers and writers of popular textbooks continue to 'use a strictly positivist definition of theory' (Griffiths 1983, p. 216) and that they work within the structural-functionalist framework. (For a reply to some of these points see Miskel 1984.)

If the Theory Movement of the 1950s and 1960s, which assumed logical positivist epistemology and considered organizations as closed systems, represents the 'old orthodoxy', then open systems and contingency theory can be said to represent the 'new orthodoxy' in educational administration from the 1970s onwards. In a later section we examine the important and influential version of the open systems view expounded in Wayne K. Hoy and Cecil G. Miskel's widely read textbook *Educational Administration: Theory, Research and Practice* (1987). In our view, it serves two purposes well: on the one hand, it allows us to demonstrate how the text continues the epistemological and theoretical beliefs of the Theory Movement, albeit in modified form; on the other, it enables us to discuss some problems of functionalism and functionalist explanation inherent in the open systems perspective.

Recent Shifts in Organizational Theory

Developments in organizational theory since the 1960s have been complex and have taken a number of different directions which cannot possibly be described here. (See Meyer 1978, Scott 1981, Burrell and Morgan 1982, Perrow 1983, Hoy and Miskel 1987.) Following Scott (1978) it is, however, safe to say that the major shift which has taken place is that the dominant closed systems model of the 1950s and 1960s was replaced by the view of organizations as open systems. Probably the most prominent organizational theory in this new perspective is Lawrence and Lorsch's (1967) 'contingency theory'. Others are the natural selection model of Hannan and Freeman (1977) and Aldrich (1979), as well as Weick's (1969) social-psychological application, and Pfeffer and Salancik's (1978) resource-dependence model. The main characteristic of all these theories is that they 'emphasize the importance for the organization of events and processes external to it' (Scott 1978, p. 21). Indeed, although closed systems thinking continues, this shift was so marked that, writing in 1978, Meyer declared the systems debate closed, 'on the side of openness' (Meyer 1978, p. 18).

These developments in the parent discipline were directly reflected, and accepted, in educational administration so that Hoy could state: 'there is now a general consensus that modern organizations, including educational ones, are open systems' (Hoy 1982, p. 2). By being able to focus on processes and activities 'outside' school organizations, the open systems, or in Willower's (1982) term 'context', perspective facilitated discussion of issues which, allegedly, did not come into the purview of the closed or rational model of the early Theory Movement. Amongst these are the role of women and racial minorities in administration, and the unions — issues raised by Griffiths (1979) — and more generally, the turbulence and political unrest experienced in the United States in the 1960s and 1970s (Hoy 1982). In fact, Bidwell (1979), in a critical reappraisal of his influential closed systems-based 'The school as a formal organization' (1965), points out that the environment of schools was relatively placid when he first wrote about formal organization, making such a perspective a plausible approach. In his updated version, he is concerned to develop a 'dynamic theory of educational production' (Bidwell 1979, p. 115) which, since it must necessarily include the school-environment nexus, is based on an open systems view. He strongly endorses modern human ecology as the 'most promising avenue for the development of dynamic open-systems theory of *any* variety of social organization (p. 116). From this new vantage point he joins the critics of closed systems thinking which has

. . . approached organizations as if they were machines. The organization-as-machine is a system that remains undisturbed by events outside its boundary, unless a prime mover of some kind — most often in these theories either an entrepreneur or top-level administrator — intervenes to change parts of the system or change the ways existing parts act on one another. . . . This Newtonian version of organizational theory sets aside problems of dynamics and environments (Bidwell 1979, p. 111).

It is also characteristic of such systems that they have only a single feedback channel which does not allow for a more complex notion of feedback from environment (p. 112).

Features of General and Open Systems

In order to evaluate the conception of open systems in educational administration itself, we first need to consider briefly some key features of general and open systems. Following Litterer's (1969, p. 4) description, the most frequently cited characteristic of a system is that it is made up of interrelated objects, attributes, and events. In the study of organizations, Litterer believes, as do Hoy and Miskel who have adopted the open systems perspective in the third edition of their text, that we need to

> . . . recognize that we are concerned with the interrelationships of people. . . . If we are going to explain adequately their various movements in regard to each other, we must determine what attributes are peculiarly involved with this interrelatedness (Litterer 1969, p. 118).

A methodologically awkward consequence of interdependence is that a change in one part of the system results in changes or adjustments in all the others. A second feature is *holism* which is often expressed by saying that the whole is greater than the sum of its parts. This feature also raises problems for systems theory, as Litterer explains:

> Is a set of bricks just a wall, or is it part of a building, is the building part of a city, is the city part of a nation? Any element contributes to a system, but all too typically that system is part of another system, and the question then is, 'What is the system under study?' (Litterer 1969, p. 4).

The answer, Litterer suggests, depends on what particular system the observer is interested in defining. General, including social, systems such as organizations, exist over time and consist in

> . . . the patterned activities of a number of individuals . . . [and] are complementary or interdependent with respect to some common output or outcome. . . . If the activity pattern occurs only once or at unpredictable intervals, we could not speak of an organization (Katz and Kahn 1983, pp. 98–99).

The observed stability of many complex systems is a third feature, often explained in terms of the system's return to equilibrium after it has been disturbed, following the second law of thermodynamics. Another way of describing this activity is to say that the system is apparently goal-oriented. Complex systems may have more than one point of equilibrium, and have thus an inbuilt potential for conflict since not all equilibria, or 'goals', can be achieved simultaneously. The fourth characteristic is that systems are self-regulating by means of either adjustment, control (involving feedback), and learning. Fifth, systems are defined by their inputs and outputs. For open systems, interaction with the environment is essential for system functioning. Sixth, the output of a system is not the same as the input received: transformation has taken place. Seventh, systems may harbour other, less complex, systems. Examining these subsystems is the main avenue for analysis in general systems theory. The eighth feature is entropy which differentiates closed from open systems. In Katz and Kahn's formulation:

> According to the second law of thermodynamics, a system moves toward equilibrium; it tends to run down, that is, its differential structures tend to move toward dissolution as the elements composing them become arranged in random disorder (Katz and Kahn 1983, p. 100).

Open systems, in contrast

> . . . which are capable of importing energy from their environment, can experience *negative entropy*. . . . By acquiring inputs of greater complexity than their outputs, open systems restore their own energy and repair breakdowns in their own organization (Scott 1981, pp. 109–110).

Ninth, it has often been noted by organizational theorists just how fundamentally organizational structures can change over time, making it difficult to determine whether new variations of the old structure are present, or whether there is in fact a new structure. It is important to stress that such diversity is derived from the system's environment, since, according to the 'law of limited variety' (Scott 1981, p. 111), a system can only ever be as complex as the environment which feeds it. The final characteristic to be described is *equifinality*. If an initial state can be defined in a closed system, then the final state is similarly determined. This is different in open systems:

> An initial state can have several possible final states. Furthermore, the same final state may be arrived at from several initial starting places (Litterer 1969, p. 6).

Summing up, the specific features and advantages of an open systems view are that it emphasizes the

... complexity and variability of the individual component parts — both individual participants and sub-groups — as well as the looseness of connections among them (Scott 1981, p. 119).

Most importantly, attention has shifted from studying 'structure' to studying 'process', from organization to organizing, both in regard to internal operations of an organization as well as to an organization's existence over time. The environment plays the most central part in this view since it provides the essential materials, energy, and information for the system to function and to survive. This latter advantage is, however, also the source of considerable worry for systems and organizational theorists. Openness to the environment is, according to Katz and Kahn, problematic insofar as a completely open system would no longer be a system which is identifiable against the background of its environment. Hence, system properties such as stable, patterned relationships and behaviours with system boundaries need to be stressed. It is also of particular importance, then, to focus on those elements in the environment that are actively selected as input, those which are ignored by the system, and those which are actively rejected (Katz and Kahn 1983, p. 101). The openness of schools, for example, is continually controlled, according to Hoy and Miskel, in that authorized persons are allowed in, and unauthorized are prohibited entry. But then there are those activities such as athletic and 'open house' events which are a 'partially controlled exchange that modifies both the system's internal and environmental components' (Hoy and Miskel 1987, p. 57). In addition to the qualified notion of openness, equifinality is an advantage when compared with the closed systems view which treats external disruptions as error variance rather than as integral to the system's functioning. And, as has been noted above, open systems views are better capable of developing the feedback, intelligence, and most crucially, learning function which was very narrowly conceived in the closed systems perspective.

Finally, there is another, and more fundamental, advantage in the new perspective. One of the traditional ways of understanding organizations is to regard them as manifestations of a leader's, or of key members' purposes, thus considering organizations primarily as teleological systems. But, as Katz and Kahn rightly point out, formal objectives and goals, while in some way expressing human purposes, are quite ambiguous. They may 'idealize, rationalize, distort, omit, or even conceal some essential aspects of the functioning of the organization' (Katz and Kahn 1983, p. 98). While individuals' purposes cannot be equated with organizational ones, it is precisely this fallacy which had been most often committed in the closed systems model. Hence, it may be more perspicacious to begin with 'concepts that do not call for identifying the purposes of the designers and then correcting for them when they do not seem to be fulfilled' (Katz and Kahn 1983, p. 98). In view of the strictures we will develop later against the uncritical use of commonsense folk theoretical explanations, this methodological caution against intentionalism seems quite reasonable, at least if we are concerned, ultimately, with building scientific theories of organizations.

Schools as Open Social Systems: Hoy and Miskel's Theory

Given the features described so far, it is easy to see the attractiveness of the open systems model for educational administration. Schools, in Hoy and Miskel's view, can readily be described as

> . . . social systems that take resources such as labour, students, and community direction, from the environment; subject these inputs to an educational transformation process to produce literate and educated students and graduates (Hoy and Miskel, 1987, p. 20).

Indeed, the argument of their text appears to be informed by the desire to recognize 'the environmental forces on educational organizations' (p. iii) which leads them to state categorically that: 'Open systems theory . . . is the *general framework* for exploring the conceptual foundations of educational administration' (p. 21).

Like Griffiths before them, Hoy and Miskel are similarly at pains to be explicit about the core theoretical assumptions of their theory of educational administration. Noting that there appears to be some agreement in the field of educational administration that Feigl's definition of theory is a suitable starting point, they then opt for Kerlinger's 'more general' definition. Their reasons for this choice are not entirely clear, but they appear to have misgivings about the 'purely logico-mathematical procedures' employed to derive empirical laws from theory as postulated by Feigl (Hoy and Miskel 1987, p. 2). Since no one else in educational administration has ever been able to live up to this particular demand of the Feigl model, their caution is both understandable and reasonable. Their assumption appears to be that Kerlinger's definition, qua social psychology orientation, is more appropriate in the social sciences. Consequently, they define theory as:

> a set of interrelated concepts, assumptions and generalizations that systematically describes and explains regularities in behaviour in educational organizations (Hoy and Miskel 1987, p. 2).

To which they add: 'Moreover, hypotheses may be derived from the theory to predict additional relationships among the concepts in the system.' The elements of theory, as described, make it clear that they place themselves squarely though not unproblematically within the broad traditional science conception of administration science that begins systematically with the Theory Movement in educational administration. Their view of research as 'guided by hypotheses that are empirically checked against observations about reality in a systematic and controlled way' (p. 5) is also based on Kerlinger's proposals. Like Griffiths, they also believe that administrative theory guides action, explains the nature of educational administration, and helps to solve problems. Their major disagreement with the early Theory Movement approach is that it entertained a closed systems perspective, and that it believed in the universal application of the theoretical knowledge provided by behavioural science. In view of subsequent theoretical developments in organizational theory, they maintain that

> . . . If the behavioural science approach is to remain productive in the late 1980s and 1990s, theory and research will have to become more refined, useful, and situationally oriented (Hoy and Miskel 1987, p. 23).

Hoy and Miskel's model attempts to satisfy the above requirements. It is based on the work of Litterer and key elements of Getzels and Guba's (1957) social system model, as well as Bidwell's 'The school as a formal organization', although we should note in passing that the latter two are, in fact, still closed systems models, and that there is no mention of Bidwell's reappraisal and abandonment of his earlier position. The two basic elements of Hoy and Miskel's system are the institutional and the individual which together 'provide the basis of a sociopsychological theory of group behaviour in which a dynamic transaction between roles and personality interact' (Hoy and Miskel 1987, p. 62). Thus:

> Behaviour (B) in the system is explained in terms of the interaction between role (R), defined by expectations, and personality (P), the internal need structure of an individual; that is, $B = f(R \times P)$ (Hoy and Miskel 1987, p. 62).

How much behaviour is determined by role or by personality factors depends on the particular type of system in which it occurs. Drawing on the work of Nadler and Tushman (1983) which is explicitly concerned with the management of organizational behaviour, they reformulate this very general social model so that it can be applied to the study of the determinants of behaviour in schools. Adding the concepts of 'work group' and 'goal' to the above mentioned, the basic elements of the model now comprise 'the concepts of bureaucracy, informal organization, work motivation, and organizational goals' (Hoy and Miskel 1987, p. 69). All of these interact not only with each other, but also with the environment. The most important issue concerns which specific features of the environment are responsible for constraining and determining behaviour. While there are both broad and more specific factors, the short answer given by Hoy and Miskel is that 'There is no quick or simple answer' (p. 69). To determine and predict behaviour in schools, the interactions between the various subsystems of schools have to be studied in terms of their *congruence*, where congruence is

> . . . the degree to which the needs, demands, goals, objectives and/or structures of one component are consistent with the needs, demands, goals, objectives and/or structures of another component. [It] therefore, is a measure of the goodness of fit between pairs of components (Nadler and Tushman 1983, p. 119).

When translated into the organizational realm, Nadler and Tushman hypothesize that:

> Other things being equal, the greater the total degree of congruence or fit between the various components, the more effective will be the organization, effectiveness being defined as the degree to which actual organization outputs at individual, group, and organizational levels are similar to expected outputs, as specified by strategy (Nadler and Tushman 1983, pp. 119–120).

Accepting this specification of congruence (Burrell and Morgan 1982, pp. 176–181) and its resultant implications for organizational effectiveness, Hoy and Miskel also adopt Nadler and Tushman's suggestion that this model can be used for organizational problem analysis. In particular, school decision makers can use it to diagnose difficulties and thus improve outcomes. They

> . . . gather information on the performance levels of their schools, compare the information with the desired performance levels, identify discrepancies and difficulties, search for causes of the problem, develop and select a plan to alleviate the problems, and implement and evaluate the plan. The model is particularly useful in diagnosing conflict or lack of congruence among the key elements of the system (Hoy and Miskel 1987, p. 81).

In order to carry out these diagnostic steps, and more specifically, to determine 'fit', one does not necessarily have to be intuitive, as 'in many cases fit is something that can be defined, measured, and even quantified' (Nadler and Tushman 1983, p. 120).

Epistemological Reflections

We expect the foregoing discussion has provided sufficient detail to enable some appreciation of perhaps the most influential modern approach to educational administration. In view of our earlier criticisms of traditional empiricist accounts of knowledge and theory, one may expect that inasmuch as these accounts penetrate open systems models, difficulties will emerge. This proves to be the case. We select two issues for special consideration. The first concerns the explanatory status of systems theory within the approach. The second concerns the use of the approach to evaluate organizational effectiveness.

We can begin by noting a distinction between ontology (the study of what exists) and epistemology (the theory of how we might come to know what exists). Evidence from attempts to construct comprehensive and predictively useful social theories suggests that, at the very least, the social reality under study is exceedingly complex. Open systems views seem to be better designed to capture and reflect this complexity of reality than closed systems views. On the other hand, traditional hypothetico-deductive methods wedded to models of theory structured into universal generalizations and their deductive consequences, seem to be fairly cumbersome instruments of inquiry and understanding. Our view is that this conception of theory places a very heavy premium indeed on the discovery or positing of new generalizations at a quite early stage of theory development. There will thus be a strain between complexity of ontology and modesty of epistemological resources. Our claim is that in an effort to meet the requirements of theory building, open system theory overreaches and ends up producing generalizations that are almost empirically vacuous.

In this respect, an examination of the more important system properties is revealing. For example, can a collection of objects ever fail to be interrelated? Since similarity is always similarity-for-us, the answer has to be no. We can just specify similarities. Thus, every physical object in the universe enjoys the relational property of spatio-temporal displacement from your nose, making the notion of system trivial. If we try to restrict relationships to just those that are of immediate causal significance, however, we get the opposite problem: very few collections, and certainly no organizations, count as systems. Lengthening permissible causal chains will let in organizations, but now we have a continuum. If everything has a common causal ancestor far enough back, every collection will again be a system. The problem is that the notion of system is vacuous pending some particular prior theoretical specification of objects and their significant interrelationships.

Capacity for feedback is another important property of systems. Unfortunately, there is an empirical difficulty with the disposition indicator term 'capacity'. What it really means is that *other things being equal* a system will use feedback to correct itself, since Hoy and Miskel want to confer system status where 'the potential is not always realized' (Hoy and Miskel 1987, p. 20). Since other things are never equal we end up with the problem of distinguishing between unrealized potential and absence of capacity. It cannot be a matter of design being thwarted by external conditions, because we are dealing with open systems. Some closer specification of feedback would help.

Consider: 'Systems that survive tend to move towards a steady state-equilibrium' (Hoy and Miskel 1987, p. 20). The word 'tend' is an empirical hedge permitting exceptions. Hoy and Miskel add a further hedge: 'This steady state however, is not static' (p. 20). A final hedge causes the story to collapse altogether when they define equilibrium in terms of maintaining a constant relationship between system parts (pp. 57–58). The collapse occurs because if a steady state is not static, the conditions for system identity look much the same as the conditions for equilibrium; namely, stability of (possibly dynamic) relationships between parts. Evidence for this reading can be found in their treatment of system disequilibrium: 'the system either changes itself or neutralizes the disruptive forces impinging on it, and restores equilibrium' (pp. 57–58). Since failure to survive is a lapse in system identity, this little circle of definitions makes their original claim a tautology.

The same point can be made against Hoy and Miskel's claim that 'open systems overcome the tendency to run down by demonstrating adaption' (1987, p. 20). If environments are assumed to change, and the maintenance of system identity in the presence of change is adaption, then all surviving systems, by definition, adapt. This criticism is not the complaint that functionally defined terms are vacuous. In defining 'heart' as 'an organ which pumps blood around the body' we do in fact have a recipe for expansion to powerful causal-explanatory theories of the heart: we proceed by way of anatomy, biology, physics, chemistry, and the like. Similarly, if 'adaption' means 'that set of behaviours a system exhibits to maintain its existence over time in a changing environment', then presumably we have another recipe. But the real explanatory punch will lie in the detailed causal theories of objects in an environment. Without these, we have little empirical funding of adaption.

Some writers in the systems tradition are aware of these difficulties. For example, after their discussion of open systems properties, Nadler and Tushman admit that while systems theory provides a

> . . . valuable basic perspective on organizations, it is limited as a problem-solving tool. The reason is that as a model systems theory is too abstract to be used for day-to-day organization behaviour-problem analysis (Nadler and Tushman 1983, p. 114).

So while electrical engineers, physicists, and chemists customarily marshall the true generalizations of science to solve day-to-day problems, it is apparently suggested that organizational theorists, who struggle to put up a single law of comparable generality, enjoy the luxury of dispensing with them when it comes to practical organizational problem solving and analysis!

A less extravagant hypothesis flowing from our current reflections is to see systems theory as vacuous rather than as too abstract.

If this kind of theoretical overreaching arises from pressure to warp suggestive metaphors into nomological, or law-like, generalizations from which testable hypotheses may be derived (pending hedges over abstractness), a few more coherentist suggestions for theory development will be helpful. For example, if we count natural science as our most powerful body of theory, avoiding contradictions with science will be an important constraint on organizational theory development. This is a much weaker and more reasonable demand than attempting to derive organizational claims from science, or attempting to mirror mistaken models of scientific theory and practice. Simplicity places further restrictions. If we take the physicalist ontology of natural science as our inventory of objects in the universe, there will be theoretical economies in accounting for people naturalistically. Further, where our current most predictively reliable theories of human behaviour, namely our commonsense folk theories, employ theoretical concepts and terms not found in science, a more parsimonious approach to reduction can fend off the temptation to posit such inelegant explanatory dualisms as reasons and causes, mind and brain, and the social and the physical. Our recommendation, elaborated later, is to treat science realistically but folk theories instrumentally, and to explore scientific accounts of the latter's predictive success. Coherentism provides more strategies, but the basic pattern is clear enough: build up administrative theory piecemeal from existing reliable theory subject to constraining the total theoretical package by coherentist criteria of theoretical excellence.

A second area where limitations in traditional empiricist accounts of knowledge and justification emerge in system-theoretic educational administration concerns the question of values. One of the major uses of administrative theory in education is to guide the evaluation of organizational effectiveness. Consider, however, the key elements of the *goal model* of organizational effectiveness that ultimately figure in Hoy and Miskel's final account of effectiveness. On the goal model 'an organization is effective if the observable outcomes of its activities meet or exceed its organizational goals' (Hoy and Miskel 1987, p. 387). Where some goals in education are considered to be values — the acquisition of worthwhile knowledge, good citizenship, love of learning — traditional theory has no contribution to make to the assessment or evaluation of the goals themselves, of saying what the goals should be. Although this narrowness of scope contributes to the separation of educational administration from educational theory, with its historically broader concerns, it is not, by itself, a problem. It becomes a problem, however, when we have trouble separating inquiry into the meeting of goals with goal evaluation. Thus one common criticism is that the procedure of not evaluating values itself expresses a value judgment. It expresses *de facto* support for the status quo.

Further criticisms emerge when we get down to the detail of discovering goals. Take the distinction between official goals, for example, 'formal statements of purpose by the board of education concerning the nature of a school's mission', and operative goals which 'reflect the true intentions of a school organization' (Hoy and Miskel 1987, pp. 387–388). Given that intentions, as mentalistic phenomena, are unobservable, what counts as evidence for operative goals? Following traditional epistemological practice, Hoy and Miskel suggested we look to 'the actual tasks and activities performed in the organization, irrespective of what it claims to be doing (p. 388). But if we do this, how do we get a mismatch between goal and actual attainment, since the epistemology collapses the distinction? All organizations come out as one hundred percent effective. On the other hand, if we retreat to observable statements of official goals, we find that they are typically 'abstract and aspirational in nature (p. 388), and so admit more conspicuously of interpretation. However, interpretation is a theory laden exercise and can be expected to draw on, among other things, theories concerning the aims of education, what schools should be doing, and a host of other value-laden matters that are embedded in the antecedent global perspective we bring to every act of interpretation. Our perspective on values thus appears to figure in, and be inseparable from, our empirical inquiry into an organization's real goals.

Positivistically inclined methodologists have a characteristic response to this line of argument; namely, to impose severe limitations on interpretation by operationalizing official, or formal, statements of organizational goals. Of the range of possibilities, Hoy and Miskel (1987) mention management by objectives, cost-benefit analysis, and behavioural objectives for instruction (p. 388). For the theoretically minded, attempts to achieve this narrowing have interesting consequences. Suppose, for example, that the operations specified are those actually performed by the organization. We then end up with the problem of perfect effectiveness by definition. The alternative is to specify the operations counterfactually. The trouble with this proposal is that we can only understand the truth conditions for counterfactuals by invoking background theory. This is the same point we made in Chapter Two when we observed that technical worries over counterfactuals damaged attempts to define theoretical terms operationally. The result was a collapse of the theory/observation distinction. In the present case of official goals, the result is an intrusion of values into the process of evaluating effectiveness.

In arguing this result, note that the term 'effectiveness' is either being used normatively to express a value or it is not. If not, it is difficult to see how we can connect up what we want of organizations, what we count as desirable in them, with the matter of effectiveness. If, on the other hand, it is being used normatively, let us assume, for the moment, that this is a value that lies outside administrative theory, that theory is simply concerned with how this given value can be realized. But we saw from our discussion of operational definition that we cannot choose just any operations, or in this case, objectives, benefits, and behaviours. What is chosen needs to bear some relation to the official goal term — say, 'quality education' — being operationalized. This means that the meaning of 'quality education', no doubt thoroughly embedded in a value-laden global theory, guides the selection of measurable objectives. Given that the reasonableness of the chosen objectives is only as good as the antecedent selecting theory and its application, evaluations of organizational effectiveness that simply take for granted the correctness of this background theory, values and all, are remarkably uncritical, especially when evaluations can often point to obvious mismatches between the external values driving the normative content of the term 'effectiveness' and the theory values that figure in the selection process. In fact Hoy and Miskel (1987) virtually concede the importance of such a critical dimension for official goals when they acknowledge the possibility of 'less attractive operative goals such as racism and sexism' (p. 388).

In the final analysis, administrators evaluating organizational effectiveness can simply elect to ignore the worth of the educational theory informing very precise specifications of an organization's official goals, and live with the moral consequences. However, when it comes to this, one particular match between the external value of doing an evaluation and the internal values of global theory will undermine the whole point of engaging in evaluations. It is when antecedent global theory itself declares that all the operational criteria for measuring a concept are so narrow that warping educational practice to meet the demands of measurement will result in a set of educational practices that are of diminished value or even not worth having. As this is always a theoretical possibility, the more so for traditional empiricist accounts of evidence, the omission of values from administrative theory is not just a theoretical liability; it can also be a moral liability.

Summary

The main argument of this chapter has been for two related conclusions. The first is that foundationalist empiricist views of knowledge associated with orthodox behavioural science of educational administration have exerted a powerful influence on the development, structure, and content of administrative theories in education. The second is that the epistemological weaknesses of foundationalism have spilled over into these administrative theories and perhaps also into the practices that they inform. We considered two periods in the recent history of educational administration: first, the earliest period of systematic theory development along behavioural science lines, known as the Theory Movement, and second, a current highly influential open systems theory, philosophically continuous with the Theory Movement, expounded in the recent work of Hoy and Miskel.

Concerning the Theory Movement, we noted the influence of logical positivism and logical empiricism, indirectly in the case of Herbert Simon's work, directly in the case of Herbert Feigl's work. An examination of Griffiths's early theoretical work suggested that Feigl's account of theory and evidence constrained administrative theorizing in at least three ways. First, it imposed a broad structuring of theory into lawlike generalizations and testable consequences. Second, it placed a premium on operational definitions. Third, it separated fact from value, eschewing values from administrative theory altogether. We then used our critique of foundationalist epistemology to criticize these constraints, and suggested some corresponding coherentist alternatives to theory building.

Concerning Hoy and Miskel's work, we outlined background developments in systems theoretic approaches to educational organizations, noting particularly the shift from closed to open systems theories. However, despite a big increase in sensitivity and sophistication of tools for understanding complex social phenomena, we observed important manifestations of the same three philosophically motivated constraints. We focused on the first, which affected the explanatory status of systems theory, and the third, which had consequences for the role of values in evaluating organizational effectiveness. Once again we argued that weaknesses in assumed empiricist philosophy created problems in theory and in the application of theory.

References

Aldrich H. E. (1979). *Organizations and Environments*. (Englewood Cliffs: Prentice-Hall).

Barnard C. (1938). *The Functions of the Executive*. (Cambridge, Mass.: Harvard University Press).

Bidwell C. E. (1965). The school as a formal organization, in J. G. March (ed.) *Handbook of Organizations*. (Chicago: Rand McNally).

Bidwell C. E. (1979). The school as a formal organization: some new thoughts, in G. L. Immegart and W. L. Boyd (eds.) *Problem-Finding in Educational Administration*. (Lexington: D. C. Heath).

Blumberg A. E. and Feigl H. (1931). Logical positivism: a new movement in European philosophy, *Journal of Philosophy*, 28(11).

Burrell G. and Morgan G. (1982). *Sociological Paradigms and Organizational Analysis*. (London: Heinemann).

Culbertson J. A. (1981). Antecedents of the theory movement, *Educational Administration Quarterly*, 17(1), pp. 25–47.

Fayol H. (1949). *General and Industrial Management*. (London: Sir Isaac Pitman and Sons, translated by C. Storrs).

Feigl H. (1951). Principles and problems in theory construction in psychology, in W. Dennis (ed.) *Current Trends in Psychological Theory*. (Pittsburgh: University of Pittsburgh Press).

Feigl H. (1953). The scientific outlook: naturalism and humanism, in H. Feigl and M. Brodbeck (eds.) *Readings in the Philosophy of Science*. (New York: Appleton-Century-Crofts).

Feigl H. (1974a). No pot of message, in H. Feigl, *Inquiries and Provocations: Selected Writings 1929–1974*. (Boston: Reidel).

Feigl H. (1974b). The power of positivistic thinking, in H. Feigl *Inquiries and Provocations: Selected Writings 1929–1974*. (Boston: Reidel).

Getzels J. W. and Guba E. G. (1957). Social behaviour and the administrative process, *The School Review*, **65**(4), pp. 423–441.
Griffiths D. (1959). *Administrative Theory*. (New York: Appleton-Century-Crofts).
Griffiths D. E. (1979). Intellectual turmoil in educational administration, *Educational Administration Quarterly*, **15**(3), pp. 43–65.
Griffiths D. E. (1983). Evolution in research and theory: a study of prominent researchers, *Educational Administration Quarterly*, **19**(3), pp. 201–221.
Griffiths D. E. (1985). Theories: past, present and future, in D. E. Griffiths *Administrative Theory in Transition*. (Geelong: Deakin University Press).
Gross B. M. (1964). The scientific approach to administration, in D. E. Griffiths (ed.) *Behavioral Science and Educational Administration*. (Chicago: University of Chicago Press).
Gulick L. and Urwick L. (1937) (eds.). *Papers on the Science of Administration*. (New York: Institute of Public Administration).
Halpin A. W. (1957). A paradigm for research on administrator behavior, in R. F. Campbell and R. T. Gregg (eds.) *Administrative Behavior in Education*. (New York: Harper and Bros.).
Halpin A. W. (1969). 'A foggy view from Olympus', *Journal of Educational Administration*, **7**(1), pp. 3–18.
Hannan M. and Freeman J. H. (1977). The population ecology of organizations, *American Journal of Sociology*, **83**, pp. 929–964.
Hoy W. K. (1982). Recent developments in theory and research in educational administration, *Educational Administration Quarterly*, **18**(3), pp. 1–11.
Hoy W. K. and Miskel C. G. (1987). *Educational Administration: Theory, Research and Practice*. (New York: Random House, third edition).
Katz D. and Kahn R. L. (1983). Organizations and the systems concept' in J. R. Hackman, E. E. Lawler III, and L. W. Porter (eds.) *Perspectives on Behaviour in Organizations*. (New York: McGraw-Hill, second edition).
Keeves J. P. (ed.) (1988). *Educational Research, Methodology and Measurement: An International Handbook*. (Oxford: Pergamon Press).
Lawrence P. R. and Lorsch J. W. (1967). *Organization and Environment: Managing Differentiation and Integration*. (Boston: Graduate School of Business Administration, Harvard University).
Litterer J. A. (1969). *Organizations: Systems, Control and Adaption*. Vol. II. (New York: John Wiley, second edition).
Mayo E. (1933). *The Human Problems of an Industrial Civilization*. (Boston: Harvard Business School).
Metcalf H. C. and Urwick L. (1940) (eds.). *Dynamic Administration: The Collected Papers of Mary Parker Follett*. (New York: Harper and Bros.).
Meyer M. W. (1978) Introduction: recent developments in organisational research and theory, in M. W. Meyer and Associates (eds.) *Environments and Organizations*. (San Francisco: Jossey-Bass).
Miskel C. (1984). Hypotheses and assumptions guiding research: a rejoinder to Daniel Griffiths, *Educational Administration Quarterly*, **20**(1), pp. 111–113.
Nadler D. A. and Tushman M. L. (1983). A general diagnostic model for organisational behaviour: applying a congruence perspective, in J. R. Hackman, E. E. Lawler III, and L. W. Porter (eds), *Perspectives, on Behaviour in Organizations*. (New York: McGraw-Hill, second edition).
Perrow C. (1983). The short and glorious history of organizational theory, in J. R. Hackman, E. E. Lawler III, and L. W. Porter (eds.) *Perspectives on Behaviour in Organizations*. (New York: McGraw-Hill, second edition).
Pfeffer J. and Salancik G. R. (1978). *The External Control of Organizations*. (New York: Harper and Row).
Popper K. R. (1959). *The Logic of Scientific Discovery*. (London: Hutchinson).
Popper K. R. (1976). *Unended Quest*. (Glasgow: Fontana)
Roethlisberger F. J. and Dickson W. J. (1939). *Management and the Worker*. (Cambridge, Mass.: Harvard University Press).
Scott W. R. (1978). Theoretical perspectives, in M. W. Meyer and Associates (eds.) *Environments and Organizations*. (San Francisco: Jossey-Bass).

Scott W. R. (1981). *Organizations-Rational, Natural, and Open Systems.* (Englewood Cliffs: Prentice-Hall).

Simon H. (1945). *Administrative Behavior.* (New York: The Free Press, third edition, 1976).

Taylor F. W. (1911). *Shop Management.* (New York: Harper and Bros.).

Taylor F. W. (1947). *Scientific Management.* (New York: Harper and Bros.).

Thompson J. D. (1958). Modern approaches to theory in administration, in A. W. Halpin (ed.) *Administrative Theory in Education.* (Chicago: Midwest Administration Centre).

Weick K. E. (1969). *The Social Psychology of Organizing.* (Reading, Mass.: Addison-Wesley).

Willower D. J. (1975). Theory in education administration, *Journal of Educational Administration,* 13(1), pp. 77–91.

Willower D. J. (1980). Contemporary issues in theory in educational administration, *Educational Administration Quarterly,* 16(3), pp. 1–25.

Willower D. J. (1981). Educational administration: some philosophical and other considerations, *Journal of Educational Administration,* 19(2), pp. 115–139.

Willower D. J. (1982). School organizations: perspectives in juxtaposition, *Educational Administration Quarterly,* 18(3), pp. 89–110.

Willower D. J. (1983). Evolution of the professorship: past, philosophy, future, *Educational Administration Quarterly,* 19(3), pp. 179–200.

Willower D. J. (1985). 'Philosophy and the study of educational administration', *Journal of Educational Administration,* 23(1), pp. 5–22.

4

The Greenfield Revolution

Up until 1974, criticisms of the behavioural science approach to educational administration were mounted largely from within the philosophical assumptions of traditional science. The shift in emphasis from closed to open systems that occurred in the 1960s is an important result of this kind of internal critique. However in 1974, Thomas Greenfield, using the occasion of an International Intervisitation Programme address in Bristol, launched a major assault on many of the philosophical and methodological assumptions that dominated traditional theory and research in educational administration (Greenfield 1975). Since then Greenfield has broadened and deepened his critique. In an impressive series of papers (1978, 1979a, 1979b, 1980, 1983, 1986) he has sought to develop a systematic view of social reality as a human invention, in opposition to the systems scientific perspective of social reality as a natural system. He has constructed strands of argument on the nature of knowledge, on administrative theory and research, on values, on the limits of science and the importance of human subjectivity, on methodology, understanding and the nature of social science, and on truth and reality. Although Greenfield is drawing on a long alternative tradition in social science — a tradition we discuss in some detail in Chapter Six — the magnitude of his undertaking and a corresponding elegance of argument make his work the most important theoretical development in recent educational administration.

Our discussion of these themes will, of necessity, be selective rather than comprehensive, and is aimed at illustrating the methods of coherentist epistemological critique and defending the possibility of a new, suitably broadened, science of administration. Within this framework our basic position on Greenfield's work can therefore be simply stated. We think that his epistemological objections to science traditionally or positivistically conceived are decisive and cannot be answered from within traditional assumptions. In what follows we sketch the more salient elements of his epistemology as he applies it to administrative theory and also consider some responses from Hills, Griffiths, and Willower. Whatever the merits of these responses, we think that Greenfield's objections do not apply to a naturalistic scientific

76

realism justified on holistic or coherentist epistemic criteria. Finally, although our account is preliminary and programmatic, we offer some suggestions for incorporating human subjectivity, intention, and interpretation within a naturalistic scientific view of organizations.

Greenfield's Epistemology

Many of the objections that Greenfield brings against traditional conceptions of scientific knowledge and epistemic practice have been touched on in earlier chapters when we have explored philosophical objections to foundationalist empiricisms. So there is much that will be familiar here. Familiar, but full of novel twists and interesting applications, and well worth retelling in Greenfield's terms.

The theoretical core of Greenfield's epistemology is his claim that all our purported knowledge of reality, natural or social, contains an irreducibly subjective component. We never see the world as it really is, but only as mediated by the interpretation our mind places on sensory inputs. For example, he claims to be following Kant in drawing

> . . . the distinction Kant drew between the noumenal world (the world as it is) and the phenomenal world (the world as we see it). For Kant, a world of reality does indeed exist but man can never perceive it directly; reality is always glossed over with human interpretations. . . . In popular form, the Kantian philosophy has been expressed as follows: 'man does not create his world but he does make it' (Greenfield 1975, p. 71).

In understanding the importance and scope of Greenfield's subjectivism, it is useful to distinguish between the place of subjectivity in knowing the natural world and subjectivity in knowing the social world, for he thinks that 'the social sciences differ fundamentally from the natural sciences' (Greenfield 1980, p. 111). His invocation of Kant's philosophy suggests an argument against traditional views of objectivity in the natural sciences. This is a significant focus of his criticisms of traditional science of administration, since if objectivity fails to hold up in natural science it is unlikely to enjoy a more secure basis in social science. Greenfield has been misunderstood on this point so we need to be clear about his strategy. He is not saying that objectivity is restricted, or applies only to, the physical sciences; that it is the social sciences that are irreducibly subjective. His point is that there is no such thing as objectivity. If he can mount a successful case against traditional conceptions of scientific objectivity he will have dealt a heavy blow to the dominant behavioural science versions of educational administration. In this section we restrict our discussion of Greenfield's epistemology to his views on our knowledge of the natural world.

In developing his case, Greenfield offers arguments for three broad epistemological conclusions. The first, as the Kant reference indicates, involves the claim that all observation is theory laden. There is no 'unvarnished news', to use Quine's delightful expression (Quine 1960, p. 2). All of our experience of the world is interpreted, or filtered through our prior cognitive apparatus. The second is the claim that all empirical test situations are complex, sufficiently so to eliminate the possibility of decisive, or crucial, tests against experience. The third is the claim that all empirical theory is drastically underdetermined by all available data, or equivalently, that any number of theories can be compatible with the same observational evidence.

In our view, Greenfield is correct in taking the first conclusion to be relatively uncontroversial:

> That we require ideas to understand our experience and to perceive reality is generally accepted as a principle of epistemology (Greenfield 1979a, p. 173).

We need theories — sources of concepts and categories — to make sense of William James's 'blooming confusion' of phenomena around us. A good example of this, suggested in Gronn's (1983, pp. 18–21) careful analysis of Greenfield's work, is the interpretation of ambiguous figures. Viewed one way, a line drawing may be perceived as a picture of an old woman; viewed another way, of a young girl. In each case the pattern of ocular irridation — what impinges on the observer's retina — is identical. What makes the difference is not a matter of observational evidence. In making inferences from observational evidence to what exists in the world, the same evidence supports divergent conclusions. One person infers a drawing of an old woman, another a drawing of a young girl. For each observer to see what the other sees, each must undergo a Gestalt-switch, a shift in interpretive perspective. Now for Greenfield, theories can provide just such a perspective, and hence can contribute just such a difference when it comes to knowing what exists. In a similar vein he remarks:

> What we see depends in large measure on what we believe we are going to see. It may be argued indeed that we see, hear, and feel nothing without first having ideas that give meaning to our experience (Greenfield 1979a, p. 173).

If this argument for theory ladenness is relatively uncontroversial, one of Greenfield's applications of it is surely not. For if empirical evidence is a standard of truth, traditional science must face the fact that the standard itself is therefore laden with interpretation:

The necessary question, then, for all scientists to face is what objective truth can mean in a world that can be perceived only subjectively (Greenfield 1980, p. 92).

The epistemological punch in all this is that the standard of truth is only as plausible as the background theories it is being invoked to adjudicate. However, as we saw earlier, this robs foundational justification schemata of their point.

Traditional hypothetico-deductive reasoning in scientific method assumes that particular scientific claims can be tested against experience, that they are open to refutation, falsification, or disproof. Greenfield's argument for the ubiquity of interpretation undermines the value of this reasoning by concluding that there are no 'hard' data to be found in experience. In siding with Kuhn and Feyerabend's critique of empiricism, he goes further and denies the testability assumption:

A long and well accepted logic in research requires researchers first to have a theoretical view of the world and then to test it stringently against reality by collecting empirical data through operationally defined procedures. In contrast, Kuhn and Feyerabend argue that theory is never disconfirmed by empirical research. If findings are inconsistent with the theory, we are likely to disbelieve them or to search for other data that fit better with the theory (Greenfield 1979a, p. 170).

Greenfield does not give a detailed argument for this conclusion, but he does give some examples, both from educational research and, following Kuhn and Feyerabend, from the history of science. He notes, from his review of empirical research in educational administration, that typically data are not used to test theories because those same theories function as a priori standards of validity (Greenfield 1979a, p. 169). He claims this is so despite the use of powerful statistical procedures designed to bring some order into vast amounts of data, and illustrates his claim with the example of (exploratory) factor analysis: 'Typically, researchers keep rotating their factors until something interpretable emerges' (1979a, p. 170). Since the antecedent conditions for interpretability are precisely those circumscribed by the researcher's theory, Greenfield's conclusion is that the data are so theoretically constructed that they cannot therefore function usefully in the process of refutation.

Turning to examples from the history of science, he cites Kuhn's claim that the Ptolemaic view of astronomy was not refuted by counter-examples, or data that would not fit (Greenfield 1979a, p. 174). It was ultimately replaced by another view — the Copernican view — which had come to enjoy, for a variety of reasons, the consensual support of the scientific community. Galileo's telescope provides another example. Citing Feyerabend,

Greenfield notes (1979a, pp. 174–175) that observations made with the telescope confirmed a heliocentric view of the cosmos but hardly provided refuting evidence against the traditional earth-centred picture. This was partly because elements of the complex test situation included assumptions about the reliability of telescopes. There was no difficulty in garnering terrestrial evidence of reliability. It was just that methodological consensus broke down over granting the reliability of extra-terrestrial observations, precisely the point at which the evidence would have been crucial.

Greenfield's argument for the underdetermination of physical theory by observational evidence is not so readily distinguished from his epistemological reflections on social theory. Nor is it clearly demarcated from his case for theory ladenness and against falsification. Nevertheless, the underdetermination of traditional science thesis is clearly presupposed in what he says. For example, while he observes that

> . . . in naturalistic science, there is usually only one theory accepted at a given time as the best explanation of phenomena in the field to which it applies . . . (Greenfield 1979a, p. 175).

Thus he follows Feyerabend in urging a proliferation of theories. This proliferation is possible, however, only if any number of theories can be consistent with the facts. That different global theories can be empirically adequate is clearly what sustains much of his talk about multiple realities and his claim that people inhabit different worlds. And in the final analysis, it is Feyerabend's anarchistic theory of knowledge that suggests the proliferation of (sometimes orthogonal, or incommensurable) viewpoints necessary to justify Greenfield's anarchistic theory of organization (Greenfield 1983).

Each of these three epistemological conclusions, if sound, implies a lapse in traditional standards of objectivity. Where such lapses occur, human choice, will, and subjectivity enter. But if subjectivity should enter in so important an area as the determination, from empirical evidence, of our best theories of natural science, we may assume that something is seriously amiss with the behavioural science approach to educational administration.

Greenfield and his Epistemological Critics

Not surprisingly, Greenfield's controversial ideas on epistemology and the nature of scientific objectivity have had their critics. For example Jean Hills's (1980) 'A critique of Greenfield's "New Perspective" ' contains a detailed analysis of many of Greenfield's characteristic theses. Daniel Griffiths (e.g. 1977, 1979) has also entered the debate on a number of issues, and Donald Willower, in a series of papers on philosophy and educational administration (e.g. 1980, 1981, 1983, 1985), has provided perhaps the most detailed and systematic response to Greenfield's position. We offer some brief commentary on Hills and Griffiths, a more extended discussion of Willower's ideas, and some further elaboration of our own epistemological perspective.

In our view, the most puzzling feature of the debate initiated by Greenfield is the fact that while almost all critics acknowledge the centrality of epistemology to its resolution, there is a conspicuous reluctance to engage in explicit epistemological theorizing. This leads to some curious results. Thus Hills agrees with Greenfield's point that systems theory 'tells us what we can never prove directly with our senses (Hills 1980, p. 31). And he makes the standard broad foundationalist point that observations are deduced from postulates which may posit an unobservable world, rather than vice versa, adding that we can switch our ontology of unobservables and still leave intact all the observations. However, agreement is engendered by his standard of proof, which is strictly foundational: direct proof from the senses requires deductions to run from observation to theory. This turns out to be not much of a concession, since while theories can never be proven, he adds: 'Greenfield's assertions to the contrary, they can be and have been disproven' (Hills 1980, p. 32). The puzzle is that in other accessible papers, including one cited by Hills, Greenfield gives examples — factor analysis and Galileo's telescope — and cites the argument of Kuhn and Feyerabend against falsification as a method of theory choice. In noting this kind of omission he complains that Hills makes 'no substantial reference to my later writings' (Greenfield 1980, p. 115).

There is further noncommunication over the question of the reality of organizations. Hills remarks:

> The standard of 'reality' generally accepted in scientific circles is 'empirical verifiability' by independent observers employing the same conceptual framework. Given that criterion, I have no hesitation in saying with reference to the school that teachers, students, principals, and custodians, for example, are real and that the division of labour and relations among them are real (Hills 1980, p. 27).

In an effort to make sense of what appears to be a challenging of the obvious, Hills suggests that Greenfield is not concerned with

> . . . the reality of the above mentioned types of entities. . . . Rather [he is concerned with] the 'reality' of some of the theoretical entities, relations, and processes postulated in order to explain them (Hills 1980, p. 27).

This is an odd response because not only is the conceptual framework of traditional scientific circles the major issue under dispute, but Greenfield's arguments for theory ladenness clearly imply that teachers, students, boards of trustees and the like are themselves theoretical entities. If this conclusion sounds implausible consider: whether someone is a teacher is not a matter discernible from the pattern of sensory nerve firings they elicit in observers. Chairs may be distinguished from tables by this test, but not teachers from non-teachers. Being a teacher, at least in the sense in which administrators are most concerned, is a matter of having appropriate qualifications, being a party to a legally binding contract, and perhaps validly being appointed to a school. To be sure, terms like 'qualifications', 'contract', and 'valid appointment' have their empirical conditions of applicability, but any simplicity thought to attend these would quickly be compromised by the complexity of associated educational, legal, and administrative theory and practice. Since all entities are theoretical, including chairs and tables, the question of the reality of organizations is really a question of whether there are any theoretical gains to be had in positing their existence over and above the existence of individuals. On this score Greenfield is a nominalist. Hills realizes that competition between theories is what is at issue, but despite Greenfield's scepticism about proof and disproof, he still insists the outcome is a matter of empirical adequacy (Hills 1980, p. 27).

Another example of epistemological debate being avoided where it needs to be engaged in concerns a criticism Griffiths makes of Greenfield's subjectivist oriented research. He cites two examples to illustrate the need to introduce new concepts into the study of administration to replace those of *role* and *bureaucracy* as commonly conceived. This need, he acknowledges, derives from attention to the perceptions and understandings of individual actors in an organization. However, after conceding 'the phenomenologist to be correct' (Griffiths 1977, p. 7) in urging a dropping of such abstractions, he concludes:

> The generalization drawn from both illustrations is that theory building without constant reference to reality is a dangerous game. In fact, theories should not be built unless they are validated through research (Griffiths 1977, p. 7).

There does not appear to be an awareness here that Greenfield is challenging what counts as a reality to refer to, that it is only through antecedent theories that we can identify and individuate entities. In what must be sheer exasperation, Greenfield responds:

> And again I ask, 'What constitutes theory, validation, and research?' Does anyone engaged in academic studies in educational administration hear these questions? I am beginning to despair that they do not, though participants in some forums seem prepared to acknowledge and consider them (Greenfield 1978, p. 7).

One critic who does hear some of these questions, and responds, is Donald Willower. For example, Willower successfully responded to Greenfield's early use of the term 'phenomenology'. As Gronn tells it, in his early work

> . . . Greenfield seems to link the method of understanding (*Verstehen*) with phenomenology. He was later to suffer for this apparent indiscretion, because it gave Willower an opportunity to point out that the term ought to be linked with Husserl, not Weber . . . (Gronn 1983, p. 11).

In any case, Greenfield abandoned the term since it was preventing rather than enhancing consideration of his subjectivist 'alternative view'.

Perhaps one unusual feature of Willower's response to Greenfield's epistemology can be traced to this switching of labels. For while Husserl's phenomenology contains an elaborate epistemology and associated methodology of inquiry, these are absent, Willower complains, in phenomenological social science. He implies that Greenfield's criticisms of scientific knowledge involve a lot of talk 'about epistemology without setting forth an epistemological position . . .' (Willower 1980, p. 8). In another paper, he reinforces this theme: 'Apart from explicitly adopting a subjectivist viewpoint, he does not discuss his epistemological position' (Willower 1981, p. 116). While there is scope for dispute over what counts as standards for adequate philosophical discussion, the pedigree of Greenfield's epistemology, especially in its more detailed presentations, seems clear enough. As we have indicated, when it comes to scientific knowledge, he endorses a number of explicit epistemological theses found in the writings of Kuhn and Feyerabend; notably, the theory ladenness of all observations, the failure of classical confirmation theory and varieties of falsificationism because of the holistic nature of empirical testing, and the underdetermination of theories by all available evidence. One might like more details after the fashion of Husserl, but it is fair to note that these theses, as elaborated and supported by Kuhn, Feyerabend, and a number of other writers, spelt the end of logical empiricism and also traditional conceptions of science and its methods, at least in philosophy. The character and content of most debate in philosophy of science changed quite substantially in the 1960s to reflect these developments. In fact, in philosophy, many of the most important criticisms of traditional empiricist conceptions of knowledge had been made by Quine during the 1950s in a series of papers (reprinted in Quine 1961), and in *Word and Object*, his most important book, published in 1960.

If there was a broad consensus among philosophers, during this period and after, that traditional empiricism was flawed, it is also fair to say that there was little enthusiasm for two substantive alternatives: Kuhn's 'mob psychology', as his critics unkindly dubbed it, and Feyerabend's 'anything goes'. Although Willower complains about a lack of explicit theorizing in Greenfield's work, he is aware of some of the weaknesses in these alternatives and offers dissent. In fact Willower seizes on two crucial claims embedded in Greenfield's critique of administrative science. The first is that traditional science of educational administration does make the epistemological errors it is accused of making. The second, and this affects the range of possible responses to Greenfield, is that the alternative epistemologies constructed by either Kuhn or Feyerabend are sound.

Concerning the first claim, Willower thinks that Greenfield is criticizing a straw man; that he tilts at a 'virtually non-existent conception of science every time he writes on the subject' (Willower 1985, pp. 19–20). The true position, Willower believes, is that:

> The interplay of the observer's ideas with what is observed is and has long been recognized as a salient feature of scientific activity. . . . To argue that there is a dominant view of science that has no place for the contribution of the puzzling, thinking scientist, is absurd (Willower 1985, p. 7).

And so it is. However, since Greenfield is not actually presuming that anyone holds to the possibility of science being conducted without scientists, the straw man charge will need to give way to some rather more intricate work in philosophy. From our discussion in the last chapter, there seems little doubt that the behavioural science approach, beginning with the Theory Movement and extending to today's orthodoxy, has been heavily influenced by foundational varieties of empiricism, especially Feigl's with its physicalist ontology of experience and theoretical entities. This influence has shaped discussion of such basic issues as the nature, content, and structure of administrative theories, and how they might be justified. Nor is there much doubt that these empiricisms are mistaken as general theories of the nature, acquisition, and justification of knowledge. The real nub of the dispute between Greenfield and Willower concerns the consequences of these mistakes, especially the role of subjectivity in determining theory choice. Looked at in these terms we have little option but to confront the second, substantive, issue of the soundness of alternative subjectivist epistemologies.

John Dewey was the most formidable early critic of empiricism in North American philosophy. Despite his change in viewpoint in the late 1880s from a theistic Hegelian to a naturalistic pragmatic perspective, his opposition to classical empiricism remained essentially unchanged. As a critic of empiricism we may expect that some of Dewey's objections would be echoed in Greenfield's writings. This turns out to be the case. In a 1979 paper, Greenfield concludes by restating one of its key aims:

It argues that our ideas about the world determine what procedures we will use for creating data and what facts we will see as important and meaningful (Greenfield 1979a, p. 187).

In a 1907 paper of Dewey's we find the following

> The fallacy of orthodox logical empiricism is right here. It supposes there can be 'givens', sensations, percepts, etc., prior to and independent of thought or ideas, and that thought or ideas may be had by some kind of compounding or separating of the givens. But it is the very nature of sensation or perception . . . already to be, in and of itself, something which is so internally fractionalized or perplexed as to suggest and to require an idea, a meaning (Dewey 1907, p. 309).

The irony is that Willower's philosophical stance is fundamentally in the Deweyan tradition. It is a small point, but it does highlight our claim that the real debate is about alternatives to empiricism, not criticisms of it. And Dewey's alternative, of course, involves a staunch defence of science. In fact in the 1929 Preface to his important work *Experience and Nature,* Dewey explained his philosophical enterprise thus:

> I believe that the method of empirical naturalism presented in this volume provides the way, and the only way . . . by which one can freely accept the standpoint and conclusions of modern science (Dewey 1929, p. ix).

It is this approach to science that marks out the main difference between Willower and Greenfield.

For Greenfield, behavioural science is traditional and positivistic, and open to the objections of Kuhn, Feyerabend and, dare we say it, Dewey. For Willower, sympathetic to a pragmatist philosophy that both celebrates science and attacks empiricism, Greenfield's objections to objectivity and science are effective, at best, against only positivistic science. Positivistic science may not be a straw man, but it has never been a vital component of Willower's conception of science. And if a workable notion of objectivity can be defended from within a pragmatist epistemology, then Greenfield's subjectivism is threatened. Our view is that such a defence is possible. Willower (1985, pp. 8–14) offers some suggestions along the lines of requiring philosophies of administration to satisfy certain criteria for communication and verification. In the end, these requirements boil down to standards of intersubjective agreement and public evidence, basic conditions for clear communication. On these standards, 'a Deweyan theory of knowledge' (Willower 1985, p. 9) fares well and subjectivism fares ill. We have not seen Greenfield's response to this argument, but his epistemology suggests the following. If public evidence is no more than shared observation, then this merely requires theories to satisfy the observation requirement, to be empirically adequate. But this is compatible with 'anything goes'. On the other hand, if we try to tighten this up by suggesting that intersubjective agreement should reflect some kind of theoretical agreement, we run the risk of begging the question, of picking criteria precisely to eliminate Greenfield's viewpoint. More debate is possible here, but the issue very quickly becomes complex. Then again, there is no reason for believing that adequately replying to Greenfield should be easy.

Our own defence of objectivity and science is also in the pragmatist tradition flowing from Dewey, but it grows out of philosophical discussions initiated by Quine. To add these considerations to our present reflections let us briefly restate the key issue. If empirical adequacy, or squaring with observation, is all there is to justification and the objectivity of knowledge as traditional empiricism claims, and if any number of exotic and divergent theories can meet this condition, as subjectivist critics maintain, then theory choice among the limitless number of suitable theories comes to depend decisively on other, nonobjective considerations. Confronted with this failure of empirical foundations adequately to confirm or disconfirm competing theories, the subjectivist response is to call for additional, subjective, foundations. Our alternative response is to locate the problem within foundationalism and foundational justification. To see how this might work over the question of objectivity, consider an example of how one interpretation of experience might be better than another. In leaving a room, most of us prefer to do so through the doorway rather than attempting to go through the wall. Of course doorways, walls, and success in getting out of rooms, are all the fruits of interpreted experience. It is just that our experience of leaving the room coheres extraordinarily well with our humdrum folk theory view that human bodies pass more readily through open doors than through what is theorized to be walls. Strictly speaking, failure to leave through the wall does not disconfirm the hypothesis that it can be done. Test situations are complex and one can elaborate the surrounding theory to prevent any kind of empirical hit on the hypothesis. The trouble with this proposal is that it makes for a very complex theory, at least in relation to empirically adequate rivals (see Lakatos 1970, Walker and Evers 1986). Since appeal to extra-empirical virtues like simplicity can winnow these alternatives, objectivity appears to be a matter of what is given by our most coherent account of our (interpreted) experience. Quine remarks that

> . . . simplicity, in a theory that squares with observation sentences so far as its contacts with them go, is the best evidence of truth we can ask;

no better can be claimed for the doctrines of molecules and electrons (Quine 1960, p. 250).

As doors and walls no more satisfy any foundational 'direct perception' requirement than molecules and electrons, the parsimony of theoretically motivated success in getting in and out of rooms is about as basic as objectivity ever gets.

In a sense, Greenfield does acknowledge certain limits to his subjectivist thesis. For example, of the realities 'out there' that are beyond our control, he identifies birth and death (Greenfield 1983, p. 294). But on this test, he could identify water flowing downhill and the resistance walls offers to the contents of rooms. For theories that deny birth and death, or assume we can pass through walls, fail to be coherent accounts of our experience. Indeed, if the limits to the subjectivist thesis are set at what lies beyond our control, the realm of objectivity expands quite dramatically, since we have virtually no control at all over the law-like features of our world, or any of the properties of its component parts. As we indicated in Chapter One, we need to distinguish between the ubiquity of interpretation in science, and what we can control. We can, of course, theorize any way we like about our experience and what gives rise to it. However, lack of control serves as a focus for objectivity because it suggests conditions under which patterns of experience may be similar for different observers. The standard simplest condition, captured by our ordinary folk-theoretic view of things, is the supposition of middle-sized enduring physical objects as the common causal source of experience. Economies, in the form of extra-empirical virtues, which accrue to theories that posit the reality of chairs and tables, sticks and stones, bricks and bones, are usually decisive when it comes to theory choice over these matters.

Once we begin to see objectivity as determined by coherence considerations, the issue of lack of control is really peripheral: it is merely an entering wedge. For the conditions which make for the objectivity of chairs and tables are, once again, the same conditions which make for the objectivity of electrons and molecules. The chief point we want to make is this. If observational evidence is all the evidence there ever is for our theories, as traditional empiricisms claim, then Greenfield's employment of arguments for theory ladenness, holistic complexity of tests, and underdetermination constitute a *reductio* argument against such empiricisms. But the correct conclusion to draw from the *reductio* argument, in our view, is that observational evidence is not all the evidence there is. As we argued in Chapter Two, we should conclude that extra-empirical conditions can constitute important evidence for the acceptability of a theory. This means that we can accept both the ubiquity of interpretation in science and also a realistic and workable notion of objectivity.

Knowledge and Organizational Reality

The foregoing discussion has focused on Greenfield's view of scientific knowledge. If there is no such thing as objectivity in the natural sciences, then it is an easy matter to extend the thesis to the social sciences. However, if all the objections to his position on scientific knowledge are sound, if objectivity does exist in the natural sciences, his most significant claims about educational administration would still appear to be largely untouched. The reason can be found in one way of characterizing his distinction between the social sciences and the natural sciences. For, interestingly, the difference can be made to depend on precisely the issue of the bounds of control. Intention, interpretation, will, values, desires, and thoughts are subjective realities that in turn are capable of influencing other subjective realities. Inasmuch as we are the originators of these realities, they lie within our control. But this is a form of control that can be extended to social realities. This is because, for Greenfield, organizations are not things, at least not as chairs and tables are things:

> They have no ontological reality, and it is no use studying them as though they did. They are an invented social reality of human creation. It is people who are responsible for organizations and people who change them. Organizations have reality only through human action, and it is that action (and the human will driving it) that we must come to understand (Greenfield 1986, p. 71).

Organizations are a form of socially constructed reality. We may perhaps concede that science can deal with brute data, with chairs and tables and 'facts that press themselves upon our understanding so forcibly that no one can question their existence' (Greenfield 1984, p. 150), but organizational reality is defined by nonbrute data, by meanings, human intentions, actions, and experiences. From this perspective Greenfield concludes that 'organizations are . . . cultural artifacts: they are systems of meaning that can be understood only through the interpretation of meaning' (1984, p. 150). Some examples might illustrate this contrast. In describing the moves in a game of chess, science appears to be limited to descriptions like: such and such a shaped piece of matter was moved from one particular position on a checkered board to another position, whereupon all the shaped pieces were swept from the board and placed in a box. With the resources of interpretation, and an understanding of the rules of chess, on the other hand, we may say that the white rook checkmated an opponent's king. In this case it seems that we cannot understand, or even predict, what is happening without a grasp of the relevant rules that constitute, or define, the practice of playing chess, of winning and losing. Or consider the case of a person, in the presence of another person, raising hand to head. Given an interpretation of what is observed as an instance of a soldier meeting a superior officer, the hand raising may be correctly described as a salute. Without the benefit of a military interpretation, however, the same pattern of sensory irridation may elicit a description of the event in terms of a metrical displacement of particular material objects. The difference in interpretation is crucial. The first version uses descriptions that make reference to human intentionality, to background rules and specific social customs; features that invoke an explanatory framework more relevant to people's reasons for doing what they do. The second version could more readily be embedded in a causal account of behaviour. But the point is that a causal account, no matter how detailed, would presumably contain different information about what was happening and why it was happening. Similarly, in organizational theory, we may regard as a brute datum the fact that a person applied chalk to a board and spoke to a group of children and adults. But whether the person is a principal, and is doing the things a principal does, are evidently matters far removed from what is given in brute data. These are social facts that draw on interpretations, and interpretations of interpretations (the double hermeneutic). For Greenfield:

> the important factors of organizational life call nonbrute data into play . . . there is therefore no ultimate reality in the understanding of organizations (Greenfield 1984, p. 151).

Now what Greenfield seems to be suggesting is this: whatever the facts are, and however reliable our knowledge of them may be, when it comes to the matter of interpretation, there is no fact of the matter, no ultimate reality to be right or wrong about, no ultimate social truth. For example, there is nothing in the physical distribution of matter bounding a game of chess in progress that is a checkmate. A checkmate is the interpretation we choose to give a certain physical configuration; it is something over and above the physical reality described by science. No scientific study of the physical players–pieces–board configuration will evidently enable us to predict the conditions under which the game terminates unless we supplement the study with an account of the rules of chess, what the various moves mean, and how we interpret the various pieces.

And so it is with organizations. For Greenfield it is a mistake to regard them as just people–environment physical configurations that interact according to sets of causal laws. Rather, they are created and sustained by the intentional, meaningful, rule-governed action of people. Social nonbrute facts that are the stuff of organizations, like signing a cheque, bidding at an auction, or issuing an order, cannot be understood except in terms of comprehensive networks of rule-governed, intentional actions. Issuing orders, or bidding, bring about the consequences they do because other people interpret these actions the way they do. If people systematically interpreted these actions differently, the physical patterns accessible to, and describable by, science would cease to bring about the consequences they do. Indeed, they would cease to be the nonbrute facts they are. Social reality itself would have altered because 'it is nonbrute facts themselves that define and constitute social reality' (Greenfield 1984, p. 151). Thus science, traditional or otherwise, inasmuch as it uses a causal/descriptive explanatory apparatus that abstracts from interpretation, cannot in principle account for the kind of social and organizational phenomena that form the locus of administrative theory. Subjectivity might conceivably come to grief in natural science where interpretations are constrained by things outside our control. But our control over the construction of social reality implies this is not the case for subjectivity in social science.

Granted this fundamental difference in orientation between the natural sciences and the social sciences, Greenfield concludes that

> . . . the purpose of social science is to understand social reality as different people see it and to demonstrate how their views shape the action which they take within that reality . . . [T]he social sciences . . . must work directly with man's definitions of reality and with the rules he devises for coping with it. While the social sciences do not reveal ultimate truth, they do help us to make sense of our world (Greenfield 1975, p. 72).

And herein lies the strength of a subjectivist methodology. For what is required for understanding and sense-making is a subjective apprehension of interpretations and a successful embedding of these into explanatory frameworks that invoke an agent's reasons and inner motivations.

In our view, Greenfield's approach to organizational theory (and the long tradition of social science in which his approach stands) admits of no easy reply. Following recent work in philosophy of mind (see Churchland 1984), we have some strategies to offer in advancing a coherentist naturalistic scientific view of social science. At this stage these strategies are programmatic rather than detailed, but as most of the current methodological debate is programmatic, we can endure to some extent a lack of detail. In general, we see the language of subjectivist explanation — talk of interpretation, intention, and the like — as a relatively autonomous domain of discourse that is both predictively useful and explanatorily economical. It is relatively autonomous in the sense that its basic concepts seem to be orthogonal to the basic concepts of physical science. Yet it facilitates mostly reliable communication between people and is an immensely serviceable language for describing and predicting what people will do. Since we imbibe such language from the beginning, when we first learn to talk, it would be fair to describe its basic concepts as part of our ordinary, everyday, folk theory of the world. Our suggestion — explored in more detail in Chapter Nine — is that this theory, which has been developed over thousands of years in almost total ignorance of the inner causal workings of people, may very well be just about optimal for a theory subject to these constraints. Our point is that this may explain its large measure of empirical adequacy. On the other hand, if humans are complex physical systems, and physical science is true (at least in its domain of application) then if the fundamental theoretical categories of folk theory are not found in physical science, folk theory may actually be false. That is, folk theory may be both empirically adequate and false.

This combination is not possible in Greenfield's epistemology because of his conflation of evidence with empirical adequacy. But if excellence of global theory includes the extra-empirical virtues of coherence, there is a premium on our best physical science somehow meshing with successful folk-theoretic accounts of human behaviour. Against the possibility of folk accounts being used to refute scientific accounts, we argue in Chapter Six, where interpretive social science is considered in more detail, for the importance of causal assumptions in folk explanations. To overcome the problem of orthogonality, we argue in Chapter Nine that the empirical success of folk theory can be accounted for by making a number of modest physicalist assumptions. And in what follows we touch on elements of both these arguments in an attempt to show that some surrendering of subjectivism, or 'anything goes', is required if subjectivist explanations are to do any epistemological work; that is, if they are to be anything other than totally arbitrary accounts of human action.

Although the issues here are complex, the key point on which we want to focus can be expressed quite simply. Either evidence for differences among competing interpretations is epistemically accessible or it is not. If not, then we have a closed and vicious hermeneutical circle which gives us no reason for supposing that interpretations can explain anything at all. If it is, then interpretations are best viewed, despite the intentional idiom, as networks of hypotheses after the fashion of scientific theories. A writer cited by Greenfield in support of a hermeneutic science is Charles Taylor, who argues that

> . . . if we have a science which has no brute data, which relies on readings, then it cannot but move in a hermeneutical circle. A given reading of intersubjective meanings of a society, or of given institutions or practices, may seem well founded, because it makes sense of these practices or the development of that society. But the conviction that it does make sense of this history itself is founded on further related readings. . . . But if these readings seem implausible, or even more, if they are not understood by our interlocutor, there is no verification procedure we can fall back on. We can only continue to offer interpretations; we are in an interpretative circle . . . a hermeneutic science cannot but rely on insight (Taylor 1979, pp. 65–66).

Not all researchers in educational administration who have been attracted to hermeneutical science have been happy with these conclusions. Thomas

Sergiovanni, who also cites Taylor on social reality and nonbrute facts, sees hermeneutics as the lesser of two evils:

> It is far better to adopt the concept of theory of practice and the hermeneutical mode of inquiry, no matter how difficult this task, than to continue with the more comfortable but less appropriate methods and images of traditional science (Sergiovanni 1984, p. 289).

Given this limited set of options he feels 'left with no other alternative but to proceed in these murky waters' (Sergiovanni 1984, p. 290). Greenfield also expresses some concern:

> The task of choosing images, metaphors, statements to represent the organization as a cultural artifact is not easy. There are no rules for such a representation, for the explication and interpretation of reality (Greenfield 1984, p. 156).

Both Sergiovanni and Greenfield are right in seeing a problem here, for if there are literally no rules — explicit, implicit, tacit, or otherwise — the task does not become difficult. Rather, there is no task to be achieved; it ceases to exist. If there is no (presumed) standard or measure of suitability of choice among images and metaphors, there is no mark to fall short of, and therefore the notion of representation becomes idle. There would literally be no such thing as a success or failure to represent. This point is apt to be disguised by talk of 'intuition', 'illumination', 'insight', or even the 'naturalness' of interpretations. But make no mistake: whatever it is that distinguishes noninsightful from insightful interpretations, it is not to be found in the distinction between fiction and nonfiction. Not unless there is more to interpretation than the methodology of the hermeneutic circle can concede. We can, of course, acquiesce in this conclusion and agree to pursue subjectivist administrative theory as something other than a non-fiction genre. A further, more radical, conclusion along the same lines would be to accept, as theoretically idle, the whole box and dice of folk intentionalist idiom, since it appears to be massively disconnected from any possible experience; there are just readings, as Taylor (1979) suggests, all the way down.

The price one pays for adopting this line, at a practical level, is that it is difficult to offer advice on everyday administrative problems and issues. Greenfield appears to admit as much, at least by implication, when he comes to the task of giving an account of how administrators should be trained. In suggesting something rather than nothing at all — spending time in a monastery, or as a patient in a mental hospital, for example (Greenfield 1980, p. 48) — he is attempting what amounts to a rough specification of some of the empirical conditions under which insight is more likely to be produced. Where his suggestions have value, they undermine the case for a hermeneutic circle. Actually, Greenfield might well raise more theoretical worries with Taylor's argument, since it runs against the chief virtues of the language of meaning, sense-making, interpretation and intention; namely, its unique combination of economy of expression and predictive power. Consider the example of bidding at an auction. In raising a hand at a strategic point in the proceedings, one can initiate a long sequence of complex events that will ultimately lead to, say, the purchase of a house. What is more, the procedure and its outcome are not unpredictable; on the contrary, they are entirely regular and uniform. Yet, as Greenfield would correctly maintain, the whole matter is held together by interpretations of behaviour and interpretations of those interpretations. Because these are the very factors which conspire to enhance predictive power — the empirical consequences of misinterpretation at an auction can be immediate and drastic, and beyond a mistaken bidder's control — there is evidently less arbitrariness about the business of interpretation than the hermeneutic circle permits.

If the evidence for competing interpretations is epistemically accessible, as these reflections suggest, in what does it consist? Unfortunately, the three epistemological considerations Greenfield raises against traditional science also apply to empirical evidence for interpretations: observations for interpretations are theory laden, tests for interpretations are complex, and all hypothesized interpretations are underdetermined by all the available evidence. Clearly, we need to invoke extra-empirical virtues if we are to distinguish among the infinite number of possibilities. Our proposal is that where empirical evidence is relevant, an interpretation is an empirical hypothesis concerning the consequences of human action. However, it is a hypothesis embedded in a reasons and motives oriented folk-theoretic account of social life. The theoretical economy of this account consists in the simplicity, comprehensiveness, and coherence of its core of subjective rationality/valuational/motivational postulates.

As we indicated earlier, any adequate reply to Greenfield's methodological bifurcation of the natural and the social sciences must adequately address the question of the combined fruitfulness and apparent autonomy of subjectivist explanation. To do this we must suppose that the basic categories of such explanations are false, but are empirically adequate because they go proxy for deep underlying causal mechanisms in human social behaviour. To see how this works, at least as an opening strategy against Greenfield's position, consider again the example of chess. Suppose we use our science to build and program two machines, A and B, to play each other at chess. In watching this active configuration of A and B plus display monitor, we may be persuaded to say that A has made a mistake, and that B will shortly checkmate A's king and win. And if we are sufficiently familiar with the ways of chess and correct in our assumption that the machines are playing rationally, our comment will no doubt enjoy high predictive accuracy. But there is nothing nonphysical, in the sense of non-causal, going on in the configuration that makes the descriptions 'mistake', 'adopted a better strategy', 'checkmate', or the prediction that B will win, particularly appropriate. Each move and counter-move has its causal antecedents if we assume, not unreasonably, that the rules of chess and certain optimizing subroutines are 'hard wired' into A and B as standing causal dispositions; and so the entire sequence proceeds according to the regularities of physical science. Winning, losing, making mistakes or deft moves all have their fine-grained physical tokens in the A plus B plus monitor system, and scientific knowledge of the behaviour of the system at this level of description will yield predictions of wins and losses that are in principle as accurate as any deterministic system permits.

The point of this example is not to imply that a science of chess — or a science of organizations — consists in giving the engineering details. At that level of detail the causal story, as it would currently be told, is too complex to be of any general use. The point worth emphasizing is that such detail is, by and large, not needed in describing and accurately predicting either chess outcomes or a great many ordinary, everyday social or organizational outcomes. This is because our ordinary, folk-theoretic ways of describing the behaviour of complex systems like chess computers — winning, losing, and making good or bad moves — already assume an underlying regularity of causal structure. Thus if machine hardware was unreliable, or arbitrary in its behaviour, we could not use our broad empirical assumption of machine rationality to predict chess outcomes. And so it is with more complex events like auctions, or vastly more complex structures like organizations. In criticizing the possibility of a naturalistic science of administration we need to bear in mind that ordinary language talk of intentions, reasons, beliefs, motives, and interpretations — in short our whole apparatus of folk psychology — assumes the regularity and reliability of equally vast amounts of causal structure in people and their environment. It is therefore a mistake, though a common one in much social theory (see for example, Giddens 1979), to say that a person's behaviour is caused only when the person does not act rationally, or in accord with subjective rationality assumptions.

Greenfield thinks that one weakness of the causal/descriptive explanatory apparatus of science is that it abstracts from human intentions, interpretations, and desires. Given the lack of any really useful empirical generalizations in social science, he is perfectly correct. But we want to suggest that the real strength of explanation in terms of these folk notions is that it abstracts from all the predictively irrelevant engineering details of complex systems. Actions our language effortlessly describes as writing a cheque, issuing an order, or bidding at an auction all presume such enormous networks of causal regularities that we could hardly begin to describe them in engineering terms. Nevertheless, the autonomy of thought and action implied by ordinary, everyday language is an illusion sustained mainly by the sheer ubiquity of the network of regularities around us. We think that Greenfield's view of interpreted social reality is therefore not an alternative to a science of organization. The whole enterprise of interpretation can only proceed on the assumption that there is a reality there to be interpreted, and that it is sufficiently stable, orderly, and regular to sustain the kind of empirical abstractions typical of interpretations.

On this view, organizations are real in the same way that chairs and tables are real. Their stability is due mainly to relatively enduring dispositions, encoded through learning, in the central nervous systems of human beings. If human memory retained information for no more than a week, or a day, and if our values and beliefs fluctuated frequently and extravagantly, organizations, at least as we currently conceive of them, would not exist. Fortunately, there are limits to the plasticity of mind as objective as any limits to the deformability of walls and doors (see Churchland 1979). Too little plasticity and we become unteachable; too much and each new experience washes away what went before, leaving no deposit. Principles governing these phenomena are becoming better understood in neuroscience (Grossberg 1982), which is the correct place to look for deep insights on the nature of introspection, consciousness, attention, selective awareness and the like. It is here that the prospects for a naturalistic account of human subjectivity look most promising. There are epistemological advantages in seeking such an account if we note that our perceptions of our inner world — our mental life — are as much laden with theory as our perceptions of the outer world. The common run of our subjective experience, for all its familiarity and ordinariness, is as much a product of the workings of a vastly complex neural machine as the more exotic experiences which dominate the clinical literature (Churchland 1986). The gains in having our observations of the external world guided by our best science are much the same as the gains to be had in accepting such guidance for our inner perceptions.

Greenfield has raised major objections to traditional views of science of administration. What is more, in drawing on the predictive and explanatory power of subjectivist theory in the form of the economical and empirically adequate accounts of human behaviour embedded in language and literature, he has made a persuasive case for the distinctiveness of social science and all his characteristic theses about organizations which flow from it. To rebut his approach decisively we would have to construct a most coherent global theory in which physical science provided the basic theoretical framework for successfully explaining and predicting social phenomena. We have not done that, and neither has anyone else. We have, however, suggested an epistemological programme for making the apparent autonomy of subjectivist theory — the chief obstacle to any unified theory — unproblematical from a naturalistic perspective; namely, treat the theory as false but empirically adequate and give a naturalistic scientific account of its empirical adequacy.

Needless to say, this represents the beginnings of a scientific account of human organizations, not the end of one.

Summary

Greenfield objects to traditional science of administration on two broad counts. First, he thinks its version of science, especially its view of objectivity, is epistemologically inadequate, even for natural science. And second, because the phenomena of administration are social phenomena, he thinks that their subjective nature puts them beyond the reach of so-called objective science. He argues the first point by adopting Kuhn and Feyerabend's objections to traditional empiricism, notably their attack on the existence of hard data: all observation is theory laden, all test situations are complex, and all theory is underdetermined by the available evidence. We agree with this attack. He concludes that since there is no hard data, anything goes. We disagree. We think there is more to evidence than data. Since all the empirical evidence for anything is soft, we think that theories admit of adjudication on extra-empirical criteria, the criteria of coherence justification. Objectivity is a matter of coherence, not hard data.

He argues his second point by distinguishing between brute data, which may even be construed as objective in traditional ways, and nonbrute data which are subjective and constructed out of meanings, intentions, interpretations, human actions, and experiences. Organizational reality is made up of nonbrute data and is like a cultural artifact. It can only be understood subjectively, by understanding interpretations and interpretations of interpretations. We suggest that if there are no limits to subjectivity in the construction of nonbrute data, subjective explanations will do no epistemological work; they will be totally arbitrary. Resulting administrative theory will admit of no distinction between fiction and nonfiction. We note that, even for Greenfield, there must be some limits to subjectivity for interpretations, meanings, and the like, to make cultural artifacts possible. These realities assume some measure of intersubjective agreement and stability over time. We conclude by exploring a physicalistic scientific account of the reality and epistemic accessibility of interpretation, meaning, and nonbrute data in general. Whether such a science will leave these folk categories intact is another matter. However, if they succumb, science of administration will be quite different to anything conceived either by its traditional supporters or its critics (see Churchland 1981, Stich 1983).

References

Churchland P. M. (1979). *Scientific Realism and the Plasticity of Mind.* (Cambridge: Cambridge University Press).
Churchland P. M. (1981). Eliminative materialism and the propositional attitudes, *Journal of Philosophy*, 78(2), pp. 67–90.

Churchland P. M. (1984). *Matter and Consciousness*. (Cambridge, Mass.: M.I.T. Press).
Churchland P. S. (1986). *Neurophilosophy*. (Cambridge, Mass.: M.I.T. Press).
Dewey J. (1907). The control of ideas by facts. III, *Journal of Philosophy*, 4(12).
Dewey J. (1929). *Experience and Nature*. (New York: Dover).
Evers C. W. (1986). Theory, politics, and experiment in educational research methodology, *International Review of Education*, 32(4), pp. 373–387.
Giddens, A. (1979). *Central Problems in Social Theory: Action, Structure and Contradiction*. (Berkeley and Los Angeles: University of California Press).
Greenfield T. B. (1975). Theory about organization: a new perspective for schools, in M. G. Hughes (ed.) *Administering Education: International Challenge*. (London: Athlone Press). We cite it as reprinted in P. C. Gronn (ed.) *Rethinking Educational Administration*. (Geelong: Deakin University Press).
Greenfield T. B. (1978). Reflections on organization theory and the truths of irreconcilable realities, *Educational Administration Quarterly*, 14(2), pp. 1–23.
Greenfield T. B. (1979a). Ideas versus data: how can the data speak for themselves? in G. L. Immegart and W. L. Boyd (eds.) *Problem-Finding in Educational Administration*. (Lexington: Lexington Books).
Greenfield T. B. (1979b) Organization theory as ideology, *Curriculum Inquiry*, 9(2), pp. 97–112.
Greenfield T. B. (1980). The man who comes back through the door in the wall: discovering truth, discovering self, discovering organizations, *Educational Administration Quarterly*, 16(3), pp. 26–59.
Greenfield T. B. (1983). Against group mind: an anarchistic theory of organization in R. L. Rattray-Wood (ed.) *Reflective Readings in Educational Administration*. (Geelong: Deakin University Press).
Greenfield T. B. (1984). Leaders and schools: wilfulness and nonnatural order in organizations, in T. J. Sergiovanni and J. E. Corbally (eds.) *Leadership and Organizational Culture*. (Chicago: University of Illinois Press).
Greenfield T. B. (1986). The decline and fall of science in educational administration, *Interchange*, 17(2), pp. 57–80.
Griffiths D. E. (1977). The individual in organization: a theoretical perspective, *Educational Administration Quarterly*, 13(2), pp. 1–18.
Griffiths D. E. (1979). Intellectual turmoil in educational administration, *Educational Administration Quarterly*, 15(3), pp. 43–65.
Gronn P. C. (1983) (ed.). *Rethinking Educational Administration*. (Geelong: Deakin University Press).
Grossberg S. (1982). *Studies in Mind and Brain*. (Boston: Reidel).
Hills J. (1980). A critique of Greenfield's 'New Perspective', *Educational Administration Quarterly*, 16(1), pp. 20–44.
Lakatos I. (1970). Falsification and the methodology of scientific research programmes, in I. Lakatos and A. Musgrave (eds.) *Criticism and the Growth of Knowledge*. (London: Cambridge University Press).
Quine W. V. (1960). *Word and Object*. (Cambridge, Mass.: M.I.T. Press).
Quine W. V. (1961). *From a Logical Point of View*. (Cambridge, Mass.: Harvard University Press).
Sergiovanni T. J. (1984). Developing a relevant theory of administration, in T. J. Sergiovanni and J. E. Corbally (eds.) *Leadership and Organizational Culture*. (Chicago: University of Illinois Press).
Stich S. P. (1983). *From Folk Psychology to Cognitive Science*. (Cambridge, Mass.: M.I.T. Press).
Taylor C. (1979). Interpretation and the sciences of man, in P. Rabinow and W. M. Sullivan (eds.) *Interpretive Social Science: A Reader*. (Berkeley: University of California Press).
Willower D. J. (1980). Contemporary issues in theory in educational administration, *Educational Administration Quarterly*, 16(3), pp. 1–25.
Willower D. J. (1981). Educational administration: some philosophical and other considerations, *Journal of Educational Administration*, 19(2), pp. 115–139.
Willower D. J. (1983). Evolution in the professorship: past, philosophy, future, *Educational Administration Quarterly*, 19(3), pp. 179–200.
Willower D. J. (1985). Philosophy and the study of educational administration, *Journal of Educational Administration*, 23(1), pp. 5–22.

5

Hodgkinson on Humanism in Administration

Although Thomas Greenfield is the best known critic of traditional science in educational administration, he is not the only theorist to have challenged its behavioural science assumptions. Christopher Hogkinson's work in educational administration is important because, like Greenfield, not only has he challenged these assumptions, he has also developed a systematic alternative perspective on administrative theory and practice (Hodgkinson 1978, 1983). In this chapter we discuss the main elements of Hodgkinson's alternative as it applies to educational administration. This last qualification is important since Hodgkinson's work is addressed to a much wider audience in administrative theory. We shall begin by locating his thought within two major approaches to the theory of knowledge, and then go on to discuss his views on the nature of administration, the place of philosophy and values in administrative theory, and possible responses to these views. We conclude by arguing that Hodgkinson's suggestions about Arrow's Theorem, when elaborated, pose a fundamental challenge to traditional science of administration, particularly over the question of goal determination in administrative decision making. Our own proposal for meeting this challenge is to suggest a realist, but fallibilist, alternative to the ethical theories that figure in Hodgkinson's analytical model. We defend our realist view later, in Chapter Eight.

Knowledge and the Politics of Administration

H. A. Alexander (1989) has recently drawn attention to two epistemological ideas that have influenced approaches to liberal education. The first goes back to Plato, and has been by far the dominant influence. The second is more recent, reflects insights from John Stuart Mill's essay *On Liberty*, and has received its strongest current expression in the work of Paul Feyerabend (1978).

Consider the central question Plato addresses in the *Republic*, namely: 'What is the nature of a just state or society?' In beginning his answer, Plato, speaking through the character of Socrates, speculates on the origins

98

of the city-state: 'the formation of a city is due, as I imagine, to this fact, that we are not individually independent, but have many wants' (Davies and Vaughan 1907, p. 53). He then identifies three of these wants as basic and in need of satisfaction by all persons: food, a house, and clothing. Of the many ways of satisfying these wants, however, Socrates speculates on what might be the most efficient. After some argument he concludes that

> . . . all things will be produced in superior quantity and quality, and with greater ease, when each man works at a single occupation, in accordance with his natural gifts. . .(Davies and Vaughan 1907, p. 55).

In the first instance, this solution to the basic economic problem requires skilled artisans, merchants, markets and a currency, retail dealers, and hired labourers. Responding to Glaucon's objection that we have here a solution adequate for a community of swine, Socrates adds artists, musicians, poets, actors, and dancers. He also applies his efficiency argument to the military needs of the state, concluding that the best solution is to have a professional army. This is controversial, since it was believed to be every man's duty to defend the state. Finally, he considers how the argument might apply to the matter of ruling the state, and concludes that because ruling is one function among others, the same efficiencies accrue to specialization here too. Since justice must reside in the relations all citizens bear to each other, the issue of state leadership, or guardianship, because it affects such relations, becomes the principal focus of concern.

What qualities must good leaders possess in order to ensure the just administration of the state, and how might these be acquired or enhanced through education? The bulk of the *Republic* is devoted to answering these questions, but to gain a perspectives on Hodgkinson's work, we need consider only one strand of Plato's thought. Socrates remarks that

> . . . the man whose natural gifts promise to make him a perfect guardian of the state will be philosophical, high-spirited, swift-footed, and strong (Davies and Vaughan 1907, p. 64).

Some emphasis on particular physical skills and qualities is to be expected as leaders are drawn from the ranks of the army. However, the most important attribute is a philosophical mind. This is essential if leaders are to apprehend the insensible forms that are the source of all knowledge of reality. And among all the forms, an apprehension of the Form of Good is the ultimate attainment:

> In the world of knowledge, the essential Form of Good is the limit of our inquiries, and can barely be perceived; but when perceived, we

cannot help concluding that it is in every case the source of all that is bright and beautiful . . . and that whosoever would act wisely, either in private or in public, must set this Form of Good before his eyes (Davies and Vaughan 1907, p. 238).

The administration of the state is fundamentally a moral activity, ideal decisions being those guided by a knowledge of the good. It is also a philosophical activity because philosophical inquiry is the source of this knowledge.

These two conclusions, applied to administration in general, reflect two central features of Christopher Hodgkinson's view. For Herbert Simon, and the theorists of the behavioural science tradition, an administrative theory is inadequate if it contains ethical claims. For Hodgkinson, as a critic of positivism, an administrative theory is inadequate precisely if it does not contain ethical claims. So if positivistic science eschews ethics, administrative theory is best viewed as a humanism not a science (Hodgkinson 1983, p. 15). His argument for this position contains two key elements which we discuss and analyse in some detail later. The first is a view of philosophy as 'in barest essence the process of correct thinking and the process of valuing: rationality, or logic, and values' (Hodgkinson 1978, p. 3). The second is a view of administration which contains philosophy as an essential component. From his analysis of the logic of administration, he concludes that two types of competence distinguish an administrative profession: an understanding of organizations and organization theory and a knowledge of the theory and practice of decision making. The second type of competence divides again into two areas of special competence: a capacity for logical analysis and a capacity for value analysis. The result is that 'the intrusion of values into the decision-making process is not merely inevitable, it is the very substance of decision' (Hodgkinson 1978, p. 39). From this he concludes that administration contains an ineliminable philosophical component, the principal reason why it is not a science at all but a humanism; hence his claim that 'administration is philosophy in action' (1978, p. 1).

Plato's epistemology comes with a politics. Leadership, as a philosophical enterprise, implies leadership by an elite, for few are able to undertake the learning required to perceive true knowledge: the forms. Interestingly, Hodgkinson would also endorse this elitism — 'meritocracy is logically preferable to democracy' (Hodgkinson 1978, p. 219) — though for different reasons. Yet, in the final analysis, it is the differences that make the comparison with Plato more suggestive than revealing. Hodgkinson has marked out his disagreements with Plato's theory, and simply does not subscribe to such an idealist epistemology. So while Plato's elitist politics of leadership depends on the rigours of knowledge acquisition, Hodgkinson's, as we shall see later, depends more on a meritocracy of the will.

If elitism is a matter of the few having access to the truth, as one might expect, the case for doubt, or uncertainty, or human fallibility, can be pressed into the service of democracy. Mill's defence of liberty against censorship is the classic formulation of this second tradition: censorship protects views that may be false (Mill 1910, pp. 78–113). The systematic and wide-ranging attack on Plato in Karl Popper's *The Open Society and its Enemies* (1945) is another fallibilist critique: open, democratic societies that foster criticism and freedom of thought are more likely to promote the growth of knowledge through the elimination of error. Paul Feyerabend's (1978) work provides another perspective on this theme. Given the 'anything goes' interpretation of Feyerabend's epistemology that, for example, Greenfield supports, with one view reckoned as good as any other, there are no errors to suppress or truths to defend. Where truth making is a matter of will, desire, and intention, the strong subjectivist seems to be the natural champion of liberty and freedom of thought and action.

Ironically, subjectivism intrudes into Hodgkinson's theory at precisely the point where philosophy has its most characteristic and important role to play in administration; namely, over the question of values. He claims that:

> The essential point to grasp in thinking about value is that values do not exist *in the world*. They are utterly phenomenological, subjective, facts of the inner and personal experience, ultimately only susceptible of location within an individual cranium. . . . The values which are immediately imputed to . . . objects, facts and events are *in principle* at the *will* of the possessors, actors, beholders, participants. The world of fact is given, the world of value made (Hodgkinson 1983, p. 31).

The most surprising feature of Hodgkinson's approach to administrative theory and practice, therefore, is the combination of elements it contains from the traditions of certitude and fallibilism; an elitist politics and view of the role of leader more akin to a tradition that sees legitimate leadership as grounded in access to objective knowledge, and a subjectivist view of knowledge of administrative values more akin to a tradition that defends democracy, participation, and a legitimate contribution by all. Surprising or not, we think that Hodgkinson is essentially correct in his insight that subjectivism at the individual level makes for elitism at the organizational level.

Philosophy and Administration

Writing in 1978, Hodgkinson observed that 'at present no distinctive philosophy of administration exists' (p. 197). One reason for this absence, he suggests, is the dominance of a positivist-inspired school of administrative thought, particularly as exemplified by its 'prototypical exponent',

H. A. Simon. According to Hodgkinson, Simon's theory implies that 'the organization is a bus and the administrator its driver. What need for philosophy in such an arrangement?' (Hodgkinson 1983, p. 11). Or less picturesquely, for Simon, the administrative process consists in selecting and implementing satisfactory means to given ends, or organizational goals, under conditions of limited, or bounded, rationality (Simon 1976, pp. 240–244). The role of philosophy is thus apparently displaced by the technical decision procedures of satisficing.

Since Simon's approach is itself the product of a definite and clearly articulated philosophy, by 'philosophy of administration' Hodgkinson clearly means more than just philosophy in the role of a constraint on the structure of administrative theorizing. Several qualifications are necessary here. For a start, he maintains a distinction between administration and management, a distinction which he claims 'can be understood in broad terms as paralleling the distinction between policy making and policy implementation' (Hodgkinson 1983, p. 1). The former involves a judgmental aspect, whereas the latter expresses organizational activity. The distinction is not sharp, and he later elaborates a view of administration and management as endpoints on a continuum, but it does highlight the judgmental aspect of administration. He also distinguishes a number of senses of 'philosophy': notably, the academic, the dualistic, the classical and the practical (Hodgkinson 1983, pp. 4–10). These senses are also not mutually exclusive, but it is the dualistic sense that best captures his particular usage:

> This understanding of philosophy would divide the domain into two parts: logic and value. The former deals with matters of fact, structures, coherence and consistency, causal chains and explanatory systems and sequences. The latter with all matters of value from the ethical and moral, through the valuational, to all the complexities of motivation. It would thus embrace all the infra- and supra-rational elements revealed by or known from depth analysis of the human psyche. Together these two fields of knowledge encompass all organizational behaviour (Hodgkinson 1983, p. 6).

Given these points about usage, philosophy is assumed to be embedded in the very process of administrative decision making. On this view, a philosophy of administration would not only provide a coordinating framework for administrative theory, it would contribute decisively to the characteristic substance of administrative practice, to decision and action.

A further qualification which needs to be noted concerns the temptation to conclude that the preceding argument is purely verbal, that the relevance of philosophy for administration flows simply from a matter of usage or definition. It does not. To see this, consider a parallel case. The administration/management distinction, when drawn very sharply, mirrors the distinction Simon draws between policy and administration (Simon 1976, pp. 52–59). That is, all the normative issues that are raised by 'administration' in Hodgkinson's sense are raised by 'policy' in Simon's sense. Moreover, ethical reasoning and ethical behaviour, as ubiquitous human phenomena, fall within the explanatory domain of even Simon's early view of philosophy. Why, then, does Hodgkinson resist concluding that Simon's work expresses a philosophy of administration? (see Evers 1985, Hodgkinson 1986). We suggest the following answer. Simon's philosophy contains a meta-ethic — a view of the nature of ethics — that rules out ethics as a legitimate body of knowledge. So this philosophy disqualifies itself from making any contribution to the determination of what ought to be done. But since ethics is not knowledge, it cannot be part of proper policy theory, or figure in its determination, either. The question of what ought to be done, as an end in policy, lies outside of policy theory. True to its epistemology, the goals of policy are determined, not by philosophy, but by empirically ascertaining and suitably aggregating people's subjective, affective, noncognitive preferences.

Now if this is the sense in which philosophy can be said to be absent from policy, and hence more readily from administration, it is hardly a verbal matter. For example, in counting ethical claims as knowledge, albeit subjective knowledge, Hodgkinson is disagreeing with Simon's positivism and its substantive meta-ethic. He would also deny the possibility of suitably aggregating preferences. And so on. So the close connection he sees between philosophy and administration is a direct result of his substantive philosophy and his philosophically motivated interpretation of the nature of administration. More specifically, he suggests that 'the most persuasive reason for doing philosophy in the field of executive action is that administrators possess power (Hodgkinson 1983, p. 13). Power, magnified by organizational size and control, also magnifies the capacity of executive action to affect the lives of others, to affect the whole of society, and to create evil. Against these possibilities inherent in modern large scale organizations, 'philosophy is a countervailing force' (1983, pp. 16–17), especially as expressed through a technique of value analysis applied to resolve value problems and conflicts, and to constrain malevolence.

The heart of Hodgkinson's distinctive approach to administration is thus a view of the place of values in administrative theory and practice. It is the ineliminability of values that makes administration a humanism rather than a science, and against Simon, it is the fact that his philosophy includes rather than excludes value claims as knowledge that enables him to deny that Simon's work counts as an adequate philosophy of administration.

Values and Administration

For Hodgkinson 'value propositions can never be labeled true or false in the same way as can propositions of logic or propositions which are empirically verifiable (Hodgkinson 1978, p. 62). And later he adds that 'it is . . . the quality of truth which most clearly distinguishes values from facts for value can *never* be true or false' (1978, p. 105). He defines value 'in a preliminary way as "concepts of the desirable with motivating force" ' (p. 105). They are subjective rather than objective, made rather than given:

> A value can exist only in the mind of the value-holder and it refers to some notion of the desirable, or preferred state of affairs, or to a condition which *ought* to be. . . . The objective terminology of science and logic deals with the true and false. The subjective terms of value are 'good' and 'bad', 'right' and 'wrong' (Hodgkinson 1978, p. 105).

These preliminary remarks on values suggest some interesting parallels with Simon's views. For example, they would both maintain that value statements can never be true or false and that the categories of truth or falsehood are most appropriate to factual statements, like those of science, or to statements of logic and mathematics. Moreover, their reasons for this stance are very similar. They both think there is an unbridgeable gap between facts and values so that the notions of truth and falsehood cannot be made to apply to values. In Hodgkinson's view, to deny that value statements can never be labeled true or false, to deny that they are

> . . . beyond the reach of quantitative methods . . . is to commit the naturalistic fallacy, the argument for which asserts that no amount of facts or 'is's' can 'prove' a value statement or an 'ought' (Hodgkinson 1978, p. 62).

In Simon's view

> . . . factual propositions cannot be derived from ethical ones by any process of reasoning, nor can ethical propositions be compared directly with the facts (Simon 1976, p. 46).

What this means is that they both support two traditional arguments for the autonomy of ethics; they believe that naturalistic attempts to define ethical terms commit what is known as the 'naturalistic fallacy', and they believe that ethical claims cannot validly be derived from factual claims. Our own view is that the 'autonomy of ethics' thesis is false, and replies to these two traditional arguments are presented in Chapter Eight.

As we have already indicated, while there may be striking similarities, a fundamental point of divergence concerns Hodgkinson's admission of the possibility of subjective knowledge, which includes values. Truth and falsehood may apply only to objective, scientific knowledge, but that is not to say that subjectivity can be ignored or denied. Stripped of considerations of truth, values are more akin to cognitive beliefs than noncognitive preferences. In fact, as his definition suggests, they are a combination, in varying degrees, of the cognitive and the affective. This is why, for Hodgkinson, values have a structure. Indeed, it is precisely their structure that needs to be considered when it comes to the adjudication of competing value claims.

As a first step in setting up the machinery for resolving value conflicts, Hodgkinson posits an analytical model for classifying all values (Hodgkinson 1978, pp. 110–121). According to this model, there are three basic types of value, and these may be grouped or ordered into a hierarchy. At the lowest level are to be found the Type III values. These values are self-justifying in that they reflect an individual's pattern of preferences. They are also primitive because they admit of no further justification. In being mere expressions of feeling and emotion, the stuff of the affective realm, they correspond to the sense of value admitted by positivists, including Simon.

At the next level are Type II values which are distinguished, in their mode of justification, by an appeal to their rationality. Two kinds of relevant reasons are sufficiently distinct to suggest that there are really two kinds of Type II values. Those that Hodgkinson calls Type IIb values are justified by an appeal to some quantitative-based consensus in a collectivity, for example, the will of the majority. Type IIa values, on the other hand, are justified by an analysis of some future set of consequences held to be desirable.

Type I values exist at the top of the hierarchy. These values are matters of principle, possessing

> . . . a quality of absoluteness which distinguishes them from the more relative Type II values and the entirely relative Type III values . . . they are based on the will rather than the reasoning faculty (Hodgkinson 1978, p. 113).

In fact, not only are they transrational, going beyond reason and not being able to be justified 'by merely logical argument' (p. 113), they may actually be irrational. As matters of principle, these values involve an act of faith or commitment.

For Hodgkinson, this model suggests three postulates, two of which have an important role to play in choosing values. The central point about adjudication is contained in Postulate 1, which explains the relevant sense of 'hierarchy'. The values that are higher in type than other values are said to be 'superior, more authentic, better justified, of more defensible grounding (Hodgkinson 1978, p. 116), thus leading to the moral decision rule

Type I > Type IIa > Type IIb > Type III (Hodgkinson 1983, p. 204)

For an administrator faced with a moral decision, the rule's application seems clear cut. In deciding to do X rather than Y, the administrator first discounts the pull of feeling, emotion, or affective preference; in short the Type III values. Consideration of consensus or majorities should also be discounted in favour of better factors, and finally, even consideration of consequences should give way to guidance by principle. Making the morally right decision thus involves more than considering feelings, counting people, or calculating consequences. It requires, ultimately, an attitude of disinterest to outcomes and nonattachment to rewards, according priority to duty and a commitment to moral principles; or in Hodgkinson's terminology, it requires the moral posture of a neo-stoic (Hodgkinson 1983, p. 221).

Problems of Application

Given the complexity of both organizational life and moral choice, we may expect that the application of the rule embodied in Postulate 1 will need to be qualified in some circumstances. Hodgkinson's Postulate 3 identifies one class of such circumstances. According to this postulate, there is a natural tendency in organizations for value conflicts to be resolved 'at the lowest level of the hierarchy possible in a given situation' (Hodgkinson 1978, p. 116). He notes that 'it is unreasonable . . . to expect to settle every issue at the highest level (1978, p. 195). Since Postulate 3 implies, contrary to Postulate 1, that there are some situations where it is better to make decisions on the basis of lower type values than on the basis of higher type values, a further consideration is called for. In *Towards a Philosophy of Administration* Hodgkinson proposes a compromise formula for the adjudication of values: they should be 'settled on the postulate of hierarchy at the lowest level of resolution consistent with authenticity and moral responsibility (1978, p. 193). This formula will work if there are ways of determining 'authenticity' and 'moral responsibility' independently of the postulates. However, where the matter is addressed, there is a tendency to offer definitions in terms of fidelity to Type I values (p. 177). In his later book, *The Philosophy of Leadership*, Hodgkinson acknowledges the difficulty more explicitly and concludes that 'any philosophy which tries to dispose of this dialectic, in one direction or another, is oversimplistic and unrealistic (1983, p. 204). We expect that he is right about the difficulties in disposing of this dialectic, but to the extent that it remains, the problem over values adjudication remains as well. This is another point on which we concede the force of Hodgkinson's reply to objections (see Hodgkinson 1986 pp. 12–13). From our correspondence with Hodgkinson we anticipate that he has made further gains on the adjudication problem in his forthcoming book *The Morality of Leadership in Education*.

A second difficulty that confronts the application of Postulate 1 is more serious and concerns both identifying and choosing among different purported Type I values. We can begin by noting that the criteria for classifying values as Type I do not specify a unique set of values; the question of content is left open. This is reasonable given the complexity and open-endedness of organizational situations but it does raise the worrying possibility that some authentic Type I values commitments can figure in the creation or maintenance of some quite disturbing states of affairs. For example, in *Towards a Philosophy of Administration*, Hodgkinson mentions the case of Eichmann and the problem posed by his Type I value of loyalty. Fortunately, he is able to dismiss the Eichmann value as a putative Type I value, suggesting instead that deeper analysis would reveal adherence to a Type III success value (Hodgkinson 1978, pp. 158–159). Problems over Watergate are dissolved in similar fashion.

In *The Philosophy of Leadership*, however, where Hitler is counted as a holder of Type I values, the problem is seen to be much more serious. In fact Hodgkinson is 'forced to the conclusion, distasteful though it may be, that megalomania and poetry can merge in the [Type I poetic] archetype' (1983, p. 184). Moreover, the problem is compounded by the admission of an epistemic difficulty in distinguishing between Type III and Type I affects in cases where a Type III value, such as personal success, becomes a dominant element in a person's life:

> One can conceive, for example, of a careerist become so committed to his personal success that this has become the dominant element in his form of life. His will committed to this value and engaged at Level I, he seeks to impose, poetically, the impress of his commitment upon the world via his organization (Hodgkinson 1983, p. 184).

In this way Type III values threaten to become Type I values, or at any rate, an epistemic indeterminancy will threaten the distinction (Evers 1985, pp. 40–41).

Hodgkinson offers two responses to this argument. First, he points out that while such examples are conceivable, they 'would, however, be unusual or exceptional' (Hodgkinson 1983, p. 184). This infrequency ameliorates the problem of values choice as a practical problem. Second, and this is a more important issue, he draws attention to the logical basis of the values hierarchy; namely, a background hierarchy of will, reason, and emotion:

will > reason > emotion

His point is that the alleged epistemic indeterminacy

> . . . is not a *logical* indeterminacy but a psychological one — an empirical-synthetic perplexity, perhaps, but not an analytic one. So as long as the faculty of will can be discriminated from the faculty of

emotion then the paradigm [the values hierarchy] holds (Hodgkinson 1986, p. 14).

This reply amounts to the claim that there is a principled distinction to be drawn even if it is difficult to draw it on occasions in practice. We note, however, that this difficulty will still add up to a problem of values choice.

Value Choice and Rationality in Administration

In the last section we have raised difficulties with Hodgkinson's theory of value as a tool for solving moral conflicts and adjudicating moral dilemmas. Our epistemological point has been the familiar coherentist one that the theory's aims outrun its available resources. However, in our view, Hodgkinson's theory admits of a very strong reply to this criticism. We must remember that the epistemological point of any criticism is to enable rational theory choice. If all serious rival theories suffer from the same problem, the criticism loses its punch. We are then obliged to look for other grounds in assessing rivals.

Recall that, for Hodgkinson, values are subjective knowledge. But the adjudication problem, conceived as a problem of deciding among competing values in an organization, amounts to a question of how individual values are to be aggregated. There is a fundamental difficulty here that Hodgkinson is fully aware of concerning the limits of collective rational choice. In a criticism of utilitarian ethics he remarks that:

> Subjective qualities are noncomparable and, indeed, from the standpoint of inter-subjective truth the *quality* of work life, the *quality* of any human and social life, can never be determined or assessed quantitatively, not even in principle (Hodgkinson 1983, p. 176).

As evidence, he cites Arrow's General Impossibility Theorem and alludes to the classic paradox of voting. We think that these two issues provide a deep basis for Hodgkinson's stance on values, leadership, and administrative theory, and therefore merit some analysis.

Consider the problem of aggregating preferences to yield a rational decision where three persons, X, Y, and Z, are to cast preferential votes, 1, 2, and 3, for three alternative choices, A, B, and C. Suppose that X's preferences for A, B, and C are expressed as the vote 1-2-3, Y's preferences as 2-3-1, and Z's preferences as 3-1-2. What does the majority prefer? Well, two out of three, X and Y, prefer A to B, two out of three, X and Z, prefer B to C, and two out of three, Y and Z, prefer C to A. Hence collectively, the majority prefers A to B, B to C, and C to A. As transitivity of preferences is reckoned to be a condition of rationality, while each individual votes rationally, the collective result is intransitive and therefore irrational. This difficulty with majority rule, first noticed by the Marquis de Condorcet nearly 200 years ago and now known as the 'paradox of voting' (Blair and Pollak 1983), is discussed in detail by Hodgkinson in his paper 'Why democracy won't work' (Hodgkinson 1973). There he cautiously concludes that for a less than perfect world 'it is probably true that all things considered, subscription to a democratic myth yields the best of the going possible worlds' (1973, p. 319), but he makes it quite clear that:

> In an ideal human arrangement I would hold with Plato that some form of aristocracy is the most desirable theory and practice for the governing of men (Hodgkinson 1973, p. 319).

Kenneth Arrow began his landmark analysis of social choice with a study of this voting paradox (Arrow 1963, p. 3). He was concerned with determining the conditions under which individual preferences could be aggregated to yield rational collective decisions. Because there can be arbitrarily many aggregation or voting procedures — sometimes in this context called social welfare functions — Arrow used an axiomatic approach, seeking to formulate ethically and rationally acceptable requirements for any procedure. He formulated and defended five such axioms:

1. Universal Scope: all possible configurations of preferences should be capable of aggregation.
2. Unanimity: if every individual prefers A to B, then the collective prefers A to B.
3. Pairwise Determination: if individuals maintain a preference for A over B, then regardless of changes in their other preferences, the collective continues to rank A over B.
4. Completeness: for every pair of alternatives, A and B, either A is collectively at least as good as B, or B is collectively at least as good as A.
5. Transitivity: the weak collective preference relation in axiom 4 is transitive (Blair and Pollak 1983, pp. 77–78).

The surprising conclusion that Arrow came to was that these axioms are jointly incompatible with a sixth nondictatorship axiom. That is, they imply that there exists some individual whose preferences determine the collective preference regardless of the preferences of all other individuals (Arrow 1963, p. 30). The relevant point for Hodgkinson's theory is that organizational decision making is a species of collective choice. Essentially, Arrow's Impossibility Theorem shows the impossibility of decisive, egalitarian, rational collective choice in general being made from a base of individual subjective values. Hodgkinson accepts this result and abandons the nondictatorship assumption. But since decisions must be made on the basis of some values, the morally significant identifying condition of leadership becomes, of necessity, the will. Mere Type III affect is not sufficient to account for decision. The jump from preference to action requires an act of will. This is why Hodgkinson posits Type I will-laden values as the essence of moral leadership in organizations. This is why his theory is both subjectivist and elitist, reflecting Plato's guardianship but without the forms as a measure of the truth or falsehood of values. And finally, this is why our earlier puzzles over values adjudication, although troublesome, do not really strike at the core of his theory.

In our view, there is no easy way of countering this argument from within a subjectivist framework of assumptions on value. Our own alternative strategy is to defend, later, an objective, coherentist account of value. But that is another story.

Summary

We began by noting that Hodgkinson's position is opposed to positivism. In particular, where positivism and its variants eschew values from administration, Hodgkinson sees values as fundamental to its nature and practice. Since he believes in a separation of fact from value, with the domain of fact being the province of science, he concludes that administration is essentially a humanism and not a science. Central to his understanding of administrative theory is an analytical model of values based on a hierarchy of will, reason, and emotion. With due allowance for moral and organizational complexity, in general, values reflecting the will — Type I values — take precedence over lower-order values reflecting reason (Type II) and emotion (Type III). Organizational leadership involves, ultimately, the expression of Type I values. We concluded our discussion by exploring Hodgkinson's suggestions for a deeper defence of his values paradigm; namely, a defence based on Arrow's Impossibility Theorem. We think this approach explains a great deal about the structure of his subjectivist theory. It also suggests that if serious rivals are to be found, they will need to come from alternatives to subjectivism in values.

References

Alexander H. A. (1989). Liberal education and open society: absolutism and relativism in curriculum theory, *Curriculum Inquiry*, **19**(1), pp. 11–31.

Arrow K. J. (1963). *Social Choice and Individual Values*. (New York: John Wiley and Sons, second edition).

Blair D. H. and Pollak R. A. (1983). Rational collective choice, *Scientific American*, **249**(2), pp. 76–83.

Davies J. L. and Vaughan D. J. (1907) (eds.). *The Republic of Plato*. (London: Macmillan, translated with analysis and notes).

Evers C. W. (1985). Hodgkinson on ethics and the philosophy of administration, *Educational Administration Quarterly*, **21**(4), pp. 27–50.

Feyerabend P. K. (1978). *Science in a Free Society*. (London: New Left Books).

Hodgkinson C. (1973). Why democracy won't work, *Phi Delta Kappan*, **54**(5), pp. 316–319.

Hodgkinson C. (1978). *Towards a Philosophy of Administration.* (Oxford: Blackwell).
Hodgkinson C. (1983). *The Philosophy of Leadership.* (Oxford: Blackwell).
Hodgkinson C. (1986). Beyond pragmatism and positivism, *Educational Administration Quarterly,* **22**(2), pp. 5–21.
Mill J. S. (1910). *Utilitarianism, Liberty, and Representative Government.* (London: Everyman).
Popper K. R. (1945). *The Open Society and its Enemies,* Vol. 1, The Spell of Plato. (London: George Routledge and Sons).
Simon H. A. (1976). *Administrative Behavior.* (London: Macmillan, third edition, revised).

6
The Cultural Perspective

The problems to be examined in this chapter are nicely posed by a tale Clifford Geertz tells in his classic text *The Interpretation of Cultures*:

> There is an Indian story . . . about an Englishman who, having been told that the world rested on a platform which rested on the back of an elephant which rested in turn on the back of a turtle, asked . . . what did the turtle rest on? Another turtle. And that turtle? 'Ah, Sahib, after that it is turtles all the way down' (Geertz 1973, p. 29).

Siding with the Indian's account of these seemingly unfathomable foundations of the world, Geertz agrees that 'Such, indeed, is the condition of things.'

In our discussion of the classical solution to the problem of knowledge in Chapter One, we argued that foundational theories of justification suffer from both a circularity and a regress problem. These problems were believed to be solvable by distinguishing between derived and immediate knowledge. Since derived knowledge had to come to an end somewhere, it was assumed that it came to rest eventually at underived knowledge. Such knowledge presented a firm foundation in virtue of which knowledge claims could be justified. In classical empiricism, these foundations were identified as either sense data, first person sensory reports, or observation statements. We also saw that the assumption of secure foundations created an incoherence, since the evidence for claiming foundations to be secure was always less secure than the foundations themselves.

What we summarily call the 'cultural perspective' in educational administration is a particular, although not entirely new, way of conceptualizing organizations such as schools. Its characteristic features are that it derives its justificatory framework from disciplines and traditions which consider themselves as alternatives to science — by which they mean empiricism — such as cultural anthropology, phenomenology, hermeneutics, and interpretive social science. (see Giddens 1977). Whereas empiricism tended to look 'outwards', the emphasis of the interpretive social sciences is on looking 'inwards'; that

112

is, to be primarily concerned with human motivation, intention, and beliefs, in short, with human subjectivity and the creation of meaning (see Rabinow and Sullivan 1977). Proponents of the cultural perspective claim that if we want to understand and improve our social environment, which includes educational organizations, then we must study the expressions of subjectivity; that is, the languages, beliefs, myths, metaphors, and rituals of organizations: their culture. This means more specifically that we need to attend to agents' interpretations of situations and actions, since whatever happens around us must be 'made sense of', and is only understandable through the subjective processes of constructing meaning. Since this is presumed to be so in the cultural perspective, it is often assumed that individuals' interpretations play the part sense data or observation statements played in empiricism; namely they are the foundations of cultural knowledge. Interpretations themselves can be queried in terms of the agent's reasons, motives, or intentions which determined this particular reading of an event. It is these 'inner', irreducibly subjective, phenomena which, according to the cultural perspective, explain an action, event, or situation. On this pattern of justification, it is desirable that they be certain and beyond doubt, because the very interpretation or reading is established or fixed in light of what an agent 'meant' by it. But very often we encounter different, and even clashing, interpretations of the same action or behaviour. For example, teachers may be asked to rate a particular form of student assessment in order to determine whether it should be continued or abandoned. It is more than likely that different views will be given. How does an administrator decide which view or interpretation to adopt as the correct one? In other words, how is rational choice possible in the cultural perspective? In order for choice to be rational, it is necessary to be able to justify it. What further justification could we have, once the teachers had stated their reasons for rating the system the way they did? Only more reasons. What warrant do we have that these additional reasons are any more justified than the first set? If we have none, the chain of providing reasons would need to continue. However, since the regress must stop somewhere, the second and more important problem is the soundness of the foundation itself which must be reached: the reasons, motives, or intentions (depending on which are employed in the context).

We want to argue that inasmuch as the justification of cultural knowledge follows this foundational pattern of justification, the assumption of the epistemic privilege of subjective, 'inner' phenomena used to avoid a regress cannot be justified given the epistemological resources of the model. If this is so, then this cultural model, despite such attractive features as being able to generate rich portrayals of situations and documenting agents' beliefs, remains unjustified on its own account. Without being embedded in a larger coherentist framework it is thus incapable of helping administrators make better, rational choices. On the other hand, in being so embedded, the requirement to cohere with natural science threatens the autonomy, or distinctiveness, of the cultural perspective. Appeals to the coherence of readings, or interpretations, have no obvious boundary of relevant considerations that prevent their meshing with naturalism.

In the following, and before we discuss the cultural perspective in educational administration itself, we want to take a brief look at the conception of culture, as it appears in the parent discipline of organization theory, in order to show the considerable variations which exist under the same umbrella term, and to demarcate the conception with which we are here concerned.

Organization Theory and Culture

It is worthy of note that the cultural model in organization theory was advocated as a successor framework to the still reigning 'new orthodoxy', or open system models (Pondy and Mitroff 1979). Such a move would emphasize the much neglected phenomena of language and the creation of meaning, a move considered most important in that it indicates the shift away from structure and technology to 'the interactive, ongoing, recreative aspects of organizations, beyond the merely rational or economic' (Jelinek et al. 1983, p. 331). The importance of this shift can clearly be seen in that the most important journal of the discipline, the *Administrative Science Quarterly*, dedicated a Special Issue to the idea of culture and organizational analysis. According to the Special Issue editors, this move demonstrated organization theory's evolution to 'more complex, paradoxical, and even contradictory modes of understanding . . . [toward] a "code of many colours" that tolerates alternative assumptions' (Jelinek et al. 1983, p. 331). The editors add that the concept of culture, as understood in this context, is employed 'as an interpretive framework for sense making (by both members and others) in organizational settings' (p. 332). The perceived benefits of linking culture and organization consist in considering the subjective, interpretive aspects of organizational life as legitimate foci for research. This is a radical departure from the traditional systems view, so it is claimed, which treated subjective elements merely as some sources of error variance. What is considered most important in the cultural view is the unveiling of 'some underlying structure of meaning that persists over time, constraining people's perception, interpretation, and behaviour' (Jelinek et al. 1983, p. 337). The editors also note, however, that while these subjective elements are rightly stressed, there remains the question of organizational outcomes. Specifically, although 'culture' enables an organization to function, it is not clear whether such functioning is 'good' or 'bad', 'effective' or 'ineffective' (p. 338).

While it appears to be clear what the concept of culture is expected to contribute to the study of organizations, we nevertheless want to follow Smircich's careful examination of the different conceptions which are gathered under the one collective expression of 'cultural perspective' (Smircich

1983). Deriving from cultural anthropology, 'culture' is a term of many meanings of that tradition. Nevertheless, within the field of organization theory, Smircich argues, it has been developed in mainly two ways: as a 'critical variable', and as a 'root metaphor' (Smircich 1983, p. 339). Smircich is concerned to underline the importance of the use of metaphors such as 'organism', 'machine', 'system', and 'culture', since they provide useful although widely diverging insights into organizational reality determined by the fact that writers hold different views on the ontological status of social reality and human nature. Indeed, she claims that the term 'organization' itself is a metaphor which characterizes 'the experience of collective coordination and orderliness' (Smircich 1983, p. 341). The critical point to remember is to examine carefully what implications and consequences flow from whatever metaphor we adopt. According to Smircich, it is the problem of social order which makes 'culture' such a fruitful conception for organization theory, since in anthropology 'culture' is already employed to explain 'the orderliness and patterning' of social life. There is a shift here. The conception of culture, on the one hand, is described as useful in organization theory because it helps to 'make sense' of organizations. Making sense of something is, however, not the same as explaining the orderliness of social life or 'the problem of social order' as sociology has it. If the conception of culture is used to denote both, then ambiguity and possible misunderstanding could result. The intersection of both themes is clearly evident in current research topics in organization and management theory and includes: Cross-cultural or Comparative Management, Corporate Culture, Organizational Cognition, Organizational Symbolism, Unconscious Processes and Organization (Smircich 1983, p. 342). In the context of the first set of studies, the concept of 'culture' remains an independent variable. Culture is something that members of an organization import qua membership. The research carried out under this theme mainly deals with differences, as well as similarities between cultures which are then somehow incorporated in discussions on organizational effectiveness. Obviously, such research is applied by multinational corporations and appears to enjoy considerable interest (see Ouchi 1981, Pascale and Athos 1981).

A different approach is that of 'Corporate Culture', since here organizations themselves are viewed as producers of cultural phenomena (see Deal and Kennedy 1982, Peters and Waterman 1982), both in the sense of producing goods and services, as well as producing more 'overtly' cultural phenomena such as myths, rituals, legends, and ceremonies. Still based on the open systems view, 'culture' in this perspective is seen as an *internal variable*, along with others such as structure, size, technology, and leadership patterns. Culture is somehow involved in helping the organization survive through its successful interaction with the other variables. It is even asserted by writers such as Deal and Kennedy and Peters and Waterman that organizations with 'strong' cultures are successful. As Smircich puts it, 'Culture is usually defined as social or normative glue that holds an organization together . . . It expresses the values or social ideals and beliefs that organization members come to share' (Smircich 1983, p. 344). Despite the variations in emphasis in the themes considered so far, there are some key features which are shared. Culture serves to provide identity for organizational members; it engenders commitment which goes beyond self-interest; it contributes to system stability, and it functions as a sense-making device (Smircich 1983, p. 346). It is also reasonably obvious that the utility of the cultural perspective can provide a new and promising tool for managerial influence, legitimation, and control, a point to be raised again later.

The problem of many cultures, as well as competing subcultures in an organization, and the required strategies for problem solving which would need to be developed, can only be mentioned briefly here. Smircich sums up the agendas of both approaches:

> Underlying the interests in comparative management and corporate culture is the search for predictable means for organizational control and improved means for organizational management. Because both of these research approaches have these basic purposes, the issue of causality is of critical importance (Smircich 1983, p. 347).

While the two perspectives described so far employ the concept of culture to draw analogies between organizations and, say, systems or organisms, culture as 'root metaphor' means that organizations *are* cultures. This view, so it is claimed, is no longer instrumental (as was the case in the 'machine' metaphor), nor adaptive (as in the 'organism' case); rather, it is mindful of 'manifestations of human consciousness' (Smircich 1938, p. 347). Organizations are studied in terms of their 'expressive, ideational, and symbolic aspects' (pp. 347–348). The research agenda which stems from this perspective is to examine organizations as subjective experience and to determine patterned social interaction. Smircich explicitly notes that the concept of culture, as developed in anthropology, serves as an epistemological device, but that given the different conceptualizations and different assumptions underlying the term, quite different modes of organizational analysis follow. She only mentions two sets of assumptions, though: the ontological (the objective-subjective question) and the 'human nature' aspect (the determinist-voluntarist question). It is significant that epistemological assumptions are not mentioned, unless these are somehow believed to be implied in the ontological issue. It would lead too far afield to discuss the other three remaining perspectives. Suffice it to characterize them briefly. Clifford Geertz's work is an example of the symbolic view which considers cultures as systems of shared symbols and meanings, whereas the last mentioned perspective is associated with the structuralist ideas of Claude Levi-Strauss who believes that culture is the expression of unconscious psychological processes (see Lakomski 1985, pp. 219–221). These ideas have not spread far into organization theory, but Geertz's views will surface again later. The main thrust of his work is the interpretation of individuals' experience and their relation to action. This perspective has, in Smircich's view, much to contribute to organizational leadership studies insofar as leadership can be described as 'the management of meaning and the shaping of interpretations' (Smircich 1983, p. 351) with the view to establish common interpretations to facilitate action.

The cognitive perspective considers culture as a system of shared cognitions or knowledge, and beliefs. Representatives of this view are Argyris and Schön (1978) and Weick (1979a, 1979b). Argyris and Schön refer to organizations as 'cognitive enterprises' which appear to be guided by some set of rules which members seem to understand and share. Summing up, different as these perspectives are in emphasis, they share a mode of thought which, in opposition to the 'culture-as-variable' view, stresses that organizations are particular forms of human expression. The 'culture-as-root' metaphor, says Smircich, denies the concrete status of the social world. It is

> . . . not assumed to have an objective, independent existence that imposes itself on human beings. Instead, the social or organizational world exists only as a pattern of symbolic relationships and meanings sustained through the continued processes of human interaction (Smircich 1983, p. 353).

While the (different) concept/s of culture, as applied in the parent discipline of organization theory, have been derived from the discipline of cultural anthropology, the 'cultural perspective' in educational administration appears to have been influenced more directly by hermeneutics and interpretive social science (at least with reference to those writers which we discuss here). Although the traditions or disciplines differ, it will soon become evident that the general assumptions, that is, about the nature of organizational reality, human subjectivity, and the need for interpretive processes, are shared in the educational variant of the 'culture-as-root metaphor'. In the following, we outline the main characteristics of this other tradition before we turn to the application of the concept of culture in educational administration itself.

Interpretive Social Science and Hermeneutics

What is commonly called the 'interpretive turn' in the social sciences serves as a broad label under which a diversity of approaches is subsumed: Symbolic Interactionism, Ethnomethodology, and Phenomenological Sociology. Symbolic Interactionism is associated with G. H. Mead and E. Goffman, Ethnomethodology with H. Garfinkel, and Phenomenological Sociology particularly with the names of P. Berger and T. Luckman.

Giddens (1977) provides a good overview of these approaches to the study of social reality in the introduction and first chapter of *New Rules of Sociological Method*. In addition to their 'anti-positivist' stance, and despite their considerable differences, these approaches are concerned with the 'essence' of social life as perceived by the actors themselves. The special contribution of hermeneutics is that it draws attention to the necessity and importance of people's interpretations of their everyday reality.

Generally speaking, interpretive social science is characterized by a number of claims. Firstly, it emphasizes that understanding (or *verstehen*) should not be treated as a special method which is to be employed by the social sciences only. Rather, interpretivists argue that it is generic to all social interaction. The concept of understanding, as the German term is usually translated, has been made prominent by Weber in his notion of interpretive social science, thus continuing the debate begun by Dilthey about the radical distinction between the natural and the social sciences (*Natur- und Geisteswissenschaften*), which culminates in the claim that the latter sciences require a special method. Modern interpretivists differ with regard to the so-called 'universality' claim of *verstehen*. Weber defined understanding as 'the observation and theoretical interpretation of the subjective "states of mind" of actors' (Weber 1947, p. 87). Secondly, it refers to 'the grasp of the meaning of logical and other systems of symbols, a meaning which is usually thought of as in some sense "intended" by a mind or intelligent being of some sort' (p. 87). A most important characteristic of *verstehen* is that, according to Weber, understanding a situation or act does not imply, or in principle lead to, its approval, or disapproval (Weber 1949, p. 41). All that 'understanding' can achieve is to enable awareness of issues and reasons which may stand in the way of agreement. Understanding and judgment are two different things in Weber's notion of social science.

Thirdly, as Giddens (1977, pp. 52–53) notes, interpretivist social scientists draw on the same resources as ordinary people when they wish to understand a particular practice or set of rules they are examining. This also means that the practical theorizing of ordinary people cannot simply be discarded as 'unscientific', since it is a constitutive part of the very conduct under investigation. Fourthly, our ordinary knowledge of the world is normally taken for granted and is thus a pragmatically oriented kind of knowledge. This means, according to the interpretivist, that we are seldom able to express it in propositional form. Consequently, the ideals of natural science are not relevant since they require precision of formulation, logical exhaustiveness, clearcut lexical definition, and so on. Finally, the concepts the social (and organizational) theorist employs are dependent upon a prior understanding of those that ordinary people use in their construction of a meaningful world.

Since it is not possible to provide a comprehensive account of the interpretive view here, we want to consider some central claims and features of hermeneutics as developed by Hans-Georg Gadamer and Charles Taylor. Both philosophers are important contemporary protagonists of this tradition whose works have significantly influenced theoretical development in the social sciences and in education. Accepting recent criticisms of logical empiricism which has 'sold us an extraordinary bill of goods about natural science', Taylor (1980b, p. 26) nevertheless rejects as a 'pleasing fancy' the view that, as a result of these criticisms, all sciences are to be considered as equally hermeneutic. While there is a place for understanding in the natural sciences, the notion of 'understanding' which is central to the 'sciences of man' is significantly different. The latter conception can best be defined, according to Taylor, as one where 'we need to grasp desirability-characterizations' (1980b, p. 30). We come to understand someone's seemingly opaque behaviour, for example, the refusal of a desirable promotion, when we understand the terms the person might apply to describe his or her behaviour, that is, as not wanting to be 'pushy' or 'insensitively self-assertive'. When we understand the meanings of these terms, then we understand someone's action, although we need not be in agreement with it. Here, Taylor clearly agrees with the Weberian distinction referred to earlier. These 'desirability-characterizations' (following Anscombe) are the key to the differences between the natural and the social sciences in that they 'belong to a range of descriptions which lie outside what has been considered the limits of natural science' (Taylor 1980b, p. 31). The latter are defined by the 'requirement of absoluteness' (a term Taylor borrows from Bernard Williams) which means that science

> . . . is to give an account of the work as it is independently of the meanings it might have for human subjects, or how it figures in their experience. An adequate scientific account should therefore eschew what one could call subject-related properties (Taylor 1980b, p. 31).

The notion of 'absolute' is not to be read as a Kantian 'in-itself', Taylor insists, but rather as something 'not relative to our interest or our context of action' (Taylor 1980a, p. 47). The business of hermeneutics is, in Taylor's well-known formulation, the

> . . . attempt to make clear, to make sense of an object of study. This object must, therefore, be a text, or text-analogue, which in some way is confused, incomplete, cloudy, seemingly contradictory — in one way or another, unclear. The interpretation aims to bring to light an underlying coherence or sense (Taylor 1979, p. 25).

Note that the special condition which first gives rise to interpretation is that the text before us must be somehow confused or unclear. This point is underlined by Gadamer (1979) who notes that 'whatever is immediately evident, whatever persuades us by its simple presence, does not call for any interpretation' (p. 111). This claim will be taken up again later on.

Gadamer's specific version of hermeneutics is the expansion of the notion of understanding to 'everything bequeathed to us by history'. Thus, he says:

> we will speak not only of the interpretation of an historical incident, but also the interpretation of spiritual and mimed expressions, the interpretation of behaviour, and so forth. We always intend by this that the meaning of what is given over for our interpretation is not revealed without mediation, and that we must look beyond the immediate sense in order to discover the 'true' hidden meaning (Gadamer 1979, p. 111).

In Gadamer's, as in Taylor's conception, the mediation between 'unclear' and 'true' meaning of a text takes place in the medium of language and its situatedness in history. This means for Gadamer that in order to study the objects of the social sciences, the observer has to enter into a dialogue with them. When we want to understand a text or period remote from our own, 'we do not try to recapture the author's attitude of mind but . . . the perspective within which he has formed his views' (Gadamer 1976, p. 118). Or, more sharply, 'the meaning of hermeneutical inquiry is to disclose the miracle of understanding texts or utterances and not the mysterious communication of souls' (Gadamer 1979, p. 147). Gadamer thus explicitly rejects Wilhelm Dilthey's conception of hermeneutics. Dilthey (1976) saw as the ultimate goal of the hermeneutic procedure to understand authors better than they have understood themselves through a kind of empathetic understanding of the individual's emotions and intentions.

Understanding for Gadamer happens through discourse, and since discourse always happens in specific historical contexts, understanding is always historically relative. This must not be mistaken to mean that Gadamer believed that all understanding is of equal value. He argues quite correctly that understanding is always bounded by the time in which we live and hence relative to that period. Unfortunately, as we will see later, he does not escape the second, vicious sense of 'relative' subject to his epistemology and despite his intentions. By saying that understanding is historically relative Gadamer means that we can never pass final judgment on history since we are always part of it. It is not possible in his view to 'step out' of history, as it were, to take a more objective look at ourselves. Such a privileged position is impossible. The fact that both interpreter and text belong to the same tradition is expressed in his adoption of Heidegger's famous hermeneutic circle (Heidegger 1962, p. 153).

What Heidegger and Gadamer want to say is that all understanding already and always presupposes some measure of understanding. Since we are characteristically historical beings, our cultural context forms the methodical premise for our interpretation of texts. To illustrate this point, consider translating a text from a foreign language into our own. It is clear that in order to attempt a translation, you must at least have a working knowledge of the language, however rudimentary, in order to tackle the task with some assurance of success. Initially, you will probably also know that the text is either a scientific treatise, a technical manual, or perhaps a novel, given the context in which you encountered it first, or the purpose for which you selected it. This provides the general context of the text whose content, however, is still unclear. You may begin by immediately identifying certain words which you take to be key words; you apply what grammatical rules, conventions and vocabulary you remember, and translate each sentence one by one. Checking as you go, you may find that you mistranslated a paragraph which does not 'make sense', does not cohere with what you thought the text was about. You reconsider and find that you misconstrued a certain phrase which then distorted the rest of the paragraph. You proceed in this fashion until the whole text is translated, checking the parts against the whole, and considering individual sections from your newly gained interpretation of the complete text. This may lead you to modify your earlier translation. As everyone who teaches a foreign language knows, the first translation is never the last. Once the 'rough' job is done, one sets about refining and polishing the text so that it expresses its meaning as clearly and elegantly as possible. In hermeneutic language this is called expressing the text in its 'authenticity'. This is, of course, a simplified account of the hermeneutic procedure, but it nevertheless presents its most important feature: the circular relation between the whole and its parts which is an ongoing process until such time as we are satisfied that we 'understand' what the text is telling us. While we normally have a number of choices of how to translate a particular phrase, or even word, and hence may choose between different meanings of the same text, we need, however, to keep an open mind if we are to be true to the hermeneutic procedure and to the possibilities inherent in the text.

This, according to Gadamer, is the 'authentic intention of understanding'. But keeping an open mind does not mean in his view that we need to pretend to be neutral about a particular text, such as a novel, for instance. As we noted earlier, we always bring to whatever we are investigating, certain attitudes, opinions, behaviours, prejudices, and knowledge that we have already acquired. The hermeneutic requirement is, according to Gadamer and Taylor, that we identify this 'fore-knowledge' by becoming conscious of it, and thus neutralize it. In this manner, the interpretivists maintain, we can keep our fore-knowledge from distorting the real authentic meaning of the text. If we manage this, then 'we grant the text the opportunity to appear as an authentically different being and to manifest its own truth, over and against our own preconceived notions' (Gadamer 1979, p. 152). In the light of this discussion, it is easy to see that the hermeneutic procedure is not simply concerned with the mastery of a language, with a system of signs or representations which 'stand for' objects, but with language itself as a 'form of life', to use Wittgenstein's expression. This means that the hermeneutic problem is one of understanding the practices and activities which are achieved through the medium of ordinary language. But what exactly does it mean to speak a language as a form of life, and hence a practice? The following example, discussed by Taylor (1979), might help (see also Ricoeur 1981).

For there to be the practice of voting, Taylor suggests, someone has to be elected, a measure has to be passed, a two-third majority must be established, and so on. If we did not have this vocabulary, he argues, there would be no practice called 'voting'. We might raise our hands, or scribble on pieces of paper, but that would not by itself count as voting. What makes it voting is that it has to

> . . . bear intentional descriptions which fall within a certain range before we can agree to call it voting . . . or in other words, that some practice is voting . . . has to do with the vocabulary established in a society as appropriate for engaging in it or describing it (Taylor 1979, p. 47).

Taylor goes on to explain this state of affairs in the following way:

> There is no simple one-way dependence here. We can speak of mutual dependence if we like, but really what this points up is the artificiality of the distinction between social reality and the language of description of that social reality. The language is constitutive of the reality, is essential to its being the kind of reality it is. To separate the two, and distinguish them as we quite rightly distinguish the heavens from our theories about them, is forever to miss the point (Taylor 1979, pp. 46–47).

Having made this point, both Gadamer and Taylor are aware that we must have some criteria which tell us when we have understood a text, situation, or social practice correctly. For Gadamer, 'getting an interpretation right' is a continuous process directed by the anticipation of 'perfect coherence'. While this is a formal feature, he claims that it is always present when we want to understand something. When we read a chapter such as this one, for example, we assume at the outset that the text is coherent, that is, that it is in principle understandable. The moment we encounter something that does not make sense to us, then critical examination begins. However, Gadamer does not tell us exactly how this is to be done: 'We need not specify here the rules of this critical examination since in every respect their justification is inseparable from the concrete understanding of the text' (Gadamer 1979, p. 154). Summing up his position, he states that the:

> original conditions of every hermeneutics . . . must be a shared and comprehensible reference to 'things in themselves'. It is the condition

which determines the possibility that a unified meaning can be aimed at, and thus also the possibility that the anticipation of perfect coherence may actually be applicable (Gadamer 1979, p. 155).

While sharing Gadamer's notion of coherence, Taylor does not consider, as the final court of appeal for the adequacy of an interpretation, the 'thing-in-itself'. He reflects on the possibility that someone might not share our interpretation and might in fact strongly disagree with it. What is to be done in this situation? The only thing we can do, according to Taylor, is to offer more interpretations. But if this fails to convince our critic, then we have unfortunately reached the end of rational argument as understood by the hermeneutician. In the end, our only chance to convince a critic is if he or she shares our understanding of the language at some point. What is fundamentally required in hermeneutics, according to Taylor, is a 'certain measure of "insight"' (Taylor 1979, p. 66). And insight cannot be formalized.

In case of disagreement, then, we might rather speak of a 'gap' in intuitions. This is quite a serious problem in Taylor's view since this 'gap' is not merely indicative of different theoretical positions or opinions, but of different options in life. Hence, to understand an interpretation or social practice, one may not only have to 'sharpen up' one's intuitions but may actually have to change one's way of doing things. This means that Taylor's hermeneutically conceived social science, which is rooted in the intersubjective meanings of agents, considers itself as a proposal for social change. In the following section we will see which of these features are taken up in the field of educational administration itself.

The Cultural Perspective in Educational Administration

Talking about the 'cultural perspective' or 'cultural analysis' in educational administration is not an easy task, mainly because we cannot yet point out a large, coherent body of literature which is representative of this movement. Nevertheless, there are some key writers who clearly identify themselves with the cultural perspective (see Sergiovanni and Corbally 1984).

In the introduction to this chapter we noted that the cultural perspective emerging in educational administration has already had some currency in the parent discipline of organizational theory. It has also had a considerable tradition in industrial research (see Gregory 1983, pp. 359–376). Similarly, it has been widely discussed in the social sciences at large (see, e.g. Bernstein 1978; Roche 1973; Willis 1978; Goffman 1959, 1961; Habermas 1972; Cicourel 1969; Fay 1975; Keat and Urry 1982), and has, in turn, shaped current debates in the field of education (Bredo and Feinberg 1982). It is in this respect a welcome development. It needs to be acknowledged, however, that 'cultural' or interpretive aspects are already found in Jackson (1968) and Wolcott (1973). For a more recent application of the concept of culture to examine the changes in a British private school, see Pettigrew (1979).

While he does not explicitly claim membership, it is fair to say that Greenfield's work is an important forerunner of the cultural model in educational administration. As we have seen, Greenfield's 'anarchistic' model attempts a radical break with positivistic administrative theory. His position has gained considerable influence among writers developing alternative proposals for educational administration theory. For example, Thomas Sergiovanni, who places himself explicitly in the interpretive paradigm, accepts a number of Greenfield's conclusions (see Sergiovanni 1984a, 1984b, 1984c; Sergiovanni and Corbally 1984).

Arguing against educational administration as applied science, where science is identified with positivism, and describing it as an art, or an 'artificial science', Sergiovanni suggests that we should view our field as a 'multiple-perspective' activity. He means specifically that theories of administration should not be pitted against one another on the assumption that one best view emerges but that we should treat theories as overlapping lenses. If we follow this path, he argues, then:

> each theory of administration is better able to illuminate and explain certain aspects of the problems administrators face but not others. Increased understanding depends upon the use of overall theories, preferably in an integrated fashion (Sergiovanni 1984a, p. 1).

He explains that proceeding in this way helps us overcome the singular use of a specific perspective which leads to the application of social scientific laws to principles of action. Educational administration, however, as an 'artificial science' is not just concerned with achieving instrumental ends, but with better ones, that is, with 'designing courses of action aimed at changing existing situations into preferred ones' (Sergiovanni 1984b, p. 278). The strength of a multiple-perspective view consists in drawing attention to the specificities of situations. While theoretical perspectives are always shaped by explicit as well as implicit assumptions, it is the latter in Sergiovanni's view which, as background assumptions, determine how administrative problems are defined and which strategies are suggested for solutions. As tacit assumptions change so do problem strategies and solutions, an assertion which leads Sergiovanni to state:

> In this sense there is no separate reality in organizational behaviour and administrative functioning. Objectivity and truth are evasive and no order exists beyond that which is created in the minds of persons and that which is imposed upon the organization by persons (Sergiovanni, 1984a, p. 2).

As we saw earlier in our discussion of organization theory, here, too, reality in the 'artificial sciences' is considered a 'human convention' which is juxtaposed with the 'natural laws' believed applicable only to 'inert nature'. The uniqueness of the human sciences, according to Sergiovanni consists in the purported fact that humans are not characterized by 'behaviour' but by their action:

> Actions differ from behaviour in that they are born of preconceptions, assumptions, and motives. Actions have meaning in the sense that as preconditions change, meanings change regardless of the sameness of recorded behaviour (Sergiovanni 1984a, p. 3).

Sergiovanni's distinction between action and behaviour is clearly analogous to that suggested earlier by Taylor.

Further in keeping with interpretive science's features, Sergiovanni also emphasizes that the cultural perspective in educational administration is concerned more with understanding than explaining, with sense-making rather than description, and with 'community' and shared meanings and values. He describes hermeneutics as going

> . . . beyond the objective identification of facts as 'is' to understanding the facts given certain combinations of circumstances and to interpreting the facts in an attempt to render them meaningful (Sergiovanni 1984b, p. 276).

Accepting the problem of institutional conflict which requires mediation of possibly antagonistic values, he maintains that articulation of such conflicts is not only necessary and possible in the cultural view but can also lead to concerted action. Indeed, the articulation of 'human consciousness', the interpretation of meanings, and the linking of organization members to those meanings becomes the primary task of the interpretive leader. These meanings are ultimately anchored in what Sergiovanni, following Shils, calls a 'centre'. Every society possesses one, that is, a realm of values and beliefs which is 'ultimate and irreducible . . . [it] is also a phenomenon of the realm of action' (Sergiovanni 1984a, p. 3). But it may occur that 'wild' centres develop which have only accidental congruence with the official organizational purposes. What is to be done in such a case? Sergiovanni's answer is congruent with the goals of the human relations school: conflicting values must be domesticated. In fact, he sees this as 'an important leadership responsibility of administrators who work within the cultural perspective' (1984a, p. 9). There are no uncertainties about the goal in his view:

> . . . leaders consciously work to build unity, order, and meaning within the organization as a whole by giving attention to organizational

purposes, the philosophical and historical traditions of the organization, and the ideals and norms which define the way of life in the organization for purposes of socialization and of obtaining compliance (Sergiovanni 1984a, p. 9).

His definition of leadership is thus quite in keeping with that advanced by Smircich. He goes even further by claiming that the 'real value of leadership rests with the meanings which actions import to others than in the actions themselves', and 'What a leader stands for is more important that what he or she does' (Sergiovanni 1984c, p. 106).

Although Sergiovanni believes that hermeneutics is an essential theoretical framework for a revitalized, relevant theory of administration, or rather theories of administration, he recognizes its limitations. While the hermeneutic process is in principle endless, old interpretations being replaced by newer and 'better' ones in the search for 'complete' meaning, the administration of schools is a practical business where problems must be solved rather than 'ever-clearer meanings and understandings' sought. The process of interpretation, in other words, has to be terminated at some point so that action can take place. Because of this 'praxis' requirement Sergiovanni believes it unlikely that educational administration can ever be a hermeneutic science in its own right (Sergiovanni 1984b, p. 284). Indeed, it will continue to avail itself of the services of descriptive and normative science without, however, being able to take refuge in either (1984b, p. 288).

Interpretive Administration and Deciding What to Do

Recall that organization theorists, interpretive social scientists, as well as educational administrators, are attracted to the cultural perspective because of the promise of 'getting at' the 'essentially human' element of action which can be accessed through interpretation. Regarding such 'inner' phenomena as motives, reasons, intentions, and 'meaning' as building-blocks of administrative theories was believed to provide a far more reliable, more authentic, basis for understanding and hence explaining events. Such profound understanding would then enable administrators to make better decisions and solve the problems they face.

Let us begin by first being quite clear about what it means to 'understand' an action or event. We noted earlier Weber's definition of this concept as *becoming aware* of issues, or in Taylor's words, as finding out 'what makes someone tick'. *Verstehen* has become one of the most central concepts in modern social science, but is not always applied as carefully as it was defined and delimited by Weber. Conceived of as the proper method of the study of cultural phenomena as opposed to the objective, scientific method, Weber described the scope of *verstehen* as follows:

The means employed by 'understanding explanation' are not *normative* correctness, but rather, on the one hand, the conventional habits of the investigator and teacher in thinking in a particular way, and on the other, as the situation requires, his capacity to 'feel himself' empathically into a mode of thought which deviates from his own and which is normatively 'false' according to his own habits of thoughts. The fact that 'error' is, in principle just as accessible to the understanding as 'correct' thinking proves that we are concerned here with the normatively 'correct' type of validity, not *as such* but only as an especially easily understandable *conventional* type (Weber 1949, p. 41).

This means, then, that the validity of understanding an act or event is a matter of subjective assessment of an individual, or a group, given prevailing attitudes in that culture or time. So we could say, for example, that we understand the principal's decision not to integrate a severely handicapped student into a classroom of students with ordinary abilities, although we actually think that the decision is wrong for both educational and ethical reasons. Similarly, we might say, 'I understand why you requested that teacher X be transferred', on hearing the reasons for the decision, and in this case, agreeing with them. The point to be made in either example is that such understanding, whether it is of a disapproving or an approving kind, does not entail any judgment of the action or event. We have merely become aware of someone else's subjective viewpoint or motives for action, we 'feel' or do not 'feel for' the decision. Whether the decision or act was correct or incorrect, or justified, is a question which cannot be settled by reference to understanding. It does not concern itself with matters of judgment, but with matters of subjective feeling. Since we have discussed some of the difficulties which follow as the result of adhering to subjectivist doctrines in earlier chapters, we need not recapitulate them here, but continue to point out the kinds of problems which arise for the making of decisions in administration.

In everyday school life we always encounter different and competing opinions, options, and values about teaching and administering. But whether we are teachers or administrators, we also have to act, a fact stressed by the cultural model. Acting means selecting some options over other, possible ones. The problem is that although we have a better 'feel' for how staff rate, for example, the new student assessment procedure — some believe it reflects students' abilities more accurately and should thus be maintained, others think it too time-consuming and want to go back to the older model, a third group does not care — we are no nearer to being able to make a decision. Who is right? We could, of course, widen our circle of informants, and ask what the students' preferences are. They actually want the new system modified. Now we have a plethora of views which could be extended still further, but still no criteria which would help us decide which option to adopt. Since the interpretivist school leader can, qua model, do no more than canvass people's subjective feelings, he or she faces the problem of either doing nothing, an option Petrie (1984) calls the danger of 'pluralistic paralysis', or selecting an option and thus making an arbitrary choice. If the administrator aligns him or herself with one of the alternatives, and a choice is made, that option does not become the better one simply by being chosen. For an option to be better than a competing one, or a rational choice, it is necessary that we can justify what we have chosen. But as we saw, subjective feelings are not the kind of thing which are amenable to justification in principle. The art of administration, as Sergiovanni has it, may well be 'celebrated in actions born of informed intuition' (Sergiovanni 1984b, p. 290), but my 'informed intuition' may well differ from yours, and result in very different, and possibly dangerous or unethical consequences or proposals for action. Intuition, like taste, is something about which there is no fact of the matter. The kind of decision making, then, which would result from the cultural perspective would rather resemble a 'hit-and-miss' approach, depending on administrators' personal, subjective, tastes.

While the inability to decide rationally among competing options is already a serious handicap for a theoretical proposal advocated because of the promise of *better* decision making, its problems worsen when we consider the so-called 'human element' believed to provide the basic foundation for human action. What makes us 'human' in the cultural perspective, is that we possess 'inner' phenomena such as motives, purposes, and intentions. These, it is believed, can be called up as 'final arbiters' to determine the meaning of an event or an action. In order to perform that role, they have to be epistemically secure, for, if they are not, we would not be able to identify any action at all. Since a given item of behaviour can be described in various ways, uncertainty functions to undermine our capacity to individuate behaviour X as a case of Y. Let us see in the final section of this chapter whether the epistemological demands made by the cultural model are adequately met by admissible evidence for 'inner' episodes.

Turtles All The Way Down?

Interpretivists are, of course, aware that a given item of behaviour can be described in different ways. Taylor's example of scribbling on pieces of paper can denote such diverse acts as filling out cheques, writing a letter, composing a shopping-list or a story, or voting. In order to know what this behaviour really means, interpretivists suggest that we ask the person concerned what he or she 'meant' or intended by it. Such an 'understanding' explanation is considered superior to the methods of the 'merely factual' sciences which, Taylor argues, exclude intersubjective meaning. The 'factual sciences' insist instead on such building-blocks as brute data which are 'data whose validity cannot be questioned by offering another interpretation or reading, data whose credibility cannot be founded or undermined by further reasoning' (Taylor 1979, p. 30). This definition suggests that Taylor relies on a foundational conception of evidence in natural science, but believes, since other interpretations and readings are always possible in principle in the understanding sciences, that the alleged imperatives of the 'brute data' approach can be avoided. In our discussion of Greenfield's work we challenged some of this reasoning. We now want to examine one methodological issue in more detail.

The dualism that interpretivists maintain between social science and natural science has sometimes depended on a commitment to *substance dualism*, particularly in the form of a distinction between mind and brain. The brain is reckoned as part of the physical, deterministic world dealt with by natural science in attempts to provide a comprehensive causal account of phenomena. The mind, on the other hand, being of different stuff, lends itself to explanation in terms of reasons, intentions, beliefs, and desires. Natural science provides an inappropriate model of explanation in the social sciences, on this view, because social phenomena are characteristically the result of mental phenomena.

This kind of dualism is now widely regarded as mistaken in philosophy, and a more subtle version has emerged in the last 25 years to underwrite the natural/social sciences distinction. We may call this second version *property dualism*. It is compatible with the view that there is only one kind of substance, but it posits a distinction between physical and nonphysical properties. The usual mental properties we use to describe social and psychological phenomena — properties like reason, beliefs, intentions, meanings, understanding, the will — are ontologically autonomous and not reducible to any physical properties like weight, size, or electric charge.

Our discussion of Greenfield's work indicates that we regard both dualisms as mistaken. The argument that follows is mainly a coherentist attack on substance dualism. Property dualism is considered more fully in Chapter Nine, in the discussion of complexity in policy analysis.

Consider the case of the 'inner' phenomenon of intention. Some philosophers, such as P.H. Hirst, for example, have argued that an activity like teaching cannot be understood except in terms of human intention (Hirst 1974, p. 106). Recently, D.C. Phillips (1981) has urged that the analysis of teaching as an intentional act be used to guide educational research. According to Phillips, and a host of others (see, e.g., White 1968), all descriptions of human action given in behavioural terms are in principle inadequate as accounts of what people are doing. If ever we are to make useful predictions about successful teaching, administration, or human conduct in general, we must consider people's intentions. However, as everyone knows, there is a fundamental problem with appeals to intention: put simply, we cannot observe a person's intentions. Intentions, like molecules, are unobservable.

What advantage is to be had, therefore, in invoking unobservables to inform our account of what makes for more effective observable teaching practices? If Quine is right, the case for molecules in physical theory turns largely on the fact that their supposition greatly simplifies such theory. Our being able to confirm predictions concerning observables, made on the basis of physical theory thus simplified, functions as confirmation of molecular theory (Quine 1976).

On the other hand, the usual case for positing intentions is based on a much used Wittgensteinian argument which may be elaborated as follows. As we have already indicated, the same item of human behaviour may be described in nonequivalent ways. For example, my arm's going up may be variously described as an involuntary movement, a Nazi salute, or 'an attempt to catch a troublesome mosquito' (Phillips 1981, p. 101). Although behaviourally identical, these actions are all different in terms of how they may be explained and predicted. They are therefore different in ways that matter. As the above examples indicate, however, the crucial differences among behaviourally identical actions can evidently be nothing more than a difference in the intention with which the act was performed. Taking account of intention is therefore important in the explanation and prediction of human behaviour.

Unfortunately, this argument assumes that we already possess knowledge of differences in intentions. But, of course, for purposes of proffering advice and counsel in teaching or administration we need to be able to individuate various acts in the required way: that is, we need a knowledge of the relevant intentions upon which the individuation of actions depends. The difficulty here is that when it comes to empirical evidence our only basis for individuating intentions, ultimately, is human behaviour and its antecedents and consequents. Wildly varying intentions that forever remain unreflected in all human behaviour are methodologically idle. If, however, our evidence for differences in intention was restricted exclusively to items of, say, teaching behaviour, then appeal to intention in this context would collapse altogether.

Fortunately, there is no reason why we cannot look to whatever behavioural clues we please if we think it will be of help in determining a person's intentions. We can, in fact, use the most comprehensive set of observable, intersubjective behavioural cues available. The worry is that a certain unreliability invests all the obvious sources. For example, one must be cautious about accepting what people state as their intentions, for there are any number of possible causes of deception and ignorance. The problem of unintended consequences should occasion further caution about inferring intentions even from quite simple behaviour (Phillips 1981, p. 105).

There is, however, a problem more serious than just the threat of an endemic uncertainty. The whole business of attributing intentions on the basis of behavioural evidence is something about which there appears to be no fact of the matter. For in trying to correlate cues with intentions, what on earth could possibly count as having got the correlation right? If all knowledge of intentions resides ultimately in some or other set of observations it makes no sense even to inquire of these observations whether they 'really' correspond to this rather than that intention. If an answer to this epistemic question requires that we first be able to match up observables, then the question outruns the capacity of our methodology to provide an answer. The argument here is parallel to Quine's objection to meaning and his arguments for the indeterminacy of radical translation:

> to accept intentional usage at face value is . . . to postulate translation relations as somehow objectively valid though indeterminate in principle relative to the totality of speech dispositions. Such postulation promises little gain in scientific insight if there is no better ground for it than that the supposed translation relations are presupposed by the vernacular of semantics and intention (Quine 1960, p. 22).

In the case of teaching acts, what we have at our disposal is a person's teaching behaviour and any observable clues, including behaviour antecedent and subsequent to this teaching behaviour, that may be relevant to our account of it. (Naturally, this will include what the teacher reports as his or her intention.) But for positing intentions this is all anyone has to go on. The same applies to our initial learning of the intentional idiom. We are coached into the ways of this vocabulary in suitably public circumstances. Appeal to intention does not therefore provide a source of knowledge over and above what is already available to the behaviourist. We do not, of course, suggest that there is some kind of one-to-one mapping of intentions onto behaviour. One of the consequences of the foregoing argument is that no such correlation is warranted. The methodological parallel to discerning intentions is the task of determining what a native really means by a foreign utterance. As Quine puts it: '. . . the arbitrariness of reading our objectifications into the heathen speech reflects not so much the inscrutability of the heathen mind, as that there is nothing to scrute' (Quine 1969, p. 5). Taylor's distinction between behaviour and action, shared by Sergiovanni and most other interpretivists, thus reflects no basic epistemological distinction at the level of observational evidence. That is, observational evidence for our positing 'inner' mental episodes in others is the same as that for positing inner physical events below the surface of the skin.

If we assume that a person's behaviour is caused, then what we are after ultimately is, in the pattern of modern materialism, a set of reliable psycho-physical laws that will link one item of behaviour to another in the same way that laws in physics integrate disparate observations into an orderly flux. If the existence of unobservables such as molecules can be sustained on the basis of their contribution to simplifying our account of observables, can the same be said for intentions? Does the supposition of intentions integrate disparate items of human behaviour in a way that enhances explanation and prediction? In practice, the folk psychological categories of commonsense are spectacularly successful on this score, but one must remember that within a physicalist monistic framework of explanation and prediction, intentions are not something distinct from the underlying mechanisms that causally link items of behaviour. (This, of course, is token physicalism. What we would really like to have is type physicalism, a vastly more ambitious philosophical aim.) In this context intention talk, where it is useful at all, functions as a kind of promissory note, going proxy for underlying mechanisms yet to be explained (Quine 1974, pp. 8–15). As should be clear, however, in this context, it is in the interests of good science progressively to eliminate intention talk rather than to champion it.

For the physicalist, a better ontological candidate for 'inner' states would be the fine-grained physical properties of human subjects (Phillips 1981, pp. 99–100). This suggestion successfully meets what is often taken to be 'the strongest argument that exists in the philosophical literature for the necessity to take "inner" variables such as intentions beliefs, and so forth into account' (Phillips 1981, p. 100); namely, the Wittgensteinean argument we sketched earlier. For why is it not unreasonable to suppose that there exist antecedent, fine-grained, electro-chemical, neuro-physiological differences to the actions 'involuntarily raising an arm', 'giving a Nazi salute', and 'attempting to catch a mosquito'? (It should be emphasized that these 'fine-grained, electro-chemical, neuro-physiological processes' are not the correlates of particular intentions.)

R.S. Peters is one philosopher of education who offers a dualist answer. He argues that there are two fundamentally different, logically distinct modes of explanation. According to Peters, the 'paradigm case of human action is when something is done in order to bring about an end' (Peters 1958, p. 4). In accounting for human action we therefore need a 'rule following purposive pattern of explanation' (Peters 1958, p. 7) not a causal story. Causal laws 'do not give sufficient explanations of human *actions*, of what human beings do deliberately, knowing what they are doing and for which they can give reasons' (Benn and Peters 1959, pp. 199–200). The point is that the presence of identical causes is no guarantee of identical outcomes. If an agent's reasons or intentions remain unreflected in the total causal fabric in which the agent is otherwise enmeshed, a causal account, no matter how complete, is in principle inadequate as an account of human action.

If Peters's answer presupposes substance dualism, we can illustrate, with the aid of an example, where the major difficulty lies. Suppose, in a certain teaching situation, X raises a hand intending to signal quiet. Suppose further that our account of X's hand raising in terms of X's intentions is logically distinct from any causal account we may give of X's hand going up. But X's hand is a physical object thoroughly enmeshed in X's causal field. If

X's muscles, bones, and nerves do not have familiar physical properties and behave in familiar physical ways, X's hand is not going to go up no matter what X intends. Indeed, the physically specifiable forces to which X's hand is subject may cause it to shoot sideways at just the time when X intends it to go up. The problem for the dualist is to explain why we should expect otherwise. Given this logical distinctness of causal explanation and intentional explanation, why should we ever expect X's body, a physical object subject to quite complex but nonetheless physical forces, to behave as X intends? For the substance dualist, such a coincidence is inexplicable (Strike 1972). It just miraculously happens.

If this is a consequence of maintaining the explanatory autonomy of 'inner' accounts of social and psychological life, then something is seriously wrong with dualism (or at least sufficiently wrong to encourage more subtle versions).

At the epistemological level, this problem lies at the heart of a criticism we have levelled early and late; namely, that interpretivist views of 'inner' episodes and the work they do in explanation outrun all available observational evidence. For evidence appears to be massively detached from the physical sources of experience. It is possible to reply that there is more to evidence than foundationally construed 'inner' events, that what counts as a valid reason or interpretation is a matter of the *coherence* of an interpretation. However, there is an ambiguity over the status of the elements that are supposed to cohere. If they all fall on the 'inner' side of the ontological divide we are left with an inexplicable link between thought and action. Indeed, there will be difficulties even in giving an account of the development of thought, of learning, or of truth and falsehood. If the elements include statements from both sides we will have trouble gaining a coherent reading in the first place.

In our view, interpretation requires us to draw on all theory that is relevant to human action. Since this manifestly includes powerful scientific physicalist theories of human behaviour, a coherentist view of evidence for interpretation, for assigning motives, beliefs, desires, and intentions, will place a premium on reducing the mental to the physical, at least at the level of substance. This, of course, will preserve the autonomy of folk theoretic description, construed as being of nonphysical properties. But if empirical adequacy is the only physical constraint there is on such theorizing, a systematic indeterminacy will invest all these descriptions because we can always posit empirically adequate but arbitrarily varying pairs of, say, beliefs and desires. For this reason we prefer a more thorough-going physicalizing of the mental and subjective categories of the cultural perspective.

While the cultural perspective in educational administration, influenced and shaped by such diverse traditions as organizational theory, interpretive social science, and hermeneutics, is right in accepting the insight of hermeneutics that our reality is always interpreted, its subjectivist and relativist conclusions overshoot the mark. Although the argument is not given here, we suggest that on our physicalist account of administration, the conception of 'culture' could still be fruitful if embedded within a theory that coheres with physical theory (Walker 1988).

Summary

In this chapter we examined what is involved in seeing administrative phenomena through a 'cultural perspective'.

Our case against this approach included discussion of the concept of 'culture' as used in organizational theory, and the presentation of key features of interpretive social science and hermeneutics from which the cultural perspective in educational administration derives its central claims as well as its justification. We discussed two prominent philosophical sources of interpretivism, the work of Taylor and Gadamer, which is used to underwrite Sergiovanni's version of the cultural perspective. While agreeing with the interpretivist insight that reality is always interpreted, we noted interpretivism's dilemma of not being able to sort true from false interpretations, a problem explicitly recognized by Taylor. We argued that the inability to determine the correct interpretation, or reading, of an action or practice is caused by just those phenomena — insight, meanings, or intentions — believed to be irreducibly subjective and autonomous knowledge foundations. Examining the case of intentions in particular, we argued that the claims to knowledge made on their behalf outran the theoretical resources required to justify them. We made the point that while we do not deny the existence of inner phenomena as causing human behaviour, it is not intentions which do the causal work but fine-grained, neuro-physiological mechanisms. Intentions, as referred to in ordinary talk, are more fruitfully conceived of as 'promissory notes' for these underlying mechanisms which, unlike the former, are, and will be, identifiable by our best science.

References

Argyris C. and Schön D. (1978). *Organizational Learning*. (Reading, Mass.: Addison-Wesley).

Benn S.I. and Peters R.S. (1959). *Social Principles and the Democratic State*. (London: George Allen & Unwin).

Bernstein R.J. (1978). *The Restructuring of Social and Political Theory*. (Pittsburgh: The University of Pennsylvania Press).

Bredo E. and Feinberg W. (1982). *Knowledge and Values in Social and Educational Research*. (Philadelphia: Temple University Press).

Cicourel A.V. (1969). *Method and Measurement in Sociology*. (New York: The Free Press).

Deal T. and Kennedy A. (1982). *Corporate Cultures*. (Reading, Mass.: Addison-Wesley).

Dilthey W. (1976). The rise of hermeneutics, in P. Connerton (ed.) *Critical Sociology*. (Harmondsworth: Penguin).

Fay B. (1975). *Social Theory and Political Practice*. (London: George Allen and Unwin).

Gadamer H.-G. (1976). The historicity of understanding, in P. Connerton (ed.) *Critical Sociology* (Harmondsworth: Penguin).

Gadamer H.-G. (1979). The problem of historical consciousness, in P. Rabinow and W.M. Sullivan (eds.) *Interpretive Social Science – A Reader*. (Berkeley, Los Angeles: University of California Press).

Geertz C. (1973). *The Interpretation of Cultures*. (New York: Basic Books).

Giddens A. (1977). *New Rules of Sociological Method*. (London: Hutchinson).

Goffman E. (1959). *The Presentation of Self in Everyday Life*. (Harmondsworth: Penguin).

Goffman E. (1961). *Encounters*. (New York: Bobbs-Merrill).

Gregory K.L. (1983). Native-view-paradigms: multiple culture and culture conflicts in organizations, *Administrative Science Quarterly*, **28**, pp. 359–376.

Habermas J. (1972). *Knowledge and Human Interests*. (London: Heinemann, translated by J.J. Shapiro).

Heidegger M. (1962). *Being and Time*. (New York: Harper and Row).

Hirst P.H. (1974). What is teaching? In P.H. Hirst *Knowledge and the Curriculum*. (London: Routledge and Kegan Paul).

Jackson P. (1968). *Life in Classrooms*. (New York: Holt, Rinehart, and Winston).

Jelinek M. Smircich L. and Hirsch P. (1983). Introduction: a code of many colours, *Administrative Science Quarterly*, **23**, pp. 331–338.

Keat R. and Urry J. (1982). *Social Theory as Science*. (London: Routledge and Kegan Paul).

Lakomski G. (1985). A metastructuralist analysis of Palermo's structuralist analysis of 'Dewey's impossible dream', in D. Nyberg (1986) (ed.) *Philosophy of Education 1985*. Proceedings of the Forty-First Annual Meeting of the Philosophy of Education Society. (Normal, IL: Philosophy of Education Society).

Ouchi W.G. (1981). *Theory Z*. (Reading, Mass.: Addison-Wesley).

Pascale R.T. and Athos A.G. (1981) *The Art of Japanese Management*. (New York: Warner).

Peters R.S. (1958). *The Concept of Motivation*. (London: Routledge and Kegan Paul).

Peters Th.J. and Waterman R.H. Jr. (1982). *In Search of Excellence*. (New York: Harper and Row).

Petrie H.G. (1984). Theory into practice: educational policy analysis and the cultural perspective, in T.J. Sergiovanni and J.E. Corbally (eds.) *Leadership and Organizational Culture*. (Urbana and Chicago: University of Illinois Press).

Pettigrew A.M. (1979). On studying organizational cultures, *Administrative Science Quarterly*, **24** (3), pp. 570–581.

Phillips D.C. (1981). Perspectives on teaching as an intentional act, *The Australian Journal of Education*, **25** (2), pp. 99–105.

Pondy L.R. and Mitroff I.I. (1979). Beyond open system models of organization, in L.L. Cummings and B.M. Staw (eds.) *Research in Organizational Behaviour 1*. (Greenwich, CT: JAI Press).

Quine W.V. (1960). *Word and Object*. (Cambridge, Mass: M.I.T. Press).

Quine W.V. (1969). Speaking of objects, in W.V. Quine *Ontological Relativity and Other Essays*. (New York: Columbia University Press).

Quine W.V. (1974). *The Roots of Reference*. (La Salle: Open Court).

Quine W.V. (1976). Posits and reality, in W.V. Quine *The Ways of Paradox and Other Essays*. (Cambridge: Harvard University Press, revised and enlarged edition).

Rabinow P. and Sullivan W.M. (1977) (eds.). *Interpretive Social Science – A Reader*. (Berkeley, Los Angeles: The University of California Press).

Ricoeur P. (1981). The model of the text: meaningful action considered as a text, in J.B. Thompson (ed. and trans.) *Paul Ricoeur – Hermeneutics and the Human Sciences*. (Cambridge: Cambridge University Press).

Roche M. (1973). *Phenomenology, Language and the Social Sciences*. (London: Routledge and Kegan Paul).

Sergiovanni T.J. (1984a). Cultural and competing perspectives in administrative theory and practice, in T.J. Sergiovanni and J.E. Corbally (eds.) *Leadership and Organizational Culture*. (Urbana and Chicago: University of Illinois Press).

Sergiovanni T.J. (1984b). Developing a relevant theory of administration, in T.J. Sergiovanni and J.E. Corbally (eds.) *Leadership and Organizational Culture.* (Urbana and Chicago: University of Illinois Press).

Sergiovanni T.J. (1984c). Leadership as cultural expression, in T.J. Sergiovanni and J.E. Corbally (eds.) *Leadership and Organizational Culture.* (Urbana and Chicago: University of Illinois Press).

Sergiovanni T.J. and Corbally J.E. (1984) (eds.). *Leadership and Organizational Culture.* (Urbana and Chicago: University of Illinois Press).

Smircich L. (1983). Concepts of culture and organizational analysis, *Administrative Science Quarterly*, **28**, pp. 339–358.

Strike K.A. (1972). Freedom, autonomy and teaching, *Educational Theory*, **22** (3), pp. 262–277.

Taylor C. (1979). Interpretation and the sciences of man, in P. Rabinow and W.M. Sullivan (eds.) *Interpretive Social Science – A Reader.* (Berkeley, Los Angeles: University of California Press).

Taylor C. (1980a). Rorty, Taylor, and Dreyfus – A Discussion, *Review of Metaphysics*, **34**, pp. 47–57.

Taylor C. (1980b). Understanding in human science, *Review of Metaphysics*, **34**, pp. 25–38.

Walker J.C. (1988). *Louts and Legends.* (Sydney: Allen and Unwin).

Weber M. (1947). *The Theory of Social and Economic Organization.* Translated and edited by A.M. Henderson and T. Parsons. (Glencoe, IL: The Free Press).

Weber M. (1949). *The Methodology of the Social Sciences.* (New York: The Free Press).

Weick K.E. (1979a). Cognitive processes in organizations, in L.L. Cummings and B.M. Staw (eds.) *Research in Organizational Behavior.* (Greenwich, CT: JAI Press).

Weick K.E. (1979b). *The Social Psychology of Organizing.* (Reading, Mass.: Addison-Wesley).

White A.R. (1968) (ed.). *The Philosophy of Action.* (Oxford: Oxford University Press).

Willis P. (1978). *Learning to Labor.* (Westmead: Saxon House).

Wolcott H. (1973). *The Man in the Principal's Office: An Ethnography.* (New York: Holt, Reinhart, and Wilson).

7

Administration for Emancipation

A major theme which runs through alternative accounts of educational administration is the criticism that orthodox, positivist, or empiricist theory of administration does not provide any help when it comes to concrete proposals for action. One attempt to overcome this deficiency is, as we saw, the 'cultural perspective' model's emphasis on human subjectivity and the creation of meaning which is seen as an indispensable foundation for the explanation of human action.

In this chapter we want to discuss two approaches which, while they also subscribe to human subjectivity in some form, push the criticisms of orthodox organization theory much further. Neo-Marxist views of organizations and critical theory emphasize the social and political context of action and explore the possibilities of social change and human emancipation. They are thus the most explicitly political alternatives to traditional approaches: theories of change *par excellence*. Given such a strong political commitment, the main problem of the orthodoxy is, as Heydebrand puts it, that it

> . . . like other theories in the social sciences, has been dominated by powerful ideological forces which, taken together, have more or less successfully reproduced and legitimized the structure of capitalist society (Heydebrand 1977, p. 83).

(For related criticisms see also Goldman 1978.) Traditional organization theory is, then, an ideology which is characterized by features such as elitism, an inadequate treatment of power, a lack of historical perspective, the inability to explain social change, and a tacit acceptance of the status quo (Jermier 1982, pp. 202–203). Above all, it blocks the development of 'praxis', which Benson describes as

> . . . the free and creative reconstruction of social arrangements on the basis of a reasoned analysis of both the limits and the potentials of present social forms (Benson 1983, p. 100).

137

For Benson, the dialectical analysis of organizations is the necessary theoretical tool by means of which organizational actors could free themselves from domination. Such analysis would concretely emphasize topics such as

> . . . the humanization of work processes, the development of systems of participation (self-management), the discovery of alternatives to bureaucracy, the removal of systems of dominance, the provision for the utilization of expert knowledge without creating technocratic elites, removing the resistance of organizations to more rational arrangements (Benson 1983, pp. 115–116).

In order to facilitate such changes, traditional theory has to be cleansed of the 'problematic of rational structuring' by which Benson understands the Weberian rational model. A more appropriate and defensible framework is one which regains the knowledge of itself as historically produced and self-reflexive, categories central to Marx's account of social production and reproduction.

Although neo-Marxist approaches to the study of organizations have not made substantive inroads into educational administration theory, neo-Marxist views are generally well represented in educational theory. The work of Bowles and Gintis, and Apple is well known in the North American and Australian education contexts, for example. It has been pointed out by Daniel Griffiths (1988, pp. 44–45) that neo-Marxist views are not well represented in educational *administration*. It is hence appropriate to introduce the work of Heydebrand and Benson in particular since they belong to the best-known advocates of neo-Marxist views in organization theory.

The second perspective — critical theory as developed by Jürgen Habermas — shares important features of neo-Marxist analysis since one of the theory's main intellectual sources is Marx's account of the production and reproduction of social life. Despite this commonality, which also culminates in the desire to bring about human emancipation, critical theory is not considered as a version of neo-Marxism. The reasons for this are complex and need not occupy us here, but they have to do with Habermas's controversial reformulation of Marx's conception of labour (Habermas 1972a ch. 3, 1974 ch. 6, 1979 ch. 4), and with criticisms raised by neo-Marxist writers themselves which include but go beyond the above mentioned category (e.g. Negt 1968, Heydebrand and Burris 1984). In addition, it may be worthy of note that Habermas concedes in a recent interview that 'my Marxist friends are not entirely unjustified in accusing me of being a radical liberal' (Dews 1986, p. 174). Although critical theory, particularly in Habermas's earlier writing (e.g. Habermas 1972b, 1976a), employs Marxian categories, it is far more comprehensive and ambitious in scope than the neo-Marxist views of organizations presented here. Unlike the latter, it has marshalled significant support among educators and educational administration theorists such as Bates, Giroux, and Foster, for example (see Bates 1982, 1983; Foster 1980a, 1980b, 1986; Giroux 1983). Although it is not expressedly a theory of administration or organizations, the critical theory of society is considered as providing a superior theoretical framework for the study of both. Writing in the context of public administration, Dehardt and Denhardt's comments express the hopes of many writers in the critical theory perspective. Voicing their concern about the increasing reliance on *technological rationality* as the standard criterion for judgment in current public administration, they note,

> . . . we focus on the execution of specific tasks but fail to examine the moral implications of our actions. The view of government as concerned merely with 'administratively soluble technical problems' is, in the last analysis, a marked departure from the ideal of public service acting affirmatively in the framework of technocratic morality (Denhardt and Denhardt 1979, p. 110).

Not surprisingly, then, expectations of critical theory are high, as Watkins outlines:

> Through the critique of ideology, a critical theory of organizations should attempt to explain why one class dominates another; it would offer an interpretive account of actions and practices; it would provide *quasi-causal* accounts of the relationships between social structures and kinds of behaviour; it would offer an historical account of how individuals come to be what they are; it would provide an ideology-critique of how people come to accept repressive social practices; it would offer a theory of crises indicating at which period in time people would be willing to listen to the ideology-critique; it would explain through a theory of communication how people have developed false consciousness and how this can be avoided; it would provide an action plan to show people how to act and organize themselves differently (Watkins 1986, p. 95).

Although it is evident that both approaches are different in several respects, they are also united in their commitment to social-political change which they want to bring about by somewhat different means. The central issue we want to discuss in this context is how well or successfully both accounts reach their aims, given the theoretical machinery they have available. That is to say, we are interested in examining both in terms of their validity as theories. The importance of this task is that since advocates of either are convinced of both their theoretical superiority when compared to traditional approaches and their practical and political desirability, they have to be able to justify their claims. Any theory, our argument goes, depends on the justification not only of its claims to knowledge but also on the grounds on which these claims are made. If these turn out to be inadequate, then any claims derived from either theory are equally unjustified. In what follows, we express some epistemological reservations over the status of both neo-Marxist and critical theory accounts of administration.

Regarding the neo-Marxist view we want to examine some of its basic categories, in particular the presuppositions of the *dialectic*, the conception of *contradiction*, and the notion of *ideology*. Similarly, our attention will be focused on critical theory's central doctrines, notably its conception of *interests*, and the notion of *communicative competence* which culminates in the *ideal speech situation*. The conception of interests is basic to Habermas's theory of knowledge, and communicative competence underwrites his approach to the so-called theory-practice problem, that is, the problem of overcoming domination. With regard to the neo-Marxist view, we argue that talk of dialectic notwithstanding, if its basic categories and distinctive claims reflect theory over and above what coheres with our best science, there is a problem in ever knowing that the theory is true. On the other hand, if its distinctive claims can be modelled in sophisticated *scientific* accounts of administration, the view appears redundant, or at best a useful heuristic to scientific administration. Critical theory, however, makes distinctions it is not entitled to make, rendering it incoherent on its own account. More specifically, its central assumptions drive it to posit a basic explanatory framework that lies beyond its resources to justify. Despite their radical consequences, we conclude that neither theory is known to advance social change.

The discussion which follows touches on many complex and big issues in social and political philosophy and theory, as well as other disciplines. These cannot be treated here and we have to remain content with providing much abbreviated discussions on central issues of Marxist and critical theory scholarship as they are brought to bear on the study of organizations.

Organizational Theory and the Roots of Crisis

In his early influential article 'Innovation and crisis in organizational theory' (Benson 1977), as well as in a later version (1983, pp. 33–56), Benson, like many other writers in the field, also attests to the crisis in the study of complex organizations. Unlike other theorists, however, he believes that the crisis is attributable to the changing structure of advanced capitalism which caused the breakdown of the dominant rational paradigm. What Benson also terms the 'rational problematic' in organizational theory was accompanied by a 'fairly simple form of positivism', by which he means that the commonsense understandings of organization members tended to be accepted as data without concern for the processes behind the actors' construction and reconstruction of organizational reality. In his view, this led to the acceptance of organizational reality as nonproblematic, or 'taken for granted'. In addition to this methodological problem, Benson argues that organizational practice was dominated by 'administrative-technical concerns', that is, with 'the essentially technical adjustments necessary to enhance the effectiveness of the organization' (Benson 1977, p. 4). Inherent in the desire for effectiveness is, he believes, an interest in administrative control.

Using the broadly Kuhnian structure of paradigm and paradigm change, Benson suggests that recent work in the field is in fact capable of bringing the dominant paradigm into crisis, although this is not widely perceived. Specifically, there are four analytical problems, or Kuhnian puzzles, which have brought the old paradigm to its conceptual limits: the problems of *action, power, levels,* and *process* (Benson 1977, p. 5). The action problem refers to the neglect of the grounding and production of organizational realities through the actions of organization members. Such attention is said to challenge conventional analysis which merely examines 'the patterned regularities characterizing organizational life at a particular time' (1977, p. 7). Closely related to the action problem is that of power, particularly the power to change paradigms, enforce rules, and redefine operating procedures in organizations. While Benson admits that power can also be examined from within standard views of organizations, such as the rational or functionalist, under the headings of organizational goals, functions, or essential output, such analysis becomes problematic when these are themselves subjected to a power analysis. The overt power of a department or unit, for example, is itself grounded in underlying power relations, a recognition which Benson considers as 'potentially paradigm-shattering' since it leads to the consideration of power as the 'essential core from which other organizational features proceed' (1977, p. 8). Failure to grasp the fact that such standard features as an organization's overt goals, technologies, division of labour, and so on are grounded in underlying power relationships — rather than their being merely orderly, or functionally related to one another — results in a seriously incomplete and biased understanding of organizations. Since these power relationships extend far beyond the organization's boundary, we have to be concerned with the relation of organizational to more comprehensive kinds of analysis. This is what the problem of levels denotes. Benson emphasizes that goals, technologies, and rules come about as a result of human action and since they are in this sense 'by-products' of such activity, they cannot claim to be considered as 'an autonomous realm capable of explanation' (1977, p. 9).

The fourth problem Benson discusses is that of process. While traditional organization theory is said to proceed on the assumption of stable organizational features, a process-oriented view is concerned to study the ongoing interactions which continuously produce and reproduce or alter an organization. This includes studying 'the transformations of context involved in major historical breaks' (Benson 1977, p. 12). These four problems push the traditional paradigm to its limits and demand new approaches of analysis in Benson's view. Although there are some promising perspectives which have been developed recently, such as conflict and action theory, the most comprehensive alternative is that which derives from dialectical Marxian formulations. Only these are in a position to provide an adequate approach to organizational analysis which needs to deal with the following substantive issues:

> (1) social production of organizational reality, including the reality-constructing activity of the organization scientist; (2) the political bases of organizational realities, including the ties of theorists to power structures; (3) the connection of organizations to the larger set of structural arrangements in the society; and (4) the continuously emergent character of organizational patterns (Benson 1977, p. 14).

Dialectical Analysis and Organizational Studies

The alternative account of organizational analysis that Benson develops is first of all characterized by the Marxian concept of the *dialectic* (see Olman 1978, ch. 5; Engels 1976, 1979). By this is meant that the social world is constantly in a state of becoming. Whatever social arrangements prevail at any given point in time, and no matter how 'natural' or fixed they appear, they are only contingent and might well have been otherwise. These arrangements will give way to new ones which originally appear as negations of the previous patterns, or, to put it another way, as being in conflict with them. A dialectical analysis is concerned to examine these changes or transformations by means of which one pattern gives way to another, and this involves 'a search for fundamental principles which account for the emergence and dissolution of specific social orders' (Benson 1983, p. 97). It is also of note, as Heydebrand points out, that dialectical analysis goes beyond negating or merely criticizing a particular arrangement. We may thus oppose orthodox organization theory but cannot remain content in only doing that. Rather, we need to transcend the criticized position and our criticism in a new synthesis:

> Concretely, this means that we will not make theoretical and methodological progress if we merely counterpose new methods to old ones, hermeneutics against causal-explanatory empiricism, interpretation against the technical-rational mode of scientific method, detached analysis against evaluation, intervention, and social action (Heydebrand 1977, p. 84).

We may do better, Heydebrand continues, 'if we retain the interpretive mode together with the "objectifying" scientific mode as natural phases of the process of inquiry' (p. 84).

Benson's dialectical analysis of organizations comprises four principles: *social construction/production*, *totality*, *contradiction*, and *praxis*. Just as the social world is constantly in flux so are organizations as part of it. More specifically, and as was noted earlier, since organizations are the product of human activity, their specific features are temporal and thus changeable. At the same time, however, they display orderly and predictable relationships or patterns which, as surface relationships, 'may be studied scientifically and empirical generalizations may be framed to describe the order' (Benson 1983, p. 101). However, this is only the beginning of inquiry since the described relationships are not determinate causal connections in Benson's view. Rather, the underlying social process needs to be studied by means of which these relationships have been produced and reproduced.

The second principle, totality, has already been hinted at in Benson's notion of levels. To study an organization as a totality means analysing it as a whole rather than abstracting it from the ongoing social activities around it. This means attending to the subtle interplay between form and content and structure and process, as well as considering organizations in relation to each other and society at large. Dialectical analysis thus provides its own answer to the traditional 'organization-boundary' problem of mainstream organization studies. Implicit in the above described categories is a distinction between what Benson calls 'morphology' and 'substructure'. The first term refers to the officially enforced and conventionally accepted view, mainly of the administrator, which, curiously enough, 'may also be somewhat accurate as a description of organizations' (Benson 1983, p. 106) since administrators are the ones who impose their definitions on the organization's form. What the second term refers to, the substructure, is, however, far more significant in Benson's view. It is the 'network of social relations' which cause the production and reproduction of the morphology. In a footnote, he explains:

> Here one encounters the bases of power, the dominance relations which establish and maintain the morphology of the organization. The orderly sequences of development, the predictable relations between components at the morphological level are grounded in and ultimately explained by the substructure (Benson 1983, p. 107).

The substructure, since it is only partially rationalized, is also the arena where oppositional forces and social systems can form within the dominant order and thus threaten its existence. It follows from what has been said so far that organizations are not necessarily 'unitary entities', 'holistic actors' or 'integrated systems'. On the contrary, they are characterized by various developing contradictions. These may occur between different levels of the organizational hierarchies but need not lead to radical transformations of an existing bureaucracy. According to Heydebrand, who borrows this insight from Habermas, contradictions 'may simply appear in the form of a political "crisis" or "legitimation crisis" . . . As such, these crises can be seen as surface manifestations of deeper structural contradictions' (Heydebrand 1977, p. 89). Depending on the kind of contradiction encountered, the existing organization may or may not be pushed to its limits. The most fundamental, generic contradiction is that between the products of human activity and the ongoing activity of humans inside their creations, whether they be factories or whole school systems. The appearance of organizations as immutable and fixed is contradictory to the continuing work of people inside them, resulting in social and political alienation in that people often feel as if they cannot change their environments. If and when they do become aware of their own alienation and powerlessness, and act to overcome them, then they are engaged in *praxis*. This most fundamental of Marx's concepts is also the most comprehensive. It applies to both historically situated individuals as well as groups, classes, and communities. Heydebrand sums it up well. Praxis includes:

producing the means of subsistence . . . producing language and the means of communication and interaction (i.e., symbolic production, consciousness as process), engaging in creative and innovative activity (material and symbolic, including artistic activity), reproducing human existence through biological, social, and ideological reproduction processes, and developing and expressing needs, including the creation of 'new needs' (Heydebrand 1977, pp. 84–85).

When applied to organizational theorizing, praxis would consist of examining the various theories developed about organizational reality by recognizing that those theories were themselves produced in certain historical situations and practical constraints. Considered thus, Benson believes that they are 'formalized solutions of certain actors (usually administrators or other dominant figures) to the technical, practical problems posed by the organization's dialectical character' (Benson 1983, p. 113). They are thus not simply to be put aside, but need to be superseded in a new synthesis. While the dialectical analysis of organizations must be reflexive, it also has to go beyond and work toward the active reconstruction of organizations. This means attending to the concrete conditions under which people may remove constraints and establish social formations in which human potential can be fulfilled.

Dialectics, Contradictions, and Scientific Explanation

Radical organization theorists such as Benson and Heydebrand claim that their neo-Marxist explanation of organizations is superior to 'orthodox' and other non-Marxist alternatives. There are a number of grounds for this claim, but in our view the central and most controversial issue concerns the role of dialectical analysis in understanding social phenomena. According to Benson, much current organizational thought ignores the 'processual perspective': the perspective dealing with 'the processes involved in the production, the reproduction, and the destruction of particular organizational forms' (Benson 1983, p. 96). So one improvement that dialectical theory might be thought to offer over modern systems scientific analyses is valid knowledge of how organizational forms change and develop. The obvious source of such knowledge in traditional Marxist thought is the dialectical laws of nature, particularly, as we saw, the law of contradiction. Indeed, the fact that nature changes at all, Engels argued, is due to an inherent contradiction in things. So as soon as we begin to consider things in their motion we immediately become involved in the study of contradictions.

Engels wanted to preserve some version of Hegel's notion of the unity of opposites whereby opposites make up the driving forces of historical change, and thus also explain the history of class struggles. 'Contradiction' would then mean the same as class conflict (see e.g. Giddens 1981). Exponents of dialectical materialism have interpreted this notion in different ways (see also Gouldner 1980, Keat and Urry 1982). What Engels ended up propounding has been regarded as controversial, or worse, almost certainly false. In order to see what is plausible in the law of contradiction, and how it might be employed in dialectical analysis, ultimately to promote an understanding of organizational change, it will be useful to examine some of these controversies.

The principal difficulty concerns the logical status of the law, for there is an ambiguity over whether it applies formally or materially. 'Contradiction', understood formally, is a property of statements, notably those that are in contradiction. Thus, 'X is eating an apple at time t' is contradicted by 'X is not eating an apple at time t'. Understood materially, contradictions are said to be states of affairs that obtain in the world. Ironically, on a standard modal semantics, a formal contradiction defines something that cannot obtain in any possible world. That is, there is no world in which X can be both eating and not eating an apple at time t. Using much the same set of modal intuitions as latter-day logicians, early critics of Engels boggled at the idea of contradictions existing in the world. The philosopher and economist Eugen Dühring had this to say:

> The contradictory is a category which can only appertain to a combination of thoughts, but not to reality. There are no contradictions in things or, in other words, contradiction accepted as reality is itself the apex of absurdity. . . . The antagonism of forces measured against each other in opposite directions is in fact the basic form of all actions in the life of the world and its creatures. But this opposition of the directions

taken by the forces of elements and individuals does not in the slightest coincide with the absurd idea of contradictions (quoted in Engels 1976, p. 150).

Engels sought to defend himself against this objection in his famous polemic *Anti-Dühring* where he argued in detail for his dialectical theory of nature. Believing motion itself to be a contradiction, he claims that

. . . even simple mechanical change of place can only come through a body being both in one place and in another place at one and the same moment of time, being in one and the same place and also not in it. And the continual assertion and simultaneous solution of this contradiction is precisely what motion is (Engels 1976, p. 152).

A more recent critic of dialectical method in general, and the law of contradiction in particular, is C. Wright Mills who comments trenchantly that

. . . for us, the 'dialectical method' is either a mess of platitudes, a way of doubletalk, a pretentious obscurantism — or all three. The essential error of the 'dialectician' is the know-it-all confusion of logic with metaphysics; if the rules of dialectics were 'the most general laws of motion', all physical scientists would use them every day. On the other hand, if dialectics is the 'science of thinking', then we are dealing with the subject matter of psychology, and not with logic or method at all (Mills 1962, pp. 128–129).

We cite this comment because Benson makes reference to it in formulating his own position on dialectical analysis. He claims, in a footnote:

My procedure is not one of relying upon dialectical laws of nature such as the transformation of quantity into quality, the interpretation of opposites, and the like. The notion of dialectical laws located in nature and expressed both in society and in physical phenomena has been rightly criticized by Mills . . . and many others (Benson 1983, p. 97).

In siding with Mills against Engels's view of dialectics we know that Benson thinks logical contradictions are not to be found in nature. Since this amounts to the requirement that descriptions of phenomena be consistent, the strongest way of construing material contradiction is as opposing causal tendencies. Familiar examples of oppositions in this sense would be an object accelerating under some force, a planet in motion around the sun, a spring being extended by a weight, and so on. This makes change the product of resultant forces. In fact the usual way of deriving the laws of motion for a body being acted upon by forces is to equate change in motion with the resultant differences between forces.

Epistemologically speaking, this makes the study of change and its reliable prediction parasitic upon reliable knowledge of forces. Physics today provides a ready source of theory for the observation, measurement, and calculation of forces for dynamic purposes. However, there is no obvious hiatus in scientific theory that might call for any special contribution from dialectical analysis construed materially. The physics of dynamics is all we need to know in the study of matter in motion. In what way, then, does a scientific study of opposing causal tendencies in social phenomena omit, in principle, explanatory and predictive material that can be provided by dialectical analysis? Given the comprehensiveness of scope that science assumes for itself, it is difficult to know where to look for the gaps.

One possibility is to see in the dialectic a place for human freedom. Benson's talk of praxis as the 'free and creative reconstruction of social arrangements on the basis of a reasoned analysis of both the limits and the potentials of present social forms' (Benson 1983, p. 100) seems to suggest this possibility. However, the Mills passage that Benson endorses is scornful of 'mere reference to "dialectical" . . . to let one out of the determinist trap' (Mills 1962, p. 128). Another possibility is to posit a principled distinction between social science and physical science. Physical science deals with opposing causal tendencies while dialectic finds its place among explanations in terms of reasons. Unfortunately, this move is compromised by Benson's positing of a partially nonrationalized substructure, necessary to explain organizational morphology. A third possibility is to see dialectical analysis as a search heuristic for 'fundamental principles' governing social change. This is certainly consistent with much of what Benson says about the inadequacies of current organizational theory. But once again we need to ask about the gaps in science. Does the heuristic guide us in the search for more causes? If so, it suggests no more than that we cast the causal net wider. Stripped of metaphors masquerading as substantive empirical theses about social change, it counsels nothing methodologically additional to what is involved in, say, the shift from a closed to an open systems perspective. On the other hand, if the heuristic guides us beyond what science can in principle yield, concerning the processes of organizational change, it is important to know precisely what more we are looking for. But apart from a major empirical theory of power and its place in social causation, which can be handled by scientific theories, it is difficult to know what more could be wanted.

In terms of our coherence criteria for theory choice, the demand for simplicity requires that justification be given for dialectical theory where it purports to yield results over and above what can be provided by good science. In the absence of a clear specification of these results, we feel that beyond its suggestive, heuristic qualities, talk of dialectical analysis as a distinctive basis of social inquiry will bring us no closer to finding the causes of social inequality and oppression.

In the following sections, we examine the other account of social change, that of critical theory.

Critical Theory and the Reconstruction of Social and Educational Studies

As a relative newcomer to Anglo-American and Australian educational theory, the critical theory of society was embraced enthusiastically. Writers such as Bredo and Feinberg (1982) argued, for example, that critical theory is able to transcend the stand-off between the dominant positivist school and its challenger, the interpretive paradigm. While both schools had come under attack — positivist research from within analytic philosophy of science and from interpretivists who criticize its reductionism — the latter school's implicit relativism obviously made it unsuitable as positivism's successor.

In educational administration, in particular, critical theory is considered to provide the appropriate theoretical framework which would help overcome domination inherent in the manipulative character of orthodox administration theory, as Bates argued so forcefully. The strength of the critical theory perspective, as expressed by Foster, is that 'it is possible to have a social science which is neither purely empirical nor purely interpretative' (Foster 1980a, p. 499), possibly on the assumption that it thus escapes the criticisms levelled at positivist and interpretivist theory respectively. According to Kemmis, critical theory is superior to its rivals for three reasons. Firstly, because

. . . Critical social scientific research, including emancipatory action research, views education as a historical and ideological process.

Secondly, because

. . . its form of reasoning is practical (like that of interpretive research) but also critical: it is shaped by the emancipatory intent to transform educational organizations and practices to achieve rationality and social justice.

And thirdly, because

. . . it is predisposed towards ideology-critique: the recognition and negation of educational ideologies which serve the interests of specific groups at the expense of others and which mask oppression and domination with the appearance of liberation (Kemmis 1985, p. 42).

What distinguishes critical theory from competitors is that it promises to solve the problems of both the empirical and interpretive sciences in a higher-order synthesis which allocates the former and latter sciences to their own, mutually exclusive, object domains, complete with their respective methodologies. From the critical perspective, the domain of the natural sciences is that of *purposive-rational* action, governed by technical rules based on empirical knowledge, and directed toward prediction about observable events, be they physical or social. The interpretive sciences, on the other hand, are characterized by symbolic interaction, or *communicative action*, which is governed by consensual norms, and is grounded in the practical interest.

In addition to relegating the sciences to their respective spheres of influence and thus settling any claims for the superiority of one or the other methodology, critical theory's political orientation is akin to that of the neo-Marxist view. It suggests that the current dominance of science and the rise of technology and bureaucracy are developmental tendencies of late capitalism which increasingly encroach on the domain of social life (see Habermas 1976a). As a result of such imperialism which is accompanied by the decline and erosion of traditional institutions and legitimations, the legitimatory vacuum thus created is filled by the new belief in science (see Habermas 1972b). What is obliterated in this process, according to Habermas, is the possibility of raising questions about social norms and values, questions about the 'good life', in the public domain. Where they are raised, they can only be perceived through the distorting lens of instrumental action, or the technical interest, which makes them appear solvable by the application of Weber's means-end scheme. Unmasking the illegitimate intrusion of science into the realm of social norms, Habermas believes, makes critical theory 'critical' in the sense Marx understood the term, since science and technology have thus been shown to be ideological. The perspective which makes such insight possible is that of critical reflection which liberates or emancipates actors from false beliefs and subsequently leads to concrete proposals for overcoming oppression.

It is not difficult to see the attraction of critical theory for those writers who, critical of positivism, wary of the implicit relativism and conservatism of the interpretive school, and disenchanted with the so-called 'economism' of Marxist education theory, as exemplified by, for example, Bowles and Gintis (1976), were searching for a more appropriate basis for a socially just education theory. Critical theory has consequently also found application in curriculum theory (Apple 1977, 1981, 1982; Young and Whitty 1977; Van Manen 1977) and action research (Carr and Kemmis 1983, Kemmis et al. 1983), and has been used to explain the crisis in formal schooling (Shapiro 1984).

It is also easy to see from the description so far where critical theory and the neo-Marxist view overlap. One important common bond is, in fact,

Habermas's thesis of the rise of technology and bureaucracy which, in turn, leads to the notions of 'legitimation' and 'legitimation crisis' employed by Benson and Heydebrand. Before we proceed to introduce and discuss the central Habermasian categories and conceptions mentioned above, recall that critical theory was described as still developing. In fact, the publication (and translation) of *Knowledge and Human Interests* denotes what Bernstein calls Habermas's 'first systematic synthesis' (Bernstein 1986, p. 8). All other work done to date is described as presenting a 'new systematic synthesis — which preserved Habermas's earlier insights, corrects its inadequacies, and points to new directions for research' (Bernstein 1986, p. 12). It culminates in the publication of *The Theory of Communicative Action* (Habermas 1984a).

Two points need to be made here. First, the administration, organization and education writers whose work is discussed here rely primarily on Habermas's work of the earlier period. This means that insofar as they enlist Habermasian categories and claims for their theories, they are as coherent or incoherent as the original theory itself. Second, the end of the 'first systematic synthesis' also denotes the end of Habermas's concern with matters epistemological. This is an important point since in the absence of further work in this regard — apart from the occasional reply to a critic (i.e. postscript to Habermas 1972a, 1982, Dews 1986) — the epistemological justification developed in *Knowledge and Human Interests* stands. Indeed, while there have been some modifications, Habermas still endorses his earlier position, specifically his theory of cognitive interests, as 'basically sound' (Dews 1986, p. 197). He does, however, add some caveats and admits difficulties. One we canvassed in Chapter One was his concern over equating physical science with narrow empiricism. Further qualifications on this theme deserve to be quoted in full:

> . . . I would be a bit more cautious now. We have all the new arguments on the table from the post-empiricists. If only for that reason, one would have to reformulate the account more carefully and leave room for historical change. Nevertheless, I hold by the fundamental idea that there are constitutive relationships between scientific enterprises and everyday orientations. These internal relationships are so strong that they can predetermine — via the formal pragmatics of research — the possible channels of application or implementation of different types of knowledge. The correlation between these knowledge-types and the various disciplines is the weakest part of the theory. There one has to admit to several sins. But I think this too could be remodelled. However, I'm no longer interested in that — at least not just now (as quoted in Dews 1986, p. 197).

Habermas also comments on his change of heart regarding the role of epistemology which, in the 1960s, he did consider important for a social theory 'which should also satisfy empirical claims' (Dews 1986, p. 152). While continuing to emphasize the basic correctness of his argumentation outline in *Knowledge and Human Interests*, he states,

> . . . I no longer believe in epistemology as the *via regia*. The critical theory of society does not need to prove its credentials in the first instance in methodological terms; it needs a substantive foundation, which will lead out of the bottlenecks produced by the conceptual framework of the philosophy of consciousness, and overcome the paradigm of production, without abandoning the intentions of Western Marxism in the process (quoted in Dews 1986, p. 152).

The reasons why Habermas so emphatically abandoned epistemology to turn instead to 'society and communicative rationality' are complex and indeed puzzling. Suffice it to observe in the present context that he acknowledges the impossibility of finding a transcendental foundation for knowledge, a *first philosophy*. Despite his modification of epistemological issues, Habermas now believes that epistemology was something of a detour which obscured the fact that *Knowledge and Human Interests* was itself dependent on the 'philosophy of consciousness' and the 'philosophy of the subject' which have their roots in the Cartesian turn to subjectivity. The more direct route, Habermas now believes, is to ground critical theory in language in general and in communication in particular (see Bernstein 1986, Giddens 1986, pp. 95–125). Indeed, he is adamant that his theory of communicative competence is neither a continuation of the theory of knowledge by other means nor a meta-theory (Dews 1986, pp. 108–109; Peukert 1984, ch. 10). Yet despite his 'linguistic turn', he stresses that he considers himself as working within the established system of scientific knowledge (although not always happily):

> When one is oriented to questions of truth and does not misunderstand oneself in the process, then one should not try, as Heidegger and Adorno both did, to produce truths outside of the sciences and to wager on a higher level of insight . . . As a professor or scholar with the authority of one who examines questions of truth, one should not say things that affect other people without at least trying to bring one's work up to the standards set by institutionalized research (Habermas, quoted in Dews 1986, pp. 127–128).

It is not the task of this chapter to examine the new thesis of the 'grounding' of critical theory, but one might well ask how Habermas would defend his turn to language when challenged by a rival theory, such as neo-Marxism, for example, since no theory can be presumed to be a true *a priori*, requiring rather the provision of evidence which, in turn, implies some theory of knowledge or other.

Having thus noted the major breaks, changes, and transformations in Habermas's work up to date which nevertheless indicate continuities especially in respect of critical theory's validity, we want to discuss the central concepts of the theory in the following sections. (For a comprehensive discussion of Habermas's work see McCarthy 1981; discussions of more select aspects of his work are to be found in Thompson and Held 1982.)

Habermasian Interests and their Epistemological Status

Central to understanding Habermas's approach to social theory is what he takes to be the fundamental problem of contemporary social science: the relationship between theory and practice (Habermas 1974). He means by this that the connection between knowledge and social action has become an instrumentalist one, a relation which assumes the neutrality of science. Because science is considered to be free of values, it cannot give us any guidance on how to conduct our lives. This development is the result of the victory of 'scientism' or positivism, which, Habermas argues, presents itself as the only valid form of knowledge. Since all valid knowledge is thus identified with natural science, whose task it is to predict and control nature, questions directed toward understanding social and political issues can hence only be posed from within the positivist framework. As a result, technical issues are not only confused with practical ones (which deal with the conduct of social life), but the latter are in fact reduced to the former, thus obliterating the very distinction. The critical theorist could argue, for instance, that the tracking of children on the basis of IQ tests is an example of such conflation. Insofar as IQ tests are considered as objective and scientific, the allocation of educational resources could also be considered as objective to the extent that it is based on the tests. IQ tests are thus technical tools applied in the just allocation of scarce resources. However, what is obscured here is that the construction of tests relies on cultural and other assumptions which have, in fact, contributed to the tests' bias in terms of class, sex, and race. Hence, the critical theorist would maintain, they are anything but just.

Habermas suggests that it has become impossible to reflect critically on current forms of domination since even they appear as problems which can be solved by merely technical means. Even worse, because science currently enjoys such high prestige, questions directed at the results of scientific research appear as illegitimate, and hence invalid, intrusions into the objective work of the scientist. Habermas argues that a social theory which is premised on the positivist self-understanding of science, and incorporates a 'technological rationality' (Habermas 1975) merely serves to increase technical control over history by perfecting the administration of society. In one form or another, it is this thesis which reverberates throughout the radical administration and organization literature. Habermas's aim is to restore to theory the dimension of reflection eclipsed by positivism and present a social theory which, as ideology-critique, reunites theory with practice.

The quest for a comprehensive theory of social evolution as a theory of rationality leads Habermas to examine recent developments in the social sciences and in analytic philosophy of science on the one hand (Habermas 1985), and to investigations in the field of philosophy of language and theoretical linguistics on the other (Habermas 1972a, 1972c, 1976b, 1979). In addition, he also reexamines the crisis potential of late capitalism (Habermas 1976a, 1976c) and the foundations of the older school of critical theory (Habermas 1982). It would lead too far afield to consider these issues here. For present purposes the conception of interests (*Interessen*) is most important since it is the cornerstone of critical theory, aiming as it does at the re-examination of the connection between knowledge and human interests in general.

Interests, Habermas contends, are not like any other contingent empirical facts about human beings; neither are they rooted in an ahistorical subjectivity. Rather, they are grounded in the fundamental human conditions of work (following Marx) and interaction. What Habermas calls a *cognitive interest* is consequently

> . . . a peculiar category, which conforms as little to the distinction between empirical and transcendental or factual and symbolic determination as to that between motivation and cognition. For knowledge is neither a mere instrument of an organism's adaptation to a changing environment nor the act of a pure rational being removed from the context of life in contemplation (Habermas 1972a, p. 197).

Cognitive, or knowledge-constitutive, interests are hence ascribed a quasi-transcendental status, an ascription Habermas acknowledges as being problematic (Habermas 1974, p. 8ff). Critical theory claims three such interests: the technical, the practical, and the emancipatory. These three are said to correspond to the three types of sciences. The natural sciences, in Habermas's view, incorporate the technical interest; the historical-hermeneutic sciences the practical interest; and the critical sciences (such as Freudian psychoanalysis and sociology) the emancipatory. The technical interest guides work, the practical interaction, and the emancipatory power. Work, or purposive-rational action, is defined as

> . . . either instrumental action or rational choice or their conjunction. Instrumental action is governed by *technical rules* based on empirical knowledge. In every case they imply conditional predictions about observable events, physical or social. These predictions can prove correct or incorrect. The conduct of rational choice is governed by *strategies* based on analytic knowledge. They imply deductions from

preference rules (value systems) and decision procedures; these propositions are either correctly or incorrectly deduced. Purposive rational action realizes defined goals under given conditions. But while instrumental action organizes means that are appropriate or inappropriate according to criteria of an effective control of reality, strategic action depends only on the correct evaluation of possible alternative choices, which results from calculation supplemented by values and maxims (Habermas 1972b, pp. 91–92).

The second cognitive interest, the practical, enables a grasping of reality through understanding in different historical contexts (Habermas 1972a, chs 7 and 8). It involves interaction patterns which provide a reliable foundation for communication. What Habermas terms interaction, or *communicative action*, is, like the technical interest, also a distinct, nonreducible kind of action which demands specific categories of description, explanation, and understanding. Habermas argues that just as human beings produce and reproduce themselves through work, so they shape and determine themselves through language and communication in the course of their historical development. While he emphasizes with Marx that the historically determined forms of work causally influence the nature and quality of interaction (Habermas 1972a, chs 2 and 3), he nevertheless insists that symbolic interaction, together with cultural tradition, forms a 'second synthesis' and is the 'only basis on which power (*Herrschaft*) and ideology can be comprehended' (1972a, p. 42). Marx is accused of not understanding the importance of communicative action since it does not play a separate role in, and is subsumed under, the concept of social labour, which, Habermas claims, fits his own notion of instrumental action. Nevertheless, undistorted communication which, in his view, is the goal of the practical interest inherent in the hermeneutic sciences, requires the existence of social institutions which are free from domination themselves. On Habermas's own admission, these do not yet exist. By adding the model of symbolic interaction, he wishes to expand epistemologically Marx's conception of social labour.

Finally, the notion of the emancipatory cognitive interest leads us to the most fundamental, yet also derivative, interest. It must be understood in the context of the German idealist tradition whose underlying theme, Habermas asserts, is that reason, once properly understood

. . . means the will to reason. In self-reflection knowledge for the sake of knowledge attains congruence with the interest in autonomy and responsibility. The emancipatory cognitive interest aims at the pursuit of reflection as such (Habermas 1972a, p. 314).

It is this interest which provides the epistemological basis for Habermas's notion of critique which is alleged to be the function of the critical social sciences. Consequently, this interest is of equal importance for education and administration theory which aims to be 'interested' in just this way. It follows that any critique directed at the former also applies to the latter.

Habermas's conception of interests was developed in critical response to positivism. The peculiar status of the interests resulted from his desire to avoid a naturalistic reduction of quasi-transcendental interests to empirical ones. Habermas wants to say, on the one hand, that humans have transformed nature, built social systems, and developed science in the course of their evolution, a process which is analogous to the evolution of claws and teeth by animals (Habermas 1972a, p. 312). On the other hand, he is not content with such naturalism and claims that these achievements of human evolution are not merely accidental or contingent but have developed the way they have because of *a priori* knowledge-constitutive interests. These cognitive interests are described as being of 'metalogical necessity . . . that we can neither prescribe nor represent, but with which we must instead *come to terms*' (1972a, p. 312). They are 'innate' and 'have emerged in man's natural history' (p. 312) and are located in 'deeply rooted (invariant?) structures of action and experience — i.e. in the constituent elements of social systems' (p. 371). But from the observation that humans have in fact transformed nature, built social systems, and created science, it does not follow that they have done so because of transcendental interests. In other words, there is no equivalence between asserting that the technical, practical, and emancipatory interests have emerged in human natural history and asserting that they provide the transcendental framework for all human knowledge. How could such a transcendental framework be justified?

Our principal worry concerns the distinction between high-level theoretical empirical claims and transcendental claims. As we know from the work of Popper, classifications of similarities and differences among objects or phenomena in the world are always made relative to a frame of reference: some animals belong to the emperor, others do not; some have backbones, others do not; some are warm-blooded, others are not, and so on. Presumably, the most fruitful taxonomies or classification schemata will be those which reflect the theoretical categories of our best theories. The same point applies to the business of classifying knowledge, interests, elements of human history and evolution, and features of social life in general. If the theory which underwrites Habermas's taxonomy is flawed, then pending better theorizing, the categories will stand in need of justification. If the process of transcendental justification is identified with, or depends on, a prior process of good theorizing, then there is no epistemologically significant distinction to be drawn between high-level empirical theorizing and the justification of transcendental claims. This is especially the case if we admit there is more to sound empirical theorizing than is captured in the methodology of varieties of positivism. Since Habermas has already admitted to adopting a too narrow view of science in his early epistemological work, we may assume that his interests taxonomy is not only questionable, but that its truth depends on nontranscendental considerations, such as the standing of substantive theories of the world. Given our views on social science, this leads, after all, to a naturalistic reduction of interests. One can, of course, maintain with Popper that some schemata must have *a priori* status. However, knowing whether these schemata are true requires a fair bit of *a posteriori* theorizing. It seems that Habermas's assertion of the existence of two categorially distinct forms of knowledge and inquiry struggles for want of adequate justification (see Dallmayr 1974).

In the following section, we argue that praxis, that is, the struggle for liberation from domination, cannot be initiated on the basis of critical theory by examining the form that 'emancipation' is expected to take in Habermas's view.

Communicative Competence and the Ideal Speech Situation

The concept of communicative competence culminating in the ideal speech situation is the centrepiece of critical theory, since here the various strands of Habermas's investigations are drawn together. Parallel to Marx's critique of political economy, Habermas attempts to elucidate contemporary forms of alienation expressed in distorted communication. He wants to show that the potential for emancipation inheres in ordinary language, which both pre-supposes and anticipates an ideal speech situation in which communication free from domination is possible. The full impact of Habermas's theory of communicative competence cannot be grasped adequately without taking recourse to its three underlying tenets which need further explication: (a) the notion of discourse and its relation to interaction, (b) the consensus theory of truth, and (c) the conception of an ideal speech situation itself.

Habermas argues that we can proceed from the fact that functioning language games, in which speech acts are exchanged, are based on an underlying consensus which is formed in the reciprocal recognition of at least four claims to validity. These claims comprise the 'comprehensibility of the utterance, the truth of its propositional component, the correctness and appropriateness of its performatory component, and the authenticity of the speaking subject' (Habermas 1974, p. 18, 1979, ch. 1). Habermas contends that in normal communication these claims are accepted uncritically. Only when a background consensus is challenged can all claims be questioned. Their justification is subject to *theoretical discourse* which is an intersubjective enterprise within a community of inquirers. This concept is adapted from Habermas's interpretation of Peirce's model of empirical science (Habermas 1972a, chs 5 and 6). Although theoretical discourse demands the 'virtualization of constraints on action', it still remains implicitly presupposed in interaction because Habermas assumes that the subjects are in fact capable of justifying their beliefs discursively. Such a capability is characteristic of a functioning language game. Yet he is also aware that there is no complete symmetry of power among the partners of communication.

If we consider a consensus to be rational and discover after further reflection and argumentation that it is not, how are we to decide what does constitute a rational consensus? Habermas claims that the only recourse we have is to discourse itself. He is aware that this answer might lead into a vicious circle and contends that not every achieved agreement is a consensus, that is, can be considered a criterion for truth (Habermas 1984b). If, for example, an agreement is reached on the basis of what Habermas calls (covert or open) 'strategic' action, then that consensus is a 'pseudo-consensus' (Habermas 1982, p. 236). Strategic action is that which is undertaken primarily to safeguard an individual's personal success by means of conscious or unconscious deception. In the case of systematically distorted communication, that is, unconscious deception, Habermas believes that:

> . . . at least one of the participants is deceiving *himself* or *herself* regarding the fact that he or she is actually behaving strategically, while he or she has only apparently adopted an attitude oriented to reaching understanding (Habermas 1982, p. 264).

Even in this case, he contends, the actors themselves can know, even though only 'vaguely and intuitively', which of the two attitudes were adopted. Both kinds are seen as 'genuine types of interaction' and may be mixed up with each other in practice. As a result, Habermas asserts, 'it is often difficult for an observer to make a correct ascription' (Habermas 1982, p. 266). If we want to reach a true (or 'founded') consensus, he argues, we must admit as the only permissible compulsion the force of the argument and consider as the only permissible motive the cooperative search for truth (Habermas 1972a, p. 363). An argument, then, qualifies as rational when it is cogent and motivates us in our search for truth. Implicit in this thesis is Habermas's belief that there must be increased freedom for discourse to reach higher levels, that truth claims and claims to correctness of problematic statements and norms must be able to be assessed discursively and, in the course of assessment, must also be able to be changed or rejected. The conditions under which such freedom can be attained are, in Habermas's view, given in the *ideal speech situation* because:

> . . . the design of an ideal speech situation is necessarily implied with the structure of potential speech; for every speech, even that of intentional deception, is oriented towards the idea of truth (Habermas 1972c, p. 144).

The ideal speech situation is attained when the requirements of symmetrical relations obtain which involve all speakers having equal chances of selecting and employing 'speech acts' and when they can assume interchangeable dialogue roles. But since practical discourse is generally distorted, according to Habermas, and since the ideal speech situation can only be anticipated, it is difficult to assess empirically whether or not, or to what extent, the conditions of an ideal speech situation actually obtain. This problem, Habermas contends, cannot be solved in any *a priori* way. There is no single decisive criterion by which we can judge whether a consensus reached is 'founded', even under ideal conditions. We can only determine in retrospect whether the conditions for an ideal speech situation have obtained. This difficulty resides in the fact that

> . . . the ideal speech situation is neither an empirical phenomenon nor simply a construct, but a reciprocal supposition or imputation (*Unterstellung*) unavoidable in discourse. This supposition can, but need not be, contra-factual; but even when contra-factual it is a fiction which is operatively effective in communication. I would therefore prefer to speak of an anticipation of an ideal speech situation. . . . This anticipation alone is the warrant which permits us to join to an actually attained consensus the claim of a rational consensus. At the same time it is a critical standard against which every actually reached consensus can be called into question and checked (Habermas, quoted in McCarthy 1976, p. 486).

When all is said and done, what does this notion amount to? Stripped of its abstractions, we are left with a procedural model of negotiation which has the following characteristics in practice: (a) not everyone can participate in a given negotiation because of the existing power differential in society; (b) even when we reach an agreement practically, we are not sure whether it really is a consensus, nor do we have the means to check this; and (c) the language we use to reach consensus is itself a carrier of ideology. While Habermas emphasizes that this model is only an 'anticipation' possessing the status of a 'practical hypothesis' which does not refer to any historical society (Habermas 1982, pp. 261–262), one is nevertheless entitled to press the point regarding its potential for realization in the here and now. Recall that the solution to this dilemma is that we can only determine with hindsight whether or not ideal conditions obtained. Recall further that these involve symmetrical relations in which all speakers have equal chances of 'selecting and employing speech acts'. But this does not solve the problem because we have to repeat the question of how we would ever know that these equal chances did obtain. Since all we have to go by are self-reports which may be consciously or unconsciously misleading, or plain false, even a retrospective assessment would need to avoid the regress problem. Pressing the issue of content further, additional problems arise such as the difficulties implied in the notion of equal chances.

The demand for equality is the demand for the levelling of differences valued by some group, differences obviously not valued by the group that wants to eliminate them. But as Gouldner (1976, p. 144) correctly notes, this equalizing is never the levelling of all differences. He points out, for example, that no one calls for compulsory plastic surgery to make all equally beautiful, nor is there a national drive for compulsory drug injections to make everyone equally great lovers and thinkers (Gouldner 1976, p. 144). The point is that both inequalities and equalities are highly selective, and the problem is with the standard of selection. If this is so, then the ideal speech situation, with its demand for equality, implies a new system for stratification since some interests are necessarily excluded. The same problem arises in relation to the fact that communicative competence entails linguistic competence. As Gouldner (1976, p. 145) notes, even in an ideal speech situation we could encounter people with different language histories, linguistic competences and codes, a point explicitly noted by Habermas (1982, p. 255). The question is, whose codes, or language, shall we accept when these differ? And furthermore, who decides, and on the basis of which criteria?

Given that we are interested in a more coherent theoretical framework for educational administration theory and practice, it is of some interest to consider the role children play or do not play in the conception of the ideal speech situation. The issue of concern is that since children have to learn to become linguistically competent, they are, at various stages of their development, more or less linguistically competent. The postulate of such competence would, then, entail exclusion of children below a certain level of development. While such exclusion may well be a defensible attitude to take, the point is that it has to be argued for on grounds other than linguistic competence, although that may well be a contributing criterion. It is not only children who are thus excluded, but anyone who is linguistically incompetent for whatever reason. The example of immigrants who have not yet mastered the language of their new country sufficiently, but may be thoroughly competent in their native tongue, comes to mind. Membership in the ideal speech situation, then, when pressed, turns out to be a rather exclusive affair, contrary to its demand for equal chances at 'conversational turn-taking'.

Habermas calls this model a 'constitutive illusion' and an 'unavoidable supposition of discourse' which, however, is possibly always counterfactual. From this, McCarthy draws the conclusion that:

Nonetheless this does not itself render the ideal illegitimate, an ideal that can be more or less adequately approximated in reality, that can serve as a guide for the institutionalization of discourse and as a critical standard against which every actually achieved consensus can be measured (McCarthy 1981, p. 309).

While this is not an uncommon defence of the ideal speech situation, it is nevertheless invalid. This is so because the ideal speech situation is in principle unrealizable. It cannot be 'more or less' adequately approximated in reality because the condition of retrospectivity does not get Habermas out of the problem of appealing to doubtful evidence for the existence of such a situation. It follows that we cannot even achieve what self-reflection and the emancipatory interest promised us: the liberation from dogmatic attitudes which is, in any case, only the formal precondition for practical, political action in Habermas's scheme of things. For critical theory to work, we must assume as already given what, on Habermas's own account, does not yet exist but is supposed to come into existence as the result of the theory being acted upon: namely, a world in which power and control are equalized. On the issue of social change, then, this theory is of little help.

It is perplexing that this model of rationality, that is, rational persons discussing their differences in an ideal speech situation, has been hailed as at least potentially the solution to the so-called theory-practice problem which holds that traditional (positivist) theory is incapable of informing and guiding practice. If the preceding analysis is correct, it seems that critical theory is similarly incapable of doing so. Indeed, Foster notes Habermas's 'Kantian swing away from the original emphasis in dialectical Marxism' and evaluates this shift in the following manner:

> This is both Habermas's strength and weakness. It is a strength insofar as it raises the level of analysis beyond the conditions in a specific society. In so doing, he allows the consideration of those factors which affect the race as a whole — science, language, moral development, and political administration. Yet this turn in his thought shifts attention away from class oppression and the resulting possibility of practical action (Foster 1980a, p. 505).

Despite this assessment, and additional problems that Foster identifies in his latest and most comprehensive treatment of critical theory, *Paradigms and Promises* (1986), he continues to support it. The irony of this assessment, which is not atypical of the kind of reception critical theory has enjoyed in Anglo-American social science, is that what is applauded as its strength is precisely what prevents the theory from becoming practical: its ahistorical nature. Foster's discussion reflects this irony in that he assumes that a position is possible which would raise 'the level of analysis beyond the conditions in a specific society'. However, no such privileged position is to be found — an assessment Habermas shares, too.

While the reasons outlined above go a considerable way towards explaining the problems of the theory of communicative competence, and hence critical theory, it finally fails because truth-as-consensus is removed from direct confrontation with the 'objects of possible experience'. In other words, the consensus theory of truth rules out the possibility of statements being true by virtue of empirical reality. If we cannot, in principle, know whether or not there is, as Habermas asserts, distorted communication and oppression in contemporary society, then we are left with mere speculation. However intuitively convincing this may be, speculation comes a poor second to knowledge. In order to understand more fully how this problem arises, we need to take a closer look at how Habermas conceives of the construction of empirical reality in his model of empirical science (see Hesse 1982, Habermas 1982).

Habermas does not accept the notion of an external reality existing independently which can serve as evidence for the truth of statements. Rather, the 'object domain' of empirical science is 'constituted' in the course of pursuing those technical interests which enable us to survive. Empirical reality is thus established pragmatically in (instrumental) action which is characterized by the unreflective 'following of the rules' and the application of the feedback methods of empirical science. All empirically descriptive and scientific statements acquire pragmatic meaning in the process of controlling external nature. The upshot of this is, as Hesse explains, that:

> the empirical meaning of a sentence is not determined . . . by the conditions under which the sentence would be said to be true, but rather by the conditions under which utterances are acceptably produced in the language community, including the conditions of learning to use the language to refer to that in the surrounding reality which is categorized as particular kinds of objects and events for technical purposes (Hesse 1982, p. 99).

Hence Habermas can say that the meaning but not the truth of an empirical proposition such as 'this ball is red' is determined by our habitual linguistic practice which, in normal circumstances, enables us to pick out this particular kind of thing or object (Habermas 1972a, p. 364).

While meaning is pragmatic, truth, as we saw earlier, is not. It is a matter for theoretical discourse and is thus asserted or denied of statements only. While Habermas does not consider truth to be applicable to the realm of unreflective action, we can nevertheless have 'opinions about objects based on experience related to action', but these are quite different and separate from 'statements about facts, founded on discourse that is free of experience and unencumbered by action' (Habermas 1974, pp. 20–21). To understand 'opinions' one needs to understand the meanings of categories of natural language. These meanings Habermas assumes as given in the habitual linguistic interactions we have with the world. The problem with this strict separation of action and discourse, premised on the twin assumptions of pragmatic meaning and consensus truth, is that if true, we could never have learnt a proposition such as 'this ball is red' in the first place. For in order to be able to account for how we learn any descriptive language at all, we must presume that there are objects and things in the world independently of us which serve initially as causal sources for learning. It is only on the assumption of an external world which remains significantly stable and endures over time that we can develop classificatory schemes to apply to our experiences at all (O'Hear 1985, ch. 1). Although Habermas explicitly rejects an external reality as evidence, it is implied in his concession that

> . . . the (discursively verifiable) fact that the ball is red can be 'grounded' in corresponding experience in handling the red ball (where the experience can claim objectivity), or else we could say, conversely, that the objective experience I have had of the red ball 'shows' the fact that the ball is red (Habermas 1972a, pp. 364–365).

In *Knowledge and Human Interests*, Habermas is rightly concerned about the errors of foundational justification. We suspect that much of the idealism in his theory which manifests itself as difficulties over theory and practice, discourse and action, and muddles over meaning, evidence, and truth, can be traced to his rejection of foundationalism. However, coherentism, as an alternative, need not be idealist, detached from the physical world. For we can combine a coherence theory of evidence with a correspondence theory of truth, as we indicated in Chapter Two. A theory of language learning will be part of our most coherent global theory. Once we have such a theory we let correspondence truth grind out its story of the referents of singular terms and predicates — in short, the theory's ontology — in order to determine what must exist for humans with our capacities to learn it. The theory posits an external source of evidence, say a red ball, but not as a foundational endpoint in the justification of a claim that the ball is red. Rather, we suppose the ball is red after coherence criteria have done their work on a global theory which includes an account of what must exist for the theory to be learned. This is arrived at by the theory's apparatus of objective reference, part of correspondence truth that is used to individuate objects in the world according to the global theory's classification schemata.

The fundamental tension in Habermas's theory between epistemological idealism and required objectivities needs to be resolved if the critical theory of society is to be relevant for this world.

Summary

The task we set ourselves in this chapter was to examine the most explicitly political challenge to orthodox, positivist, administration theory. This challenge, we argued, consists of two, related, forms: the neo-Marxist perspective and Jürgen Habermas's critical theory. While the first view was developed specifically in relation to the study of organizations, the second was not, although — as a general theory of society — its concepts can be applied to the study of organizations and administration, as indeed they have been. For this reason we chose to examine the original version of Habermas's critical theory, rather than the reading given it by writers in educational administration or organizational analysis. While there are significant distinctions between them, both approaches are concerned to argue that theory development must be put in the service of human betterment or emancipation. Achieving this goal is made dependent on unveiling the essentially manipulative character of science with its hidden agenda of (administrative-technical) control.

In regard to neo-Marxism as represented in the work of Benson, Heydebrand, and Denhardt, we argued that the view failed to make good its claim to offer a substantive contribution to organizational theory over and above what could be given, at least in principle, by good science. Insofar as organization theory needed to assume a wider class of relevant causes, no new approach was needed. Insofar as more than causes were required, no new approach seemed warranted.

Our strategy in relation to Habermasian critical theory consisted in analysing those concepts which, on the theory's own account of itself, were to give it validity as a theory. These are the notion of interests which underwrite critical theory as knowledge, and the concepts of communicative competence and the ideal speech situation. The latter two are Habermas's solution to the so-called theory-practice problem, and constitute his proposal for social change and emancipation. Using the theoretical machinery of our coherentist epistemology, we concluded that critical theory overreached itself in terms of the explanatory resources at its disposal. According to the theory's own argument, we could never know whether or not the ideal speech situation was actually obtained. We concluded that the radical challenge in both forms presented here falls short on its own account of itself when considered in light of some modest constraints of good theory.

References

Apple M.W. (1977). Ivan Illich and deschooling society: the politics of slogan systems, in M. Young and G. Whitty (eds.) *Society, State and Schooling*. (Guildford, Surrey: The Falmer Press).

Apple M.W. (1981). Reproduction, contestation, and curriculum: an essay in self-criticism, *Interchange*, **12** (2–3), pp. 27–47.

Apple M.W. (1982). *Education and Power*. (Melbourne: Routledge and Kegan Paul).

Bates R.J. (1982). Towards a critical practice of educational administration. (Armidale, Australia: Commonwealth Council for Educational Administration).

Bates R.J. (1983). *Educational Administration and the Management of Knowledge*. (Victoria, Australia: Deakin University Press).

Benson J.K. (1977). Innovation and crisis in organizational theory *The Sociological Quarterly*, **18**, pp. 3–16.

Benson J.K. (1983). Paradigm and praxis in organizational analysis in B.M. Staw and L.L. Cummings (eds.) *Research in Organizational Behavior* **5** (Greenwich, CT: JAI Press), pp. 33–56.

Benson J.K. (1983). Organizations: a dialectical view. Cited as reprinted in W.P. Foster (ed.) *Loose Coupling Revisited*. (Victoria, Australia: Deakin University Press).

Bernstein R.J. (1986). Introduction, in R.J. Bernstein (ed.) *Habermas and Modernity*. (Cambridge, Mass.: The M.I.T. Press, reprinted).

Bowles S. and Gintis H. (1976). *Schooling in Capitalist America*. (New York: Basic Books).

Bredo E. and Feinberg W. (1982) (eds.). *Knowledge and Values in Social and Educational Research*. (Philadelphia: Temple).

Carr W. and Kemmis S. (1983). *Becoming Critical: Knowing Through Action Research*. (Victoria, Australia: Deakin University Press).

Dallmayr W. (1974) (ed.). *Materialien zu Habermas' 'Erkenntnis und Interesse'*. (Frankfurt am Main: Suhrkamp).

Denhardt R.B. and Denhardt K.G. (1979). Public administration and the critique of domination, *Administration and Society*, **11** (1), pp. 107–120.

Dews P. (1986) (ed.). *Jürgen Habermas Autonomy and Solidarity*. Interviews. (London: Verso).

Engels F. (1976). *Anti-Dühring*. (Peking: Foreign Languages Press).

Engels F. (1979). *Dialectics of Nature*. (New York: International Publishers, ninth printing).

Foster W.P. (1980a). Administration and the crisis of legitimacy: a review of Habermasian thought, *Harvard Education Review*, **50** (4), pp. 496–505.

Foster W.P. (1980b). The changing administrator: developing managerial praxis, *Educational Theory*, **30** (1), pp. 11–23.

Foster W.P. (1986). *Paradigms and Promises*. (Buffalo, N.Y.: Prometheus).

Giddens A. (1981). *A Contemporary Critique of Historical Materialism*. (Berkeley and Los Angeles: University of California Press).

Giddens A. (1986). Reason without revolution? Habermas's *Theorie des kommunikativen Handelns*, in R.J. Bernstein (ed.) *Habermas and Modernity*. (Cambridge, Mass., M.I.T. Press).

Giroux H. (1983). *Critical Theory and Educational Practice*. (Victoria, Australia: Deakin University Press).

Goldman P. (1978). Sociologists and the study of bureaucracy: a critique of ideology and practice, *Insurgent Sociologist*, **8**, pp. 21–30.

Gouldner A. W. (1976). *The Dialectic of Ideology and Technology*. (New York and Toronto: Oxford University Press).

Gouldner A. (1980). *The Two Marxisms*. (New York: The Seabury Press).

Griffiths D. (1988). Administrative theory, in N.J. Boyan (ed.) *Handbook of Research on Educational Administration*. (New York and London: Longman).

Habermas J. (1972a). *Knowledge and Human Interests*. (London: Heinemann, translated by J.J. Shapiro).

Habermas J. (1972b). *Toward a Rational Society*. (London: Heinemann, translated by J.J. Shapiro).

Habermas J. (1972c). Towards a theory of communicative competence, in H.P. Dreitzel (ed.) *Recent Sociology No. 2 patterns of Communicative Behavior*. (New York: Macmillan).

Habermas J. (1974). *Theory and Practice*. (London: Heinemann, translated by J. Viertel).

Habermas J. (1975). Rationalism divided in two, in A. Giddens (ed.) *Positivism and Sociology*. (London: Heinemann).

Habermas J. (1976a). *Legitimation Crisis*. (London: Heinemann, translated by T.A. McCarthy).

Habermas J. (1976b). Systematically distorted communication, in P. Connerton (ed.) *Critical Sociology*. (Harmondsworth: Penguin).

Habermas J. (1976c). *Zur Rekonstruktion des Historischen Materialismus*. (Frankfurt am Main: Suhrkamp, zweite Auflage).

Habermas J. (1979). *Communication and the Evolution of Society* (Boston: Beacon Press, translated by T.A. McCarthy).

Habermas J. (1982). A reply to my critics, in J.B. Thompson and D. Held (eds.) *Habermas: Critical Debates*. (London: Macmillan).

Habermas J. (1984a). *The Theory of Communicative Action I: Reason and the Rationalization of Society*. (Boston: Beacon Press, translated by T.A. McCarthy).

Habermas J. (1984b). Wahrheitstheorien, in J. Habermas *Vorstudien und Ergänzungen zur Theorie des kommunikativen Handelns*. (Frankfurt am Main: Suhrkamp).

Habermas J. (1985). *Zur Logik der Sozialwissenschaften*. (Frankfurt am Main: Suhrkamp, erweiterte Ausgabe).

Hesse M. (1982). Science and objectivity, in J.B. Thompson and D. Held (eds.) *Habermas: Critical Debates*. (London: Macmillan).

Heydebrand W. (1977). Organizational contradictions in public bureaucracies: toward a Marxian theory of organizations, *The Sociological Quarterly*, **18**, pp. 83–107.

Heydebrand W. and Burris B. (1984). The limits of praxis in critical theory, in J. Marcus and Z. Tar (eds.) *Foundations of the Frankfurt School of Social Research*. (New Jersey: Transaction Books).

Jermier J.M. (1982). Infusion of critical social theory into organizational analysis: implications for studies of work adjustment (I) in D. Dunkerley and G. Salaman (eds.) *The International Yearbook of Organization Studies 1981*. (London: Routledge and Kegan Paul).

Keat R. and Urry J. (1982). *Social Theory as Science*. (London: Routledge and Kegan Paul, second edition).

Kemmis S. (1985). Action research, in T. Husen and T.N. Postlethwaite (eds.) *International Encyclopedia of Education: Research and Studies*. (Oxford: Pergamon).

Kemmis S., Cole P., and Suggett D. (1983). *Towards the Socially-Critical School*. (Victoria, Australia: Victorian Institute of Secondary Education).

McCarthy T.A. (1976). A theory of communicative competence, in P. Connerton (ed.) *Critical Sociology*. (Harmondsworth: Penguin).

McCarthy T.A. (1981). *The Critical Theory of Jürgen Habermas*. (Cambridge, Mass, and London, England: The M.I.T. Press).

Mills C.W. (1962). *The Marxists*. (Harmondsworth: Penguin).

Negt O. (1968) (ed.). *Die Linke antwortet Jürgen Habermas*. (Frankfurt: Europäische Verlagsanstalt).

O'Hear A. (1985). *What Philosophy Is*. (Harmondsworth: Penguin).

Ollman B. (1978). *Alienation*. (Cambridge: Cambridge University Press, second edition).

Peukert H. (1984). *Science, Action, and Fundamental Theology – Toward a Theory of Communicative Action*. (Cambridge, Mass.: The M.I.T. Press, translated by J. Bohman).

Shapiro S. (1984). Crisis of legitimation: schools, society, and declining faith in education, *Interchange*, **15** (4), pp. 26–39.

Thompson J.B. and Held D. (1982) (eds.). *Habermas: Critical Debates*. (London: Macmillan).

Van Manen M. (1977). Linking ways of knowing with ways of being practical, *Curriculum Inquiry*, **6** (3), pp. 205–228.

Watkins P. (1986). From managerialism to communicative competence: control and consensus in educational administration. *The Journal of Educational Administration*, **24** (1), pp. 86–106.

Young M. and Whitty G. (1977). *Society, State and Schooling*. (Guildford, Surrey: The Falmer Press).

8

Ethical Theory and Educational Administration

We have now seen a number of approaches to administration where a view of ethical knowledge has been of decisive importance in determining the nature and scope of administrative theory, especially in relation to science. For Christopher Hodgkinson, science deals in factual claims that are quite separate and distinct from value claims. And since administrative practice is irreducibly value laden, no science of administration can ever be adequate or complete. Herbert Simon, accepting equally the distinctness of ethics from fact, argues in *Administrative Behavior* for the opposite conclusion. Ethical claims are not testable, that is, they do not admit of confirmation or disconfirmation, and so do not count as cognitively significant knowledge. No adequate or complete science of administration could include value claims. For Thomas Greenfield, the primary issue of concern is between the objective and the subjective. Traditional science and its methods claims to deal with the objective. Values, along with human action, choice, and intention — the basic stuff of organizational reality — are subjective, and so beyond the reach of such a science or an administrative theory based thereon. Critical theorists, who argue for a closing of the gap between fact and value, who acknowledge the value ladenness of administration, and who see empirical science as eschewing values, defend a hermeneutical and critical theory of administration, in part because they believe that a hermeneutical analysis of communication displays an implicit value structure.

It seems to us that what all these approaches have in common is an epistemological assumption that the justification of scientific and ethical claims proceeds along different lines; that evidence for one cannot function as evidence for the other. In this chapter we propose to develop and apply our holistic epistemology to argue against this view and for a unified approach to the justification of scientific and ethical claims. Our aim is to show that ethics can be a legitimate part of a global theory of administration. After examining a number of influential ethical theories we then show how our epistemological argument can be extended to suggest, at least in outline, a substantive ethics for educational administration.

The 'Autonomy of Ethics' Thesis: The Is/Ought Dichotomy

Two important arguments have traditionally been associated with the 'autonomy of ethics' thesis: the thesis that ethics is somehow distinct or separate from empirical knowledge. The first is the 'is/ought dichotomy', which in its usual formulations amounts to the claim that ethical conclusions cannot be derived from factual premises (see Hudson 1969). The second is the 'naturalistic fallacy', which denies that ethical terms can be defined naturalistically, or at least in terms of the subject matter of natural science (Frankena 1939). Despite a tendency in the administration literature to run these two arguments together, they are different, and in what follows we shall treat them separately.

Concerning the claim that one cannot derive an 'ought' from an 'is', the classic text is David Hume's *A Treatise of Human Nature*, where he says:

> I cannot forbear adding to these reasonings an observation which may, perhaps be found of some importance. In every system of morality, which I have hitherto met with, I have always remark'd, that the author proceeds for some time in the ordinary way of reasoning, and establishes the being of a God, or makes observations concerning human affairs; when of a sudden I am surpriz'd to find, that instead of the usual copulations of propositions, *is*, and *is not*, I meet with no proposition that is not connected with an *ought*, or an *ought not*. This change is imperceptible; but is, however, of the last consequence. For as this *ought*, or *ought not*, expresses some new relation or affirmation, 'tis necessary that it should be observ'd and explain'd and at the same time that a reason should be given, for what seems altogether inconceivable, how this new relation can be a deduction from others, which are entirely different from it (Hume 1988, p. 469).

What Hume evidently finds of some importance in this observation is that, were it heeded, 'all the vulgar systems of morality' would be subverted (Hume 1988, p. 470).

On the standard interpretation of this passage, Hume is making a comment on the validity of a certain class of arguments. Putting the matter more generally, his claim seems to be that statements expressing values cannot validly be derived from statements expressing only matters of fact. Since in logic, however, invalidity, understood either syntactically or model-theoretically, is a property of the form of an argument rather than its nonlogical subject matter, if there is any mistake in trying to derive an 'ought' from an 'is' it is going to show up in the syntax of such arguments. Thus, consider the argument

Poverty causes much human suffering.
  Therefore: Poverty ought to be eliminated.

We may reckon this argument as invalid because in the sentence 'if poverty causes human suffering then poverty ought to be eliminated' the nonlogical words occur essentially and not vacuously. We say that a word occurs essentially in a statement 'if replacement of the word by another is capable of turning the statement into a falsehood. When this is not the case, the word may be said to occur vacuously' (Quine 1940, p. 2). On the other hand, the argument

All Fridays are rainy.
Therefore: Last Friday was rainy

is valid since only the logical particles occur essentially. Now at first sight, it looks as though the appearance of any nonlogical words in the conclusion of an argument, which do not appear also in one or more of the premises, is going to be a fairly extravagant way of generating essential occurrences among nonlogical words. And if this is so, there is a simple test — call it the vocabulary criterion — for the invalidity of an argument. Let 'P$_1$ and P$_2$ and P$_3$ . . . and P$_n$. Therefore C' be an argument, and let V be the nonlogical vocabulary used to state the premises P$_1$ to P$_n$. Then — so the suggestion runs — the argument is invalid if C contains nonlogical words not included in V. So, in the case of deriving judgments from matters of fact, the error appears to occur because the conclusion, C, contains words like 'ought', 'good', 'bad', 'right', and 'wrong' that are not to be found in V. According to this diagnosis there is nothing special about the is/ought fallacy. It is simply an instance of a very general type of fallacy which we may call the *deductive* fallacy.

Unfortunately for Humean and other defenders of this argument, the vocabulary criterion is unreliable as a test for invalidity. A.N. Prior (1960), for example, has noticed that it is possible validly to derive statements containing an 'ought' from purely 'is' statements. This is so simply because elementary logic sanctions what amounts to a denial of the vocabulary criterion. For example the rule known as 'addition' in the propositional calculus (written as p⊃pvq) permits the deduction

Snow is white.
Therefore: Either snow is white or we ought not to kill.

Peano's principle of the factor (written as (p⊃q)⊃(p.r⊃q.r) likewise permits the vocabulary of the conclusion of a valid argument to be expanded extravagantly. Max Black, following Prior, gives a more complex example:

Vivisection causes gratuitous suffering to animals.

Therefore: If nothing that causes gratuitous suffering ought to be done, vivisection ought not to be done (Black 1964).

And David Kurtzman, in seeking to overcome Black's objection that such deductions are trivial, gives us

No one can lift the Pentagon.

Therefore: Everyone is such that either he is not obligated to lift the Pentagon or not everyone who is obligated to perform something can perform it (Kurtzman 1970).

It is possible to argue that these deductions are trivial. However, the critic who demands nontrivial valid deductions may have so defined terms that what is demanded cannot be obtained. This would be the case, for example, if validity was a test or sufficient condition for triviality. In this case nontrivial deductions of 'ought' from 'is' would be invalid by definition. We do not propose to press the point further. It is sufficient for our purposes merely to note that there is an awkward complexity involved in specifying a version of the 'is/ought dichotomy' once it is admitted that one can validly derive statements containing 'oughts' from statements containing only 'is's'.

The 'Autonomy of Ethics' Thesis: The Naturalistic Fallacy

The second, and in our view, more important argument for the autonomy of ethics, or at least its separation from science and scientific evidence, is the argument known as the naturalistic fallacy, first introduced into philosophy by the Cambridge philosopher G.E. Moore. To see how it works, consider the following simple utilitarian argument for the goodness of pleasure:

(1) Pleasure is desired by all humans.
(2) What is desired by all humans is good.
Therefore: (3) Pleasure is good.

The argument is formally valid. A claim about 'good' is derived from (1) an empirical premise, and (2) what purports to be a definition of 'good'. Let us call this utilitarian premise (2) the naturalistic premise. We call it this because it purports to define 'good' in terms of some natural quality or property; in this case, what is desired by all humans. Other naturalistic definitions would be:

Good is that which promotes happiness.
Good is that which promotes the general welfare.
Good is that which promotes growth.

Moore (1903, chs 1 and 3) argues that all naturalistic definitions of 'good', like premise (2) above, are mistaken. His argument is not directed at the validity of the utilitarian argument; it is directed at the truth of the conclusion. That is, we are invited not to accept the truth of the conclusion because one of the premises in the argument is false, namely, premise (2). Premise (2) and all other naturalistic definitions of 'good' are mistaken because, according to Moore, they commit the naturalistic fallacy. Precisely what this fallacy is supposed to be can be seen from a reconstruction of Moore's argument for his view that good is a simple nonnatural property.

He begins by asking how 'good' may be defined (Moore 1903, pp. 8–12). This leads to a discussion of the nature of definition, and as part of this discussion he considers three ways we can understand the term 'definition'. What way we understand it will have important consequences for how we try to define 'good'. Moore first distinguishes the *arbitrary verbal definition*. We give arbitrary verbal definitions when we stipulate that one word or set of words (the definiendum) is equivalent to, or can be used in place of, or can be understood in terms of, another set of words (the definiens). 'Good' is not indefinable in this sense of definition. Secondly, we may give *verbal definitions*. This is the lexicographer's job and consists of listing strings of words (the definiens) which most speakers of the language would find an acceptable substitute for some other word or set of words (the definiendum). Here we are concerned with how most people actually use words; with ordinary language. 'Good' is not indefinable in this sense of definition either. Finally, and what Moore considers the most important sense of 'definition', is definition that describes *the real nature of an object*, or notion denoted by a word, that says what an object really is, rather than what some person through sheer stipulation says it is, or what the bulk of people, inured through callow usage, say it is. In this robustly essentialist sense of definition, 'good' is, according to Moore, indefinable. Getting down to detail (Moore 1903, pp. 5–15) he thinks that:

(1)   A correct definition of X, in the important sense, can only be given if X is complex; if X has enumerably different parts and properties.

(2)   Definitions in this sense are always analytic and never synthetic.

(3)   An analytic statement is one that cannot sensibly be denied or cannot intelligibly be queried. To illustrate: a triangle is a complex of three sides and a bounded area, so it can be defined. A correct definition is: a triangle is a plane figure bounded by three straight lines. We cannot intelligibly query this; it is just what a triangle is. If it were anything else it would not be a triangle (to echo Bishop Butler).

(4)   But with any naturalistic definition of 'good', for example, 'good is that which promotes happiness', we can always ask 'Is good really that which promotes happiness?' A purported definition that can sensibly be queried is one that can be reparsed as an open question.

Thus all naturalistic definitions of good can be reworked as open questions.

Therefore:

(5) No naturalistic account of good can be a correct definition. (This is the main conclusion from the 'open question' argument.)

(6) But with every definition of 'good', we can reparse it as an open question.

Therefore:

(7) 'Good' is indefinable.

Therefore:

(8) Good is neither complex nor a simple natural property.

Therefore:

(9) Good is a simple nonnatural property.

The naturalistic fallacy occurs, according to Moore, when we equate or confuse a simple nonnatural object (like good) with a natural or complex object (like pleasure).

It will come as no surprise that we think this argument fails because it depends on a distinction between analytic and synthetic statements. Following Quine, our earlier arguments for a holistic epistemology specifically deny that such a distinction can be drawn. It is an unwarranted dogma of classical empiricism. In our view, definition merely reflects the degree of substitutivity of one set of expressions for another throughout a theory. More precisely, we should add, an extensional theory. (In an extensional theory co-referring singular terms may be interchanged without affecting truth. The same condition applies also to co-extensive predicates. See Quine 1960, p. 151.) For theories structured in a tightly deductive way, such as mathematical theories, or theories of physics, complexity and variability of context are usually no bar to truth-preserving substitution. In the loosely structured, multi-purpose theories of ordinary language, on the other hand, context is vital and only the most entrenched substitutes will be appropriate in all contexts. Thus, to use the philosopher's favourite example, the expression 'unmarried adult male' will probably substitute for 'bachelor' in all (extensional) contexts in which that word appears. And it is, perhaps, this feature which gives the impression that the sentence 'a bachelor is an unmarried adult male' is an analytic truth, true in virtue of the meanings of its (nonlogical) vocabulary. For other definitions, appropriateness of substitution rapidly shades off beyond a few local contexts, or controversy sets in. Terms like 'education', 'administration', 'teaching', or 'leadership' do not readily admit of definitions in Moore's third sense, that is, essential definition. Some philosophers explain this by saying these are 'essentially contested' concepts (Gallie 1955–56). But a simple explanation is to say that lack of agreement, or differences in definition, reflect differences in embedding theories. There are simply different, in some cases incompatible, theories of education, administration, and the like (see Evers 1979). Agreement over a term like 'bachelor' reflects, therefore, not evidence for analytic truth, but evidence for shared, common, or touchstone theory, even at the level of theories embedded in commonsense or ordinary language. However, as we remarked in our critique of ordinary language views of knowledge, degree of entrenchment and truth are different matters. Epistemologically speaking, the touchstone theories of language, or folk theories, with their relatively well-entrenched usages, are still in need of justification and can still compete unfavourably with other, perhaps scientific, theories.

If this perspective is sound, Moore's open question argument shows no more than that we can ask whether a particular theory of good is really justified. It does not show that the mere asking of this question demonstrates that such a theory can never be justified. In fact, not only is the matter of justification methodologically open, but in our view a particular naturalistic theory of good is more coherent than its major rivals, and hence to be preferred. Such a theory could be construed as offering a reduction of good to some natural quality.

Before we go on to consider some coherentist methodological aspects of defending ethical theories, we should note that while we have dealt in some detail with Moore's version of the 'naturalistic fallacy' argument, there are other, later versions (e.g. Hare 1952, pp. 79–93; Williams 1985, pp. 120–131; Begum 1979) that we have not touched. To argue a general case against this kind of defence of the 'autonomy of ethics' thesis, we would have to consider these other versions too. Against this omission we settle for expressing the belief that the whole strategy of defending partitions in knowledge is extremely difficult given our holistic theory of knowledge.

Reduction, Coherence and Varieties of Utilitarianism

Our attack on Moore's argument for a naturalistic fallacy boiled down to denying epistemic privilege to the entrenched statements of ordinary language, or at least the class of purported analytic truths. Our claim is that it is better to see familiar everyday discourse as expressing, or being underpinned by, some theory or theories. What overall consistency, structure, or pattern there is to be found in discourse reflects the systematic properties of underlying theory which, in turn, is not immune from review, criticism, feedback, refutation or, most drastically, elimination and wholesale replacement by other theories.

Some theories make for radical revisions of our ordinary moral judgments and some do not. Writers as diverse as Skinner and Rawls attempt to explain moral terms by reducing them to some other terms. An example of a reducing theory, proposed by B.F. Skinner, seems drastic enough to require the wholesale elimination of familiar moral usage:

Good things are positive reinforcers . . . When we say that a value judgment is a matter not of fact but of how someone feels about a fact, we are simply distinguishing between a thing and its reinforcing effect. Things themselves are studied by physics and biology, usually without reference to their value, but the reinforcing effects of things are the province of behavioural science, which, to the extent that it is concerned with operant reinforcement, is a science of values . . . To make a value judgment by calling something good or bad is to classify it in terms of its reinforcing effects (Skinner 1971, pp. 103–104).

Skinner has analogous reductions/eliminations for 'justice', 'right', and 'ought', as well as behaviouristic causal analyses for a variety of moral judgments. If this theory is true, there would be so little of worth left in our familiar categories of moral appraisal and their relations to one another, that a moral assessment of what, say, administrators do would be as inappropriate as a moral assessment of the doings of some complex piece of machinery.

Not all reducing theories have such drastic consequences. Varieties of utilitarianism that define good in terms of maximizing human happiness, for example, are often tested for adequacy against our ordinary moral language and experience, against the qualified judgments of our folk moral theory (Brandt 1959, pp. 241–270). Of course, some utilitarians (e.g. Smart 1956), like Skinner, recommend revising folk theory where conflicts occur. A more generous accommodation with folk moral theory can be found in the theory of justice developed by Rawls (1971). It asserts that our best moral judgments are likely to be those that result from a kind of 'reflective equilibrium' between folk theory and the dictates of a proposed theory's formal principles of justice. Accordingly:

From the standpoint of moral philosophy, the best account of a person's sense of justice is not the one which fits his judgments prior to his examining any conception of justice, but rather the one which matches his judgments in reflective equilibrium (Rawls 1971, p. 48).

In ethical decision making in administrative contexts of great complexity, the process of seeking a reflective equilibrium is quite commonplace. It usually consists of trying to find the most coherent trade-off between some general moral principles and apparently justifiable exceptions; or perhaps trying to resolve a case that pits one rule or principle against another. Precisely what broad theory acts as a source of moral principles will vary from person to person, but the utilitarian tradition has historically been a very pervasive source. So much so that John Rawls remarks on ethical decision making that:

Most likely we finally settle upon a variant of the utility principle circumscribed and restricted in certain ad hoc ways by intuitionistic constraints (Rawls 1971, p. viii).

In the remainder of this section we give a brief account of how attempts to achieve an overall coherence, or satisfactory equilibrium, have been reflected in the development of different strands of utilitarianism.

Ethical theories characteristically divide into a theory of value — usually concerned with the nature of good, or right, or justice — and a theory of obligation, which sets out what we must do, or what we are obligated to do (Frankena 1963, pp. 1–46). Teleological or consequentialist theories usually define 'good' as some quality, natural or nonnatural, and then evaluate actions in terms of the amount of good produced, or the resulting balance of good over evil. These theories also tend to be monistic, with 'right' or 'just' being defined, derivatively, in terms of 'good'.

The most influential teleological theory has been utilitarianism, or better, varieties of utilitarianism, since it exits in a number of forms. A number of classifications of these forms are possible, but for our purposes we distinguish hedonistic from preferential theories, and within each of these, rule from act theories. With regard to the first division, the Bentham–Mill tradition adopts a theory of value that equates good with maximizing human happiness or, more precisely, the greatest balance of pleasure over pain. Mill (1861) makes the identification at one remove, equating good with what is desirable and pleasure with what all people desire and consequently, as the example of our previous discussion showed, incurs the wrath of those sensitive to the naturalistic fallacy of equating what is desirable with what is desired. In any case, on this theory of value, pleasure and happiness — and these are to be understood very broadly — function as intrinsic goods.

On the question of obligation, what ought to be done, what constitutes the right thing to do, is that course of action which brings about the largest amount or quantity of human happiness. Although there may be problems determining when this condition is met, nevertheless, theoretically there is a fact of the matter about whether an action is right or wrong. The next problem is the epistemological one of knowing what the relevant quantities are prior to their summation. This problem is made severe by noting that happiness may not be a sensation (with intensity and duration) that lends itself to quantitative summation. For example, pleasures appear to be qualitatively different. Mill expresses his concern over this point by claiming that Socrates dissatisfied is better than a fool satisfied (Mill 1861, p. 9). Unfortunately, pleasures that are qualitatively different do not lend themselves to addition. Is the pleasure derived from an elegant proof of a theorem comparable to the pleasures of good food? If the latter is a sensation, then it is doubtful that the former is, or at least not the same kind of sensation; that is, it differs on more than just intensity and duration. However, even if all happiness, even broadly construed, is sensation of the same kind, then being essentially a matter of private experience, it would seem impossible to know the amount of sensation involved beyond one's own experience. The assumption of intersubjective equivalence seems at odds with behavioural manifestations of great variety in tastes and preferences.

Assuming that these problems can be solved, we then confront difficulties over the nature of the utilitarian reduction of folk morality. If it is construed as a largely conservative reduction (as most theorists do), then it will be presumed to leave intact the bulk of our ordinary moral judgments. We must then make the two sources of judgment cohere where there appear to be conflicts. For example, if utilitarianism is concerned exclusively with maximizing happiness, then that is a consideration that appears to be independent of the distribution of happiness. Indeed, some ways of maximizing happiness can be profoundly unjust. The classic case is scapegoating, perhaps the sacrificing of an innocent person in order to placate an angry mob. Other examples include breaking promises or telling lies, which are sanctioned every time an increase in utility results.

To avoid this sort of difficulty, it is standard to distinguish act utilitarianism from rule utilitarianism. The above conflicts with folk morality appear to be generated by applying the principle of utility to each individual act. However, the rule utilitarian requires only that moral rules or principles be justified by the principle of utility (Rawls 1955, Mabbott 1956). On this theory, in deciding what we ought to do in a given situation, we look for moral guidance from a set of rules that are in turn justified. And here justification consists in showing that following some favoured set of rules will produce more happiness than following any other set. Thus a society with a rule of justice requiring fair distribution of happiness is happier than one without such a rule. And similarly for justification of truth telling and promise keeping.

This sounds well but complications emerge when we consider problems created by exceptions. For example, why cannot we permit exceptions to a rule where the exceptions are justified by the principle of utility? Truth telling may be a justifiable practice in general but there are clearly cases where breaches will engender much greater happiness. The same point holds, perhaps to a lesser extent, with the practice of justice, or promise keeping (Smart 1956). The challenge for the rule utilitarian here is to devise some way of either admitting exceptions without rule utilitarianism collapsing back into act utilitarianism, or prohibiting exceptions without undermining the point of utilitarian justification, namely the appeal to human happiness.

One important move is to claim that just as, say, truth telling is a practice, so truth telling with exceptions is an alternative practice. The rule utilitarian then attempts to adjudicate the merits of these distinct practices on the basis of the principle of maximizing utility, usually deciding in favour of exceptionless practices. Some writers have observed, however, that this move rests on a confusion between constitutive rules and regulative rules (McCloskey 1957). Constitutive rules define a practice, and make it what it is, for example, the rules of chess, or golf. Regulative rules, on the other hand, do no such thing; they are like rules of thumb, functioning to regulate behaviour. Critics of pure rule utilitarianism deny that truth telling, promise keeping, and the like are practices defined by constitutive rules which admit exceptions only in the form of alternative, constitutively defined, practices. These practices may reflect agreed social practices or conventions, but they are regulative nonetheless. It is worth noting that in either case, if the rule utilitarian is after a conservative reduction, there is considerable scope for conflict with our ordinary moral judgments.

For someone like Smart, who favours a more radical reduction, conflicts with folk morality are not so important. Where the appraisals of his act utilitarianism run counter to the demands of commonsense morality, Smart concludes instead, 'so much the worse for our ordinary moral judgments'. His point is that we should be using utilitarianism to inform and correct our folk morality rather than vice versa (Smart 1973). The main worry with this bold approach is that any number of moral theories can entail major differences with folk theory. Why should we choose act utilitarianism? This, in a nut-shell, captures the basic methodological issue. If the principal test for a moral theory is coherence with folk morality, then only fairly conservative theories will be acceptable. Indeed, departures from commonsense morality will come out justified only where they result in increasing the systematic virtues of folk moral theory. In our view, defenders of more radically divergent moral theories need to argue for more than coherence with folk morality. They need to argue, in addition, that their theories cohere with the most reliable body of knowledge we possess: our best scientific theories. This cannot be the whole story, but it will help, and it is easy to point to obvious moral advantages, whether they are to be found in the theories of Skinner and Smart or not.

Consider an earlier criticism we made of Hodgkinson's moral theory. The theory accorded moral priority to Type I values over values of Types II and III. Yet the theory implied that a leader such as Hitler was a source of Type I values. The political philosopher Hanna Arendt, in her classic study *Eichmann in Jerusalem*, draws attention to . . . 'the totality of the moral collapse the Nazis caused in respectable European society . . . ' (Arendt 1963, p. 111), that 'evil in the Third Reich had lost the quality by which most people recognize it – the quality of temptation . . . ' (p. 134) and finally to 'the lesson of the fearsome, word-and-thought defying *banality of evil*' (p. 231). In short, she draws attention to a monumental shift that took place in ordinary moral consciousness. But moral consciousness and its informing folk theory is not so fragile as to be distorted by alternative moral pronouncements, however authoritative their source. A more reasonable view is that such distortions feed on lies and misrepresentations and false theories; they need to cohere with particular theories of race and religion, of economics and political power and national destiny. Against the sheer ordinariness of this kind of systematic moral corruption, there are gains to be had in being able to speak scientific truthfulness. For us, the soundness of topic-specific theories that contribute to a person's global perspective, is a fairly basic requirement for sound moral reasoning within that perspective. So the reductions proposed by Skinner or Smart, for example, would need to show some further theoretical gains to global theory to be ultimately persuasive.

Preferential Utilitarianism

One theoretical gain made by the preferential utilitarian tradition is a by-passing of the epistemological problem of knowing magnitudes of sensations for summing intersubjectively. Instead, preferential utilitarianism deals in expressed preferences. Beauchamp and Childress sum up this approach as follows:

> The major alternative approach is to appeal to the language of individual preferences. For this approach, the concept of utility refers not to experiences or states of affairs, but rather to one's actual preferences, as determined by one's behaviour. To maximize a single person's utility is to provide what one has chosen or would choose from among the available alternatives that might be produced. To maximize the utility of all persons affected by an action or policy is to maximize the utility of the aggregate group (Beauchamp and Childress 1984, pp. 46–47).

These remarks are very general. To give a more detailed account of how modern preference utilitarianism works, as well as some of its theoretical advantages and limitations, we sketch some of the main features of an influential version developed by John Harsanyi.

In the case of maximizing a single person's utility, Harsanyi (1977, p. 43) considers three broad conditions under which the rationality of expressed preferences can be defined:

(i)   Under conditions of uncertainty, where some or all probabilities are unknown, and
(ii) Under conditions of risk, where all probabilities of outcomes are known, an individual's preferences are assumed to maximize expected utility.
(iii) Under conditions of certainty, where all outcomes are known, an individual's preferences are assumed to maximize utility.

Decision theory deals with the problem of maximizing expected utility under conditions of risk and uncertainty, although for Harsanyi, more is required for moral decision making. Where a person is engaged in rational interaction with one or more other persons, each rationally pursuing their own objectives, the problem of determining strategies or preferences, which are assumed to maximize expected utility, is a matter for that part of decision theory known as the mathematical theory of games. Again, Harsanyi does not consider game theoretic constraints sufficient to constitute moral decision making.

What he requires for ethics is 'a theory of rational behaviour in the service of the common interests of society as a whole' (Harsanyi 1977, p. 43). Thus, consider a person x, rationally deciding which of two social systems or arrangements to prefer. If x knows what position he or she would occupy in each system then x would presumably decide on the basis of the expected utility maximization decision rule. But while this is certainly a judgment of personal preference, it is hardly a moral value judgment. However,

> . . . in contrast, most of us will admit that he would be making a moral value judgment if he chose between the two social systems without knowing what his personal position would be under either system (Harsanyi 1980, p. 45).

Under this condition of ignorance, however, where each society has, say, n individuals in positions from the worst-off to the best-off, x must assume that the probability of being in any position in either society is 1/n, a condition Harsanyi calls the *equi-probability assumption*. He then goes on to argue that an individual who chooses between the two systems on the principle of maximizing expected utility, but under the assumption of equi-probability

> . . . would always choose that social system which, in his opinion, would yield the higher *average utility level* to the individual members of the society (Harsanyi 1980, p. 45).

Applied to individuals in society, what this means is that making rational moral judgments will involve maximizing the average utility level of all individuals in society. According to Harsanyi, on this criterion rule utilitarianism is rationally (and morally) preferable to act utilitarianism, so in practice it is best to interpret the principle of maximizing societal utility as a constraint on proposed moral rules.

It is easy to see the attractiveness of this approach to systematic administrative theory. It coheres with approaches to rational choice theory in economics and the decision sciences. It continues, at a more sophisticated level, a tradition in administrative theorizing that goes back through logical empiricism to logical positivism, and ultimately the early work of Herbert Simon, but without the assumption that ethical claims have no cognitive content and with more ambitious assumptions about the powers of human reason than Simon's model sanctions. It locates ethical decision making within a general theory of rationality. And finally, it purports to offer applicable criteria for making moral choices. This last point must be of particular concern to practising administrators who constantly face and answer the question 'What should I do?' under conditions of risk and uncertainty.

In our view, this is a research programme of some promise and deserves more thorough treatment than we can provide here. However, we are cautious over two central claims. First, to formulate moral decision criteria, the theory assumes a particular normative view of rationality, known as Bayesian rationality. The axioms are plausible and weak, but in being normative they are assumed to be independent of how people actually do think. As Harsanyi says:

> all we need is the requirement of consistent preferences (complete preordering), a continuity axiom, the sure-thing principle (avoidance of dominated strategies), and the requirement that our preferences for lotteries should depend only on the possible prizes and on the specific random events deciding the actual prize (Harsanyi 1977, p. 48).

Second, to be applicable we need to assume some theory of social causation so that we can work out the effect of choices on utility aggregates, represented by social welfare functions. Since the evidence suggests that people do not always behave in Bayesian rational ways (see Tversky and Kahneman 1981, Stich and Nisbett 1980, Davidson 1974), the theory of social causation, which must attend to these matters, becomes detached from the normative theory of rationality driving the decision criteria. This is not disastrous but it does limit the applicability of preference utilitarianism. We discuss some of these limits in more detail in the next chapter when we consider objections to the use of social welfare functions in determining policy alternatives. However, one example can easily be given. Bayesian rationality assumes a stable, consistent preference structure. Unfortunately, preference, as an outcome of human reasoning, is an intensional notion; that is, it is sensitive to how options are described. Since the same finite set of options, or courses of action, can be described in arbitrarily many and various ways, all subject to sundry further shifts (systematic or otherwise) as a result of further learning, thought, and experience, it is not obvious that either stability or consistency of beliefs and values can be so readily assumed.

This weakness in the rationality assumption can, under certain conditions, make problems for the theory of social causation, notably where ignorance of causal detail and associated theory are being compensated for by assuming that people behave rationally. In our discussion of the Theory Movement, one of the grounds we saw for preferring an open systems approach to administration over a closed systems approach was precisely the large number of often attenuated causes influencing human behaviour. Whether or not the theoretical successors to the Theory Movement can deal adequately with such external influences as class, gender, race and ethnicity, it is clear that these networks of causes undermine the credibility of Harsanyi's broadly liberal model of society as an arena for the rational pursuit of individual life plans.

Rawls's Theory of Justice

Another important moral theory that draws heavily on a normative theory of rationality is that developed by John Rawls in his *A Theory of Justice*. Although of similar structure to Harsanyi's theory, Rawls's theory is deontological rather than consequentialist. Generally speaking, deontological theories of moral appraisal hold that some actions are right or wrong independently of their consequences. The usual pattern of deontological moral justification is to show how right actions are those that are entailed or sanctioned by a theory of reason. Thus Kant, a rule deontologist, held that moral rules were justified if they conformed to a single categorical imperative, which required that rules should be universalizable. And to be universalizable, a rule must be able to be conceived and willed to be acted upon by all without contradiction. An example of Kant's should illustrate how he supposed his theory of reason could guide ethics. Consider his objections to a rule for making promises that will later be broken:

> How would things stand if my maxim became a universal law? I then see straight away that this maxim can never rank as a universal law of nature and be self-consistent, but must necessarily contradict itself. For the universality of a law that everyone believing himself to be in need can make any promise he pleases with the intention not to keep it would make promising, and the very purpose of promising, itself impossible, since no one would believe he was being promised anything, but would laugh at utterances of this kind as empty shams (Kant 1785, pp. 85–86).

This kind of approach for determining moral rules has had its critics, but Rawls's theory, which is in the Kantian tradition, is a more powerful and sophisticated version not open to the usual criticisms.

What Rawls is primarily concerned with is demonstrating what principles of social justice would be chosen by rational persons reasoning in an impartial way. To simulate impartiality he conducts a thought experiment where people are to choose the basic principles of justice regulating social life from behind a 'veil of ignorance' (Rawls 1971, pp. 136–142). This amounts to Harsanyi's condition of not knowing what one's social position will be in the span of options from the worst off to the best off. However, the principle of rationality for Rawls is not Bayesian rationality; rather it is the *maximin* rule. According to Rawls:

The maximin rule tells us to rank alternatives by their worst possible outcomes: we are to adopt the alternative the worst outcome of which is superior to the worst outcome of the others (Rawls 1971, pp. 152–153).

Essentially, the effect of this rule is to guide the choice of principles of justice in such a way that we who choose, because of our hypothetical ignorance of the social positions we will occupy, will hedge against the worst possible alternatives, since we may end up occupying these ourselves.

Rawls argues that persons choosing rationally (according to maximin) and impartially (under a veil of ignorance) would choose to regulate their social life according to the following two (ordered) principles of justice:

(i) Each person is to have an equal right to the most extensive total system of equal basic liberties compatible with a similar system of liberty for all.

(ii) Social and economic inequalities are to be arranged so that they are both
(a) to the greatest benefit of the least advantaged consistent with the just savings principles, and
(b) attached to the offices and positions open to all under conditions of fair equality of opportunity (Rawls 1971, p. 302).

The central idea of this theory is that:

all social primary goods — liberty and opportunity, income and wealth, and the bases of self-respect — are to be distributed equally unless an unequal distribution of any or all of these goods is to the advantage of the least favoured (Rawls 1971, p. 303).

It is easy to see how these principles could be applied to administrative contexts in education. Indeed, Rawls himself draws a number of conclusions:

Thus, for example, resources for education are not to be allotted solely or necessarily mainly according to their return as estimated in productive trained ability, but also according to their worth in enriching the personal and social life of citizens, including here the less favoured (Rawls 1971, p. 107).

He also observes that his derivative 'difference principle', that is, choosing an equal distribution unless another distribution makes all parties better off, ' . . . would allocate resources in education, say, so as to improve the long-term expectation of the least favoured' (p. 101). Historically, deontological arguments have tended to support minimum standards of basic educational provision for all, and equality of opportunity for all where further educational provision is scarce. In these broad moral aims they cohere with much that is found in our ordinary folk morality. Perhaps because of this agreement, dissent from Rawls's theory is often directed at the sorts of things we queried in Harsanyi's preference utilitarian model: namely, theory of rationality and theory of society.

To see just how unusual maximin reasoning can be, consider how it guides action in a simple case. You have a choice of carrying an umbrella to work or not. If it rains and you are without your umbrella you could catch cold and may even become seriously ill. On the other hand, if you carry the umbrella and it fails to rain you have merely the inconvenience of extra baggage. Since the worst outcome of carrying an umbrella is always superior to the worst outcome of not, rationally, you should always carry an umbrella to work. This is an odd result because it is insensitive to the probability of rain. Maximin grinds out the same result whether you work near a rain forest or in an arid desert. But correspondingly, hedging against being in the worst off social position by framing one's ethical principles accordingly may be as reasonable as carrying an umbrella in a region of negligible rainfall. This suggests that the reasonableness of maximin depends on making assumptions about the distribution of probabilities for social positions. So the 'veil of ignorance' condition for generating impartiality imposes *de facto* a model of society for generating moral rules.

We should note that once again, inasmuch as the model is counterfactual, or sharply divergent from the circumstances of our own society, the theory of rationality comes apart from the best theories we might use to describe our society. Part of the problem is due to the way 'impartiality' is specified. For example, there are alternatives to methodological ignorance that will permit impartial judgment to be combined with a knowledge of probabilities; averaging different points of view is a case in point. Note, however, that admitting probabilities is tantamount to permitting elements of a substantive social theory to figure in an account of rationality. Not only do we find this conclusion congenial, but we think it is entirely to be expected for two very general reasons.

First, methodologically, theories of rationality involve a study and refinement of folk theoretic rational practice, the fundamental example of which is goal-directed behaviour. But generating a theory of rational behaviour that is relatively free from specific contexts and problem situations in which people act, calls for a fair measure of abstraction. Not surprisingly, an empirical gap emerges between content-specific problem-solving practices and decision making, and the dictates of abstract rationality. One solution to this gap problem is to see the abstract theory as a normative theory that may be called upon to correct or improve our content-laden reasoning. A better solution, in our view, is to deny the distinction between rationality and content, or substantive theory. Where a particular type of reasoning appears ubiquitous we have, instead, evidence of common or touchstone theory. Where ubiquity lapses, content exerts its pull. Promoting good standards of rationality is therefore a matter of promoting the kind of reasoning employed in and exhibited by our best theories. Indeed, it will involve a further willingness to engage in epistemological practices aimed at improving those theories.

Second, since the growth of reasoning occurs along with the growth of knowledge, indeed is part of that process, empirical theories of human reasoning and knowledge growth — how people actually learn and think — assume a fundamental importance. In what follows we offer a view of moral knowledge that coheres with our preferred non-foundational epistemology.

Acquiring Moral Knowledge

In Chapter Two we argued, following Popper (and Quine), that an organism's capacity to recognize perceptual similarities is a condition for successful reinforcement which, in turn, is required for the simple conditioning of responses for elementary learning. If there were no perceived similarities between perceptual episodes there would be no basis for reinforcement, no basis for making the kind of systematic discrimination among future episodes that is the hallmark of learned behaviour. This is because, from a purely theoretical point of view, one episode shares with a second episode as many similarities as it does with any distinct third episode: two swans have as many common properties as a swan and a duck. What makes initial learning possible in this circumstance is our innate bias in grouping properties into kinds. According to Quine, however, similarity is not enough. For him, 'the two factors that make for learning, in general, are perceptual similarity and the pleasure principle' (Quine 1974, p. 49). Of this 'bipartite equipment' Quine says: 'the similarity standards are the epistemic component of habit formation . . . the reward–penalty axis is the valuative component' (Quine 1978, p. 37). He states finally that, 'some such equipment . . . must precede all learning; that is, it must be innate' (1978, p. 37). Prior to any learning, we possess a primordial apparatus for valuation; that is, a set of innate dispositions that encourages a partition of certain stimulations into those that count for us as rewards and those that count as penalties. Such then is the biological basis for our initial preferences, our values. Without discrimination on this basis, reinforcement, which is essential for subsequent learning, could not occur.

Strictly speaking, our innate bipartite equipment constitutes our first theory of the world. Its elements are the first strands of our expanding web of belief. As such, they are our initial source of hypotheses by which, through testing, conjecture and refutation, and revision, we develop our beliefs. As our corporate body of beliefs faces the tribunal of sensory experience, over time we may be required, in the interests of greater coherence, to alter and abandon certain of these initial beliefs. So our unlettered grouping of whales with fish yields, in the fullness of time, to the taxonomically more informed similarity grouping of whales with kangaroos. Systematic theory intrudes to alter our standards of similarity in ways that make for better prediction, understanding, and problem solving.

Our suggestion is that analogous considerations apply in the case of values. Consider the following Quinean naturalistic and holistic account of learning a moral term like 'good', remembering that our initial values are no more than biologically programmed reactions to certain stimuli. 'Good', said of things to eat, is learned on a par with other observation terms like 'red'. The child learns to assent to it in the presence of certain foods which are pleasurable to the infant palate. What is interesting about this case, however, is that pleasure does double duty, serving as both the reinforcement and the similarity basis. In Quine's view the same circumstances attend the learning of the moral 'good':

> . . . we find the same convergence of factors here as before: the similarity basis of the term 'good', morally applied, is the reward itself. Obedience brings pleasure much as toffee does (Quine 1974, p. 50).

This is just in the beginning, though, and it is a mistake to see the meaning of 'good' as identifiable with the class of pleasurable stimuli. Complexity of learned theory intervenes often to sever this initial connection, or *stimulus meaning*, altogether. For language learning, which is also theory learning, is an empirical matter and proceeds, in the first instance, via the direct ostention of short, sometimes one word, sentences with their intersubjectively observable instantiations. But thus begun, the child's linguistic repertoire expands apace, with sentences being learned contextually as part of a linguistic whole. Where this occurs, connections between word and object are already tenuous and subject to realignment through systematic shifts in the associations among sentences, such as those brought about by revisions of theory. The upshot, as we saw in our earlier discussion of epistemology, is that there need be no fixed pattern of observations, or stimulations, that constitutes a sentences's empirical content. The notion of stimulus meaning has no clear application here. So even if a one word sentence like 'good' is first learned under conditions of original associations between word and object, these associations are only temporary. Once sufficient language (or theory) is built up to permit a word to function in a wider linguistic context, the resultant pull of various intra-linguistic associations may shift the conditions of assent away from the initial stimulus meaning of the word. As our theory of the world grows and develops, coherence considerations of simplicity, scope, consistency and the like can make for major revisions in the word/world associations that were the entering wedge of infant language learning. In this way values get revised and worked into the flux of ongoing theory development.

How then do we justify or improve our values? The short answer, we suggest, is by justifying or improving our total or global theory of the world. Since, as Quine remarks, '. . . the paths of language learning, which lead from observation sentences to theoretical sentences, are the only connection there is between observation and theory . . .' (Quine 1975, p. 79) then the only evidence we have for our moral beliefs is evidence which is on a par with the evidence we have for our so-called empirical beliefs. From the point of view of coherence justification, the various definitions, embedded in systematic theoretical packages, offered by utilitarians, other consequentialists, as well as deontologists, are justified according to the virtues of system that accrue to the global theories of which they are part. Value terms in ethical theories are thus best regarded as theoretical terms within the web of global theory. Because humans are complex physical systems living in a physical world, we assume the most parsimonious accounts of our moral beliefs will be naturalistic accounts, since these will cohere most economically with our best physical science. Attempts within biology to use evolutionary theory to explain our current folk moral dispositions are a case in point (Ruse and Wilson 1986).

In view of the many divergent perspectives that can meet this parsimony constraint, considerable further work seems to be required to argue for a preferred normative ethic for educational administration. The short answer we attempt here is only a prelude to a much longer and vastly more complex and controversial set of considerations. Our proposal, at least to give a point of entry for future developments, is to focus on what we take to be some of the touchstone conditions for adjudicating moral theories.

A Normative Framework for Administrative Practice

In confronting a welter of conflicting moral viewpoints and the sheer complexity of administrative decision making, we suggest that the basic normative framework for educational administrators is provided by the general requirement that decision and action should be, in the long term, educative; that the growth of knowledge be promoted. (A more eclectic example of such an approach being applied systematically in educational administration can be seen in Duignan and Macpherson 1987.) This is a fundamental Deweyan insight that we wish to defend and elaborate.

Whatever particular problems we need to solve, from the universal ones of supplying food, clothing, and shelter through to more arcane and specialized ones, the touchstone, or common epistemological need is reliable knowledge. But we have seen that all our knowledge is fallible and grows from a broad process of conjecture and refutation. With few exceptions there are therefore advantages in maintaining and promoting the social conditions for learning from this broad process. That is, almost regardless of the nature of problems and the range of solutions under consideration, there are large scale touchstone gains to be had in supporting the option of improving our theories whatever they may be. The exceptions we hedge against are not those of sacrifice, which are aimed at overcoming the problems of others, but rather the possibility of legitimate despair where the best informed, but fallible, reason sees no solutions consistent with further inquiry forthcoming, and waiting on inquiry is itself a burden.

Since, from an epistemological viewpoint, it is not important to distinguish what are reckoned to be ethical claims from empirical claims, maintaining the social relations of inquiry is as relevant to moral theory as it is to empirical theory. Crucially, the networks of social relations most conducive to the growth of knowledge can also be described in characteristically moral terms. Inasmuch as people are prepared to see virtue in being able to pursue their theory-informed goals and plans, the claims in which these moral terms figure are common, or touchstone, moral claims. The moral theory that best systematizes these claims is thus a form of *rule consequentialism*. That is, the hypothesized common theoretical virtues of problem solving and promoting the growth of knowledge are used to adjudicate rules or principles of social and administrative practice against the standard of whether they are fundamentally *educative*.

Although a consequentialist, or teleological theory, it is not a form of utilitarianism, unless the term is used so widely as to include any consistent behaviour. It is pragmatic and fallibilist in that it coheres with the claim that all our beliefs are in principle open to revision. It is holistic in that principles of revision include consistency, simplicity, comprehensiveness and all the rest of the coherentist criteria. On theory of value we follow Dewey (1929, ch. 10) in identifying good naturalistically with problem solving — a value we think is arguably touchstone for any comprehensive account of the human condition — though we think our holism and a rule consequentialist approach will fend off the usual objections to Deweyan ethics (for example the kind of worries generated by distinguishing between growth and direction of growth).

Does this approach make for radical revisions to folk moral judgments, as distinct from folk ethical theory? In general we think it does not, although we would like to think there are some roundings out and improvements accruing from greater systematicity. Despite developing a rigorously naturalistic philosophy after a short Hegelian period, Dewey's later normative ethics had much in common with his earlier Christian-based ethics. In looking at inquiry as a social and organizational phenomenon, the conditions for enhancing the process of trial and error, conjecture and refutation, suggested by Karl Popper's social and political philosophy, are also, in the main, congenial. Popper's (1945) defence of the 'open society' carries over in some respects to a defence of the open organization and community, where there is concern primarily for democratic reform, for maximizing provision for the correction of policy and practice through informed participative feedback from those most concerned with the consequences of policy and practice; and, in general, where there is a premium on freedom, trust, and truthfulness as conditions for full participation in a fundamentally epistemic community governed by the social relations of effective inquiry. (We discuss more of Popper's ideas on social theory in the next chapter, when we consider some of their consequences for policy analysis.)

Finally, some recent work in educational theory by J.C. Walker (1987b) on the connection between values and feedback models of knowledge growth, offers a number of plausible specific educational prescriptions. According to Walker, we know that some distributions of knowledge diminish opportunities for learning. For example, knowledge vital to the solution of community-wide problems may be concentrated in certain specialized groups, such as professions, or kept exclusively in the hands of experts where its further distribution is subject to non-educative regulation. Yet the powerful coping resources of a well-educated community constitutes an important consideration for making knowledge as widely available as possible. Even where it is arguable that expertise only develops under conditions of restricted distribution, it does not follow that opportunities to gain expertise should be restricted. Fleshing out these considerations, Walker develops moral critiques of professionalization, educational research methodology, and the social control of schooling (Walker and Evers 1986; Walker 1985, 1987a). He also observes that participation in the social relations of effective inquiry carries some moral obligations. For example, respect and tolerance for different points of view are the cornerstone of a theory that sees criticism as the key ingredient in the growth of knowledge. Like-mindedness may be a virtue in consolidating, or even developing to a certain point, a particular perspective, but without criticism the fallibility of our knowledge implies that errors will remain to live on in like-minded 'solutions'.

There is nothing decisive in these moral conclusions squaring with many of our ordinary sentiments and we put forward these ideas merely as a framework for moral decision making in education. However, if they continue to hold up in greater detail as the theory of knowledge behind them meshes with the comprehensive range of theories comprising our most economical global perspective, familiarity with recognized folk theoretical examples of moral excellence can be a bonus. In seeking to develop a moral theory for educational administration that also coheres with a perspective on educational theory we observe a small irony. In educational administration it has seemed to us that quite often the only thing educational being referred to has been the particular organizations under study: schools, government departments of education, institutions of higher education, and so on. The varieties of administrative theory in use have been, in the main, insensitive to the educational aspects of these organizations. In proposing a theory of moral

value whose benchmark for administrative choice is educative administration — administrative choices which promote greater learning — we hope
to contribute towards redressing this balance.

Of course, some administrative theories do embody a characteristically
fallibilist epistemic structure and therefore permit a greater congruence
between administrative practice and moral gain within the naturalistic global
context we favour. We conclude this chapter by describing some features
of one well-known theory that we first introduced in Chapter One. Just
as Herbert Simon proposes organizational structures that enhance decision
making, so Chris Argyris proposes organizational structures that enhance
organizational learning. In a series of studies of a large range of organizations, Argyris and associates have distinguished two main categories of
organizational learning. In *single loop* learning:

> there is a single feedback loop which connects detected outcomes of
> action to organizational strategies and assumptions which are modified
> to keep organizational performance within the range set by organiza-
> tional norms. The norms themselves — for product quality, sales, or
> task performance — remain unchanged. . . . In order for *organiza-
> tional* learning to occur, learning agents' discoveries, inventions and
> evaluations must be embedded in organizational memory (Argyris and
> Schön 1978, p. 19).

Organizational learning can occur by so structuring the possibility of individual learning that certain shared perceptions of the organization — the
organization's theory-in-use — are changed.

Argyris regards single loop learning as being quite inadequate for the
decisions and problems most organizations face (Argyris 1982). For example,
while such a design makes it possible for organizations to '. . . create continuity, consistency, and stability, and to maintain the status quo in order to
achieve objectives within desired costs . . .' (Argyris and Schön 1978, p. 123)
it contains no provision for the correction of its goals and values, or the basis
of weightings used to structure decision alternatives. So while participation
in decision making is enhanced through the process of organized feedback,
the scope of error elimination falls short of values. Single loop organizational
learning underwrites 'dynamic conservatism', a condition inimical to long-
term success or survival in a changing internal or external environment. It
is a learning structure ill-suited to coping with discontinuity, instability, and
changes in the status quo. As such, it is unable to use to the full extent the
epistemic possibilities inherent in learning through conjecture and refutation.

The second type of learning, which Argyris regards as the most appropriate
given the conditions under which most organizations exist, is called *double
loop* learning. This applies to

. . . those sorts of organizational inquiry which resolve incompatible organizational norms by setting new priorities and weightings of norms, or by restructuring the norms themselves together with associated strategies and assumptions (Argyris 1982, p. 24).

In systems that employ double loop learning structures, goals, aims, objectives, moral values, in fact all knowledge that figures in the making of a decision, is subject to revision through error elimination.

We do not propose to press this point further. (For further developments see Evers 1990.) Suffice it to note that in our view, administrative structures are not morally neutral. In education especially, where many outside the formal schooling structure have a legitimate and informed interest in educational outcomes, systems that permit feedback and scrutiny of guiding moral goals and assumptions enjoy epistemic, and therefore moral, advantages over systems that do not.

Summary

Ethics is often supposed to be distinct and separate from administrative theory. However, we find two key arguments for this claim — the 'is/ought dichotomy' and the 'naturalistic fallacy' — unconvincing, largely for epistemological reasons. This opens the way for a variety of accounts, or reductions, of moral terms, including naturalistic accounts, which we favour because of their links with wider physical theory and explanatory advantages. In this way coherence criteria gain some purchase on adjudicating rival moral theories. We next considered some varieties of utilitarianism and also, equally briefly, Rawls's deontological theory of justice, as examples of normative ethical theories that might be considered to have developed under pressure of (admittedly more narrowly applied) coherence criteria. Of the two theories we considered in most detail, namely those of Harsanyi and Rawls, we expressed reservations over what appeared to be an unwarranted distinction between their accounts of rationality used to justify moral principles, and substantive theories of society necessary to apply their moral theories.

Our alternative approach simply permitted the distinction to collapse. We identified 'good' naturalistically as growth in knowledge and then proposed using the definition as a constraint on the construction of moral rules; a form of rule consequentialism. For us moral reasoning is embedded in theory laden reasoning in general, and develops most readily along with our overall theory of the world. Such global theories will also include systematic accounts of administration, and to enhance parsimony, and especially coherence with our ethical views, we favoured administrative theories that embody sound epistemic practice. As an example we suggested the work of Argyris on organizational learning. We noted the corollary that organizational structures are not neutral but admit of moral appraisal.

References

Arendt H. (1963). *Eichmann in Jerusalem*. (London: Faber and Faber).

Argyris C. (1982). *Reasoning, Learning and Action*. (San Francisco: Jossey-Bass).

Argyris C. and Schön D. (1978). *Organizational Learning: A Theory of Action Perspective*. (Menlo Park: Addison-Wesley).

Beauchamp T. and Childress J.F. (1984). Morality, ethics and ethical theories, in P.A. Sola (ed.) *Ethics, Education and Administrative Decisions*. (New York: Peter Lang).

Begum H. (1979). Moore on goodness and the naturalistic fallacy, *Australasian Journal of Philosophy*, 57(3), pp. 251–265.

Black M. (1964). The gap between 'Is' and 'Should', *Philosophical Review*, 73, pp. 165–181.

Brandt R.B. (1959). *Ethical Theory*. (Englewood Cliffs N.J.: Prentice-Hall).

Davidson D. (1974). Psychology as philosophy, in S.C. Brown (ed.) *Philosophy of Psychology*. (London: Macmillan).

Dewey J. (1929). *Experience and Nature*. (New York: Dover, 1958 edition).

Duignan P. and Macpherson R.J.S. (1987). The educative leadership project, *Educational Management and Administration*, 15, pp. 49–62.

Evers C.W. (1979). Analytic philosophy of education: from a logical point of view, *Educational Philosophy and Theory*, 11(2), pp. 1–15.

Evers C.W. (1990). Schooling, organizational learning and efficiency in the growth of knowledge, in J.D. Chapman (ed.) *School Based Decision Making and Management*. (London: Falmer Press).

Frankena W.K. (1939). The naturalistic fallacy, *Mind*, 48, pp. 464–77.

Frankena W.K. (1963). *Ethics*. (Englewood Cliffs N.J.: Prentice-Hall).

Gallie W.B. (1955–56). Essentially contested concepts, *Proceedings of the Aristotelian Society*, 56, pp. 167–198.

Hare R.M. (1952). *The Language of Morals*. (Oxford: Oxford University Press).

Harsanyi J. (1977). Morality and the theory of rational behaviour, in A. Sen and B. Williams (eds.) *Utilitarianism and Beyond*. (London: Cambridge University Press).

Harsanyi J. (1980). Can the maximin principle serve as a basis for morality? A critique of John Rawls' theory, in J. Harsanyi, *Essays on Ethics, Social Behaviour, and Scientific Explanation*. (Dordrecht: D. Reidel).

Hudson W.D. (1969) (ed.). *The Is/Ought Question*. (London: Macmillan).

Kant I. (1785). *Groundwork of the Metaphysics of Morals*. (London: Hutchinson, 1947 edition, translated by H.J. Paton).

Kurtzman D.R. (1970). 'Is', 'Ought', and the autonomy of ethics, *Philosophical Review*, 79, pp. 493–509.

Mabbott J.D. (1956). Interpretations of Mill's 'Utilitarianism', *Philosophical Quarterly*, 6, pp. 115–120.

McCloskey H.J. (1957). An examination of restricted utilitarianism, *Philosophical Review*, 66, pp. 466–485.

Mill J.S. (1861). *Utilitarianism*. (London: Collins, 1962 edition).

Moore G.E. (1903). *Principia Ethica*. (London: Cambridge University Press).

Popper K.R. (1945). *The Open Society and its Enemies*, Vols. 1 and 2. (London: George Routledge & Sons).

Prior A.N. (1960). The autonomy of ethics, *Australasian Journal of Philosophy*, 38(3), pp. 199–206.

Quine W.V. (1940). *Mathematical Logic*. (Cambridge, Mass.: Harvard University Press).

Quine W.V. (1960). *Word and Object*. (Cambridge, Mass.: M.I.T. Press).

Quine W.V. (1974). *The Roots of Reference*. (La Salle: Open Court).

Quine W.V. (1975). The nature of natural knowledge, in S. Guttenplan (ed.) *Mind and Language*. (London: Oxford University Press).

Quine W.V. (1978). On the nature of moral values, in A.I. Goldman and J. Kun (eds.) *Values and Morals*. (Dordrecht: D. Reidel).

Rawls J. (1955). Two concepts of rules, *Philosophical Review*, **64**, pp. 3–32.

Rawls J. (1971). *A Theory of Justice*. (Cambridge, Mass.: Harvard University Press).

Ruse M. and Wilson E.O. (1986). Moral Philosophy as applied science, *Philosophy*, **61**, pp. 173–192.

Skinner B.F. (1971). *Beyond Freedom and Dignity*. (Harmondsworth: Penguin).

Smart J.J.C. (1956). Extreme and restricted utilitarianism, *Philosophical Quarterly*, **6**, pp. 344–354.

Smart J.J.C. (1973). An outline of a system of utilitarian ethics, in J.J.C. Smart and B. Williams, *Utilitarianism: For and Against*. (London: Cambridge University Press).

Stich S.P. and Nisbett R.E. (1980). Justification and the psychology of human reasoning, *Philosophy of Science*, **47**, pp. 188–202.

Tversky A. and Kahneman D. (1981). The framing of decisions and the psychology of choice, *Science*, **211**, pp. 453–458.

Walker, J.C. (1985). Materialist pragmatism and sociology of education, *British Journal of Sociology of Education*, **6** (1), pp. 55–74.

Walker J.C. (1987a). Democracy and pragmatism in curriculum development, *Educational Philosophy and Theory*, **19**(2), pp. 1–10.

Walker J.C. (1987b). Materialism and the growth of knowledge in education, in C.W. Evers (ed.) *Moral Theory of Educative Leadership*. (Melbourne: Victorian Ministry of Education).

Walker J.C. and Evers C.W. (1986). Theory, politics and experiment in educational research methodology, *International Review of Education*, **32**(4), pp. 373–387.

Williams B. (1985). *Ethics and the Limits of Philosophy*. (London: Fontana).

9

Policy Analysis: Values and Complexity

In his review of the state of the art in educational policy analysis, Mitchell notes at the outset that:

> the vast literature on the topic of educational policy has produced no standard textbooks, little agreement on the methods or goals of educational policy research, and few 'classic' or exemplary studies for defining the area's central thrust or overall theoretical perspectives (Mitchell 1984, p. 130).

Mitchell's assessment is echoed, as well as qualified, in Boyd (1988). Whether described as fragmented, or just diverse in perspective, educational policy analysis, as part of the larger policy arena, is currently debating what should be its proper conceptual foundations, and how the professional practice of policy analysis should be conducted. These concerns include consideration of the relation between policy analysis and policy making which represents a 'continuing conflict' (Shapiro and Berkeley 1986, p. 88) insofar as policy analysis is seen as scientific and value free by some, and political and value laden by others. Both conceptions are assumed to be mutually exclusive. It is nevertheless agreed by most policy analysts of either shade that scientific policy analysis has had a low, or even distorting, impact on policy making, thus producing 'something of a crisis in the professional practice of scientific policy analysis' (Mitchell 1984, p. 135).

We want to argue in this chapter that some important problems which currently concern policy analysts and policy makers have their origins in an older theoretical dispute concerning the most appropriate methodological framework for the conduct of policy analysis. The older dispute concerns the merits of a *synoptic* as opposed to a limited, piecemeal, or incremental approach to policy (see Braybrooke and Lindblom 1963, Garson 1986).

In particular, we want to examine two current methodological problems:

(i) How may value considerations be integrated into the process of policy analysis? and

(ii)   What is the most reasonable general strategy for overcoming our ignorance of the workings of the very complex (human) systems that are the usual objects of policy?

These two problems are clearly epistemological in character, and have been recognized as such in the policy studies literature, particularly the literature arising out of the synoptic/anti-synoptic debate, as well as in recent contributions from interpretive social science. Since issues in the theory of knowledge are of decisive importance here, we shall draw on our coherentist epistemological framework and its associated methodology, especially our findings on ethics in the last chapter, to suggest ways in which a coherentist approach to these problems can yield a more comprehensive and flexible framework for a science of policy analysis. Not surprisingly, the intellectual diversity now characteristic of educational administration is mirrored, to some extent, in policy studies where there can now be found competing scientific, interpretive, and critical theory perspectives on policy and policy analysis. In our discussion of values, we explore two of these perspectives: the scientific tradition to which Harold Lasswell made such an important contribution, and a more recent interpretive approach associated with the work of Bruce Jennings. We conclude by arguing for a fallibilist, coherentist view of values within a much broadened scientific view of policy and decision. We then explore ways in which this fallibilist coherentist epistemological approach can be applied to the problem of complexity, and what constraints it imposes on both policy making and policy analysis.

Policy Science, Policy Analysis, and Values

Perhaps the most influential figure in the development of a synoptic tradition in policy is Lasswell who, with Daniel Lerner in the early 1950s, introduced the ambitious notion of 'policy sciences' (Lerner and Lasswell 1951). According to Lasswell:

> the most fruitful policy science idea is . . . that all the resources of our expanding social science need to be directed toward the basic conflicts in our civilization which are so vividly disclosed by the application of scientific method to the study of personality and culture. . . . The basic emphasis of the policy approach, therefore, is upon the fundamental problems of man in society, rather than upon the topical issues of the moment (Lasswell 1951, p. 6).

What Lasswell had in mind, however, was more than just a distinctive breadth of purview for the policy sciences, although breadth was certainly required to create 'world-encompassing hyptheses' to deal with 'events on a global scale' (Lasswell 1951, p. 11). He aimed also for a principle of integration to draw together relevant contributing disciplines into a coherent and systematic body of policy knowledge. Thus for Lasswell, the policy sciences include both knowledge of the policy-making and policy-executing processes, and also the resources for assembling and evaluating the whole range of specialisms that have a bearing on the solution of policy problems (Lasswell 1951, p. 14). They require a unified view of social science and a general theory of choice (Lasswell 1951, pp. 3–4, Garson 1986, pp. 541–542).

Lasswell's chief argument for a synoptic approach to policy lay in an acknowledgement of the complexity of social life, especially its international complexity. Problems addressed by policy analysis in the service of government, pursuing a government agenda, were less likely to be understood and dealt with effectively in the absence of a comprehensive global perspective. This argument also formed part of a common rationale offered during the 1950s and 1960s for policy analysis to be conducted within the framework of General Systems Theory: 'A core problematic concern of the systems approach is the understanding, analysing and managing of complexity' (Backoff and Mitnick 1986, p. 25).

In using the resources of the social sciences to provide a synoptic framework for acquiring knowledge of complex systems, however, Lasswell's vision of the policy sciences was compromised in familiar ways. For the dominant view of science informing methodology and theory construction, certainly in the 1950s and 1960s, was based on a narrow empiricism which placed a premium on behavioural and statistical analyses. Typical of the epistemological doctrines associated with this style of empiricism, as we should expect, are:

1. A sharp separation of observation from theory;
2. Evidence for a claim consists in a correspondence between claim and observation;
3. Evidence against a claim consists in a mismatch between claim and observation; and
4. A fact/value dichotomy.

The first three doctrines will not pose noticeable methodological barriers to a unification of the sciences for policy if they are shared by all the contributing sciences; the whole synthesis merely ends up containing whatever methodological infirmities accrue to this kind of empiricism. So if mastering complexity through comprehensiveness requires at least a bringing to bear on problems of every relevant science, a ubiquitous notion of science (whatever its merits) is an advantage.

Unfortunately, what is gained by way of this synoptic view of science is lost when it comes to values; that is, when it comes to using what science yields to guide the making of policy choices. The point is that while evidence admissible by the scruples of the first three doctrines can be applied directly to the range of sciences, maintaining a sharp fact/value distinction has the effect of robbing value claims of the very possibility of empirical support. So while scientific assertions face the tribunal of observational evidence, the adjudication of values presumably takes place in an empirical vacuum.

An example might help to illustrate the epistemological basis of the division in justification. Within this tradition, we may suppose that there is a knowable fact of the matter concerning whether a particular course of action will result in, say, a particular distribution of income, or a particular pattern of access to higher education, or whatever. Let us suppose that there exists just the right amount of evidence for reasonably claiming what social state will follow from this course of action. Let us make the additional (though moral) claim that what follows is unjust (or perhaps wrong, or bad) and is therefore grounds for eschewing a policy choice with these consequences. What is the evidence for this additional claim of injustice? If it is merely the same as the evidence for the first (though factual) claim, the additional claim is either evidentially unjustified or says no more than the first. But if more empirical evidence is supplied, all it can ever yield is more detail about consequent states of affairs, or resulting facts of the matter.

Arguing in this fashion it is not surprising that empiricist writers located the grounds for our moral beliefs, our beliefs about what constitutes injustice, or good, or right, not in empirical evidence itself, but in our subjective responses, or attitudes, to that evidence; and in theory of choice, the most important of these attitudes is *preference* (usually measured as expressed preference). Thus in his classic paper, Lasswell takes the term 'value' to mean 'a category of preferred events' (Lasswell 1951, p. 9).

Given that so much powerful analysis can go into determining the supposed consequences of an action, it is perhaps something to be lamented that what can be decisive at the point of policy choice is a person's unanalysed moral tastes. To be sure, much modern normative decision theory attempts to determine the bounds of taste by appeal to the bounds of reason; to make them less subjective. (A point we argued in detail in Chapter Eight.) Within preference utilitarianism – which is the decision-theoretic ethical perspective most often associated with varieties of empiricism – Harsanyi, defending one version, argues that 'rational moral value judgments will involve maximizing the average utility level of all individuals in society' (Harsanyi 1980a, p. 97). However, these approaches usually involve funnelling empirical evidence, by way of a concern for consequences, into ethical judgment by assuming that one behaves according to the dictates of a particular theory of rationality. Since theories of rationality are meant to be relatively content free, ethical claims can appear as hypothetical imperatives of the form: 'if you want X, do Y'. A fact/value distinction is thus maintained by positing values as the basis for each antecedent, and moral tastes are shaped by a process of rational mutual adjustment.

Within the synoptic tradition C. West Churchman, an influential systems theorist, in his reflective *The Systems Approach and its Enemies* seeks a rapprochement between systems theory and four identified enemies, of which morality is one. His task of providing a comprehensive decision framework for the ideal planner, however, is not made any easier by proclaiming his belief that 'ethics is not a body of theory substantiated by facts' (Churchman 1979, p. 118). Indeed, when he comes to elaborate his own views of morality, he admits: 'This has been for me the most difficult chapter to write, because it has never developed a coherent theme' (p. 165).

Lasswell also gets into difficulty over values, though not without first attempting some ingenious manoeuvres. For example, he distinguishes what he calls the content approach from the procedural approach. In justifying the content of particular propositions, he notes that we can appeal to their 'empirical grounding', that is, those relevant empirical events that we are able to observe with our ordinary psychophysical equipment (Lasswell 1958, p. 89). Values fare ill on this score, but do better with a metaphysical or theological 'transempirical grounding'. In general, however, Lasswell disapproves of the policy scientist trading in transempirical justifications. Does this stand preclude a person from identifying with value goals? 'Definitely not', Lasswell says (1971, p. 41). The (partial) solution he offers is that the procedures of policy science call for personal goal clarification since policy outcomes 'affect value realizations' (1971, p. 41). Yet no amount of value clarification, however necessary because of the ubiquity of values in policy choice, can dispose of the fundamental problem of value adjudication. Lasswell and others in this empirical tradition acknowledge that persons may feel some of their preferences to be better than others they hold. But the relation 'better than' ultimately reduces to a second order preference that ranks preferences.

There is a long tradition within empirical democratic conceptions of policy studies for avoiding this problem by treating the 'public interest' as a fundamental policy goal. The public interest is here determined by suitably aggregating individual preferences of arbitrary merit. This principle of aggregation, known as a social welfare function, operates as follows. Let $S_1, \ldots, S_m$ be the set of possible social states that would correspond to m policy alternatives. Let R_1 be the preference ordering of all S_m made by the ith individual, and let $R_1, \ldots, R_m$ be the set of all such orderings for all individuals. Then a social welfare function defines R, an ordering of all S_m, for all R_m (Arrow 1963, pp. 22–25; Braybrooke and Lindblom 1963, pp. 12–16). For a particular example, consider again Harsanyi's utilitarian theory. The ith individual ranks social states, $S_1, \ldots, S_m$, according to his or her individual utility function, although all individuals may produce different rankings, $R_1, \ldots, R_m$. This principle of aggregation produces a ranking R of social states, and hence preferred policy options, according to the numerical value of the arithmetic mean of the utility levels of all individuals for each social state (Harsanyi 1980b, p. 65). Notice that this version of a social welfare function is also Harsanyi's definition of what is involved in rational moral choice.

Anti-synoptic Objections

In mounting a detailed critique of the synoptic approach to policy, Charles Lindblom has often drawn attention to many of the practical difficulties involved in being comprehensive in the face of complexity. This is a point that he has made particularly in relation to the construction of social welfare functions.

Consider, by way of example, a government policy proposal to change the basis of funding for higher education in order that higher education might more directly contribute toward meeting certain national economic objectives. In comparing just two social states we run into the problem of multiplicity of values created by the multiplicity of differences between the two states (Braybrooke and Lindblom 1963, pp. 23–26). There are shifts in goal values resulting from a coordinated shift in a range of previous objectives, as well as shifts in input values associated with the use of resources and means for meeting new objectives. Permuted by the number of different individuals, this makes for a very large number of values. More worrying, though obvious to anyone hearing the competing rhetorics over universities, is the fact that values are sensitive to the way things are described. Since there is no natural upper bound here, talk of enumerating values for quantitative purpose seems extravagant. Like most of our beliefs, values can also be unstable, especially in the light of experience. The mere experiencing of a new order in higher education can force revisions on the values that originally sanctioned it. Maintaining a sharp distinction between fact and value does our capacity to learn new values from experience a disservice. And once acknowledged, this capacity undermines the point of decision making by hypothetical preference. A third problem, which can also exist at the level of individual values, is value conflict. One can applaud the short-term economic advantages that may accrue from more rapidly meeting economic objectives, while, say, lamenting a possible redirection of support away from the humanities. According to Lindblom, these problems make the task of knowing and somehow accumulating individual preferences in a way that permits an aggregate based ranking of policy alternatives, impossible to accomplish. Arrow's Impossibility Theorem, which we discussed in Chapter Five, raises further, though quite fundamental difficulties for egalitarian ways of incorporating individual preferences into a rational framework of social choice.

In exploring some of the difficulties over values arising out of the earlier synoptic tradition, one strand of criticism, ironically, has been the tradition's failure to be comprehensive enough. In trying to account for all relevant policy knowledge, a belief in the fact/value distinction has comprehensiveness falling just short of values.

In addition to the kind of criticisms raised by Lindblom noted above, as well as by Arrows Theorem, concern over the alleged value neutrality of policy analysis has accompanied the synoptic movement from its beginnings. Dwight Waldo, long-time editor of the *Public Administration Review*, denied as early as 1952 that 'efficiency is a value-neutral concept or . . . that it is antithetical to democracy' (Waldo 1952, p. 97). While not being specific on the relationship between facts and values, Waldo believed that 'there is no realm of "factual decisions" from which values are excluded. To decide is to choose between alternatives, to choose between alternatives is to introduce values' (1952, p. 97). And in an interesting aside he acknowledged Herbert Simon's outstanding contributions to administrative theory, but felt compelled to add 'These contributions have been made, however, when he has worked free of the methodology he has asserted' (p. 97).

The subsequent complex, and often contradictory, anti-synoptic history of policy analysis, drawing largely on the humanist tradition, has repeatedly emphasized that value-free scientific assessments of policies were 'a mis-guided attempt to side-step the more fundamental issues of societal values (Garson 1986, p. 539). In his influential review of the policy and policy-making literature, Lowi concluded that the approaches to policy analysis were

> . . . essentially technocratic and instrumental in values, in analysis, and in ultimate impact. When one assumes that 'policy making is policy making is decision making' and therefore does not enter into *a priori* analysis of the character of the choices being made, one almost inevitably becomes incrementalist and manipulative. . . . If one does not analyse the character of the choices made, one need not ask any question about the impact of those choices (taken as variables) upon the processes themselves or upon the society at large (Lowi 1970, p. 318).

Neglecting to put social values at the centre of policy analysis, which showed in the split between 'value-laden' politics and 'rational' scientific administration, policy analysis came to be described as the 'handmaiden' to policy makers. Coined originally by Irving Horowitz and James Katz (1975, pp. 156–157), the term was meant to indicate that policy analysis had become a degenerate activity in the eyes of some, directly geared to satisfying the informational needs of policy makers and thus only serving narrow, particularistic interests.

While the synoptic tradition continues to be influential, both in its empha-sis on policy analysis as science and in its role as 'handmaiden' to policy makers, however valued, recent developments are increasingly critical both of the scientific status of the field and the role of policy analysis in a democratic society. Policy analysis as a field of study and a set of practices is, like educational administration, in the process of redefining itself. The 1970s in particular, saw a rise in more systematic attempts at theory building in policy analysis. According to Jennings, the development of theory 'has been a remarkably neglected enterprise considering the way the field has grown in size and influence since the 1960s' (Jennings 1987, p. 122). Prominent among these recent normative models is Aaron Wildavsky's *Speaking Truth to Power: The Art and Craft of Policy Analysis* (1979). It is an example of what Jennings calls an 'advocacy' model of policy analysis, which, as the title indicates, takes a diametrically opposed view to the science tradition discussed so far, and assumes a 'version of epistemological skepticism' (Jennings 1987, pp. 122–123).

In Wildavsky's view, policy analysis is an art as well as a moral enterprise. It 'is about improvement, about improving citizen preferences for the policies they — the people — ought to prefer' (Wildavsky 1979, p. 19). In his conception, policy analysis is both descriptive and prescriptive insofar as it explains policy failure and advises what should be done (Wildavsky 1979, p. 14). Its objectivity consists in obtaining intersubjective agreement about the consequences of various alternatives, and depends on argumentation to urge acceptance of one specific policy over a competing one. And since it is particular people who, in the light of their interests, choose the problems to be solved, as well as the alternatives to be considered, policy analysis is also subjective. Wildavsky wonders whether it is indeed a 'union of opposites — prospective and retrospective, objective and subjective, descriptive and prescriptive — or, different things under different circumstances?' (1979, p. 15). His answer is that it is both.

While Wildavsky's almost anarchistic conception of policy analysis lies squarely in the anti-synoptic tradition, it also reflects the relatively recent influence of social science without, however, explicitly discussing it. Just as orthodox educational administration was challenged by (interpretive) administrators because of its positivist, 'technical' orientation which split values from facts (see Chapter Six), so policy analysis has similarly come under scrutiny by political scientists and other writers who believe that the interpretive social sciences can help overcome the current diversity and fragmentation of their field. (For recent discussions on the role of values and the interpretive social sciences see Dunn 1980–81, 1983; Dallmayr 1980–81; Callahan and Jennings 1983; MacRae 1971; Nielsen 1983, pp. 133–157; Rein 1983, pp. 83–111; Fischer and Forester 1987.)

Interpretive Social Science, Policy Analysis, and Values

In the following section we want to consider in more detail a proposal for policy analysis advocated by Bruce Jennings: *policy analysis as counsel* (Jennings 1983, pp. 3–35; 1987, pp. 121–134). Jennings presents possibly the most systematic recent attempt at reconceptualizing policy analysis from within the interpretive perspective on the basis of epistemological criticisms raised in relation to empiricist science in general, as well as Laswellian policy science in particular. As an expressedly normative enterprise, policy analysis as counsel thus promises to provide a more satisfactory answer particularly to the first question we raised at the beginning of this chapter. For if values, which remained outside of the scientific approach, are rather to be considered as the very foundation for policy analysis, then it might be supposed that policy analysis would become more relevant as a social activity; that is, it would

> . . . raise the question of a policy's effect on community and would take the fostering of community and the mitigation of alienation and anomie to be fundamentally legitimate and important policy considerations (Jennings 1983, p. 28).

Rather than ending up being dismissive of values, as was the case in the synoptic tradition, values would be part of the very fabric of policy analysis and thus correct the problems of the scientific approach. While this is a plausible supposition, it is, however, already clear that insofar as this conception bases itself on the major features of interpretive social science, it must expect to run into the same problems encountered in the cultural perspective model in educational administration. More specifically, while the synoptic tradition turned out to be less than comprehensive by eschewing values, Jennings's conception, although 'comprehensive' by being value-based, also ends up without clear empirical constraints on policy analysis. This is due in part to the hermeneutic tradition's theory of meaning. If our argument is correct that policy analysis as counsel ends up incapable of making policy choices, then the gains — explicit consideration of values — are outweighed by the losses, by an incapacity adequately to deal with the empirical world.

Critical of the Laswellian conception of policy science, Jennings believes that this positivistic

> . . . 'engineering model' of applied social science, supplemented by techniques such as decision theory or cost benefit analysis . . . does not accurately represent — and cannot methodologically or ethically guide — the actual or potential practice of policy analysis (Jennings 1987, p. 122).

The reasons for his rejection of the synoptic tradition are based on some epistemological criticisms recently levelled against logical positivism and empiricism.

These he cites as

. . . the theory-ladenness of observation, the inherently metaphori-
cal, nonformalizable character of scientific languages, the imagina-
tive dimension of scientific discovery, the non-referential meaning of
scientific terms (Jennings 1983, p. 6).

While Jennings agrees with the notion of policy analysis as advocacy insofar as
it has drawn one important lesson from these criticisms by having recognized
the 'value-bias implicit in all analytic techniques' (Jennings 1987, p. 123) and
consequently rejected the distinction between social science and ideology,
he nevertheless criticizes it for having replaced scientific objectivity with a
procedural solution akin to the adversarial legal system. In the face of the
turn to advocacy, Jennings believes that it is still possible to have a rational
and objective conception of policy analysis. He draws his own conclusion
from the recent criticisms of empiricism, one of which is fundamental for
the justification of policy analysis as counsel:

a new link is being forged between the *Naturwissenschaften* and the
Geisteswissenschaften — a link reminiscent of the logical positivists' original programme of a unified science, now constituted not by a logic of
deductive-nomological explanation but by a common hermeneutic of
nature and of culture (Jennings 1983, p. 6).

It thus follows for Jennings that an adequate conception of policy analysis
must be based on a hermeneutic conception of social science. As he rightly
observes, there is no neutral observation language in science and social
science, and he concludes, erroneously, that hence science cannot provide
the objective knowledge base presumed by the synoptic approach. He thus
continues the mistaken practice of equating science with narrow, discredited,
forms of empiricism. As a consequence, Jennings turns away from the fact
side. Indeed, the fact/value distinction has become untenable for him since,
according to hermeneutics, all of science is theory laden and interpretive.
Hence, a unified science is still possible, but now only by accepting hermeneutics and its foundations as the proper ones for natural science as
well. Scientific objectivity, which Jennings equates with positivist notions
of objectivity, consequently makes way for 'post-positivistic' objectivity, a
notion to which we will return. While Jennings is aware of some of the
shortcomings of the interpretive perspective — its inbuilt conservatism is
cited as an example — he nevertheless believes that interpretive policy
analysis will be superior to the synoptic, as well as the advocacy approach,
because it emphasizes community, 'traditions of shared meaning and belief,
and intentional agency' (Jennings 1983, p. 11) which are constitutive of the
uniqueness and complexity of social life. These features are particularly
important in such areas as social welfare policy and foreign policy 'where

a subtle and sympathetic appraisal of the intentions and self-understandings of the agents involved is crucial to the policy's effectiveness and justice' (1983, p. 10).

Since Jennings is concerned to link knowledge with action, an objective familiar from the works of Habermas and others discussed earlier, this notion of policy analysis as counsel is, not surprisingly, also derived from the older tradition of political philosophy which wanted to unite political knowledge with political action through the application of practical reason, or *phronesis*. Policy analysis thus conceived has a threefold task:

> (1) to grasp the meaning or significance of contemporary problems as they are experienced, adapted to, and struggled against by the reasonable, purposive agents who are members of the political community; (2) to clarify the meaning of these problems so that strategically located political agents . . . will be able to devise a set of efficacious and just solutions to them; and (3) to guide the selection of one preferred policy from that set in light of the more general vision of the good of the community as a whole as well as the more discrete interests of the policy makers themselves (Jennings 1987, p. 123).

One of the key concepts underlying policy analysis as counsel is that of intention. Intentions, Jennings is careful to point out, are not to be taken as internal mental events or private wants, but are rather 'the purposes that an agent constructs . . . using the publicly available concepts and meanings of his or her culture' (1987, p. 129). Nor is it to be assumed that the agent's own point of view is to be accepted uncritically. Rather, his or her views must be transcended by a broader and more critical perspective, which requires

> . . . an empirically accurate description of the factual circumstances surrounding the action, and . . . an understanding of the norms and values operating in the cultural context to make the action 'appropriate' (Jennings 1987, p. 130).

Policy analysis as counsel stresses the notion of coherence, desiring to explicate a particular event within the network of relationships in which it is embedded.

These characteristics have specific implications and consequences for the practice of interpretive policy analysis. First of all, because interpretations are inherently value laden, they are fundamentally contestable. In addition, it is much more difficult to select between competing interpretations because criteria for choice are more 'akin to the evaluative criteria in certain disciplines in the humanities' (Jennings 1987, p. 131). Successful interpretations depend crucially on the insight, creativity, personal and intellectual characteristics of the policy analyst. His or her business is largely rhetorical or persuasive, involving literary, figurative, and stylistic skills. According to Jennings, none of these features necessarily imply lack of objectivity. This is because he thinks that 'post-positivistic objectivity' consists in the fact that the concepts and categories employed by agents are

> . . . 'publicly available' . . . drawn from a common, intersubjectively meaningful set of cultural norms, traditional values, and serviceable common-sense understandings of what human beings need and how they react to various circumstances. . . . This sort of objectivity will not give policy makers an understanding of the policy options that is based on science, but it will give them one based on *phronesis* – prudence and practical rationality. And that is the understanding that policy analysts as counsellors aim to provide (Jennings 1987, p. 131).

Since meanings are intersubjectively shared, forming the stock-in-trade of policy counsellors, Jennings believes that they thus speak in the public interest when presenting a particular assessment which, he admits, is only ever one of the possible perspectives which can be presented. It is this feature which, according to Jennings, raises policy analysis as counsel above the particularistic and group-specific interests of the advocacy model, making it the ethically preferred option. The decision procedure in this model, then, relies on the successful arbitration between competing perspectives on the public interest, and somehow rendering these coherent by finding a complementary 'fit' among them on the basis of the above given criteria.

Science, Meaning, and Values

Central to policy analysis as counsel, as indeed to the advocacy model and interpretive social science at large, is the assumption that natural science is 'technical', oriented toward control of nature, and social science 'practical', aiming at understanding the special meaningfulness of social phenomena. This conception of the division of labour between the sciences, advocated by Weber, but made most prominent in the writings of Habermas, is the cornerstone of much contemporary social, political, and administrative theory (see Habermas 1974, Introduction and ch. 1; also Fay 1975, especially ch. 2). However, the distinction relies on an unnecessarily narrow and now rejected instrumentalist conception of natural science. For example, it entails a definition of science as accumulating knowledge of observables, rather than as being concerned with explaining the hidden nature of the world. As Hesse explains:

> This is the kind of knowledge that issues in technical application, the cumulative character of which cannot be in doubt. Thus the claim

of science to yield objective knowledge comes to be identified with the cumulative possibilities of instrumental control rather than with theoretical discovery (Hesse 1980, pp. 174–175).

When measured against this conception of objectivity, it is not surprising that social science is found wanting in the eyes of writers such as Jennings and other hermeneutically inclined administrators and policy analysts.

The difficulties we canvassed in our discussion of subjectivism concerning knowledge of intentions also apply to knowledge of intersubjective meanings, for it is the intersubjectively observable cues that form the basis of our empirical evidence for shared meanings. But if meanings are publicly available, why not just keep the cues that constitute the public evidence and let the meanings go? As we have been emphasizing, the answer, of course, is that the evidence is bound together by a folk-theoretic account of human behaviour. We are assumed to act with reasons to fulfil purposes. Success at identifying the right purpose in Jennings's case depends heavily on such personal characteristics as insight and creativity. And because it is the agent's 'own' intentions, or purposes — correctly identified by the cultural administrator or policy analyst — which are the purportedly solid grounds for action, interpretive administration and policy counsel are said to be more democratic, and even emancipatory. The argument for the emancipatory potential of policy analysis, infused by critical theory, is presented by, for example, Dallmayr (1980–81) and Nielsen (1983). While we do not argue the point here, suffice it to note that the problems encountered by a critical theory version of policy analysis are likely to make it founder on the same rocks on which its educational administration cousin came to grief. Although Jennings rightly rejects a Diltheyan introspectivism by resorting to purposes, 'publicly available concepts and meanings' still have their problems.

We have already noted that familiar criticisms of empiricism lead to identical problems in specifying the content of folk-theoretic notions, resulting in a systematic indeterminacy of interpretation. However, suppose individual meanings could be identified correctly, as claimed by the special method of understanding. We would still have to single out the correct (representative) one since there is always more than one interpretation of, or perspective on, what Jennings calls the 'public interest'. This identification, in turn, depends on the personal characteristics of the analyst. Since these differ between people, we could end up with as many views as the number of analysts consulted on a particular policy. In the absence of clear adjudication criteria a certain arbitrariness invests decision making in interpretive policy analysis, and it is difficult to see how the claim to be ethically superior could be maintained.

Jennings is aware of the need to specify the relationship between data and decision making in post-positivist interpretive social science. For example, he acknowledges that such interpretation

. . . is not a nonempirical or antiempirical mode of analysis. The notion that it is rests on a simple confusion between empirical analysis and empiricism as an epistemological doctrine. Interpretive social science is incompatible with the latter but not with the former. The real question raised by interpretive social science is not whether empirical data are relevant to the analysis — that is taken for granted, without data there is nothing to interpret — but what kinds of data are useful and how they are to be interpreted (Jennings 1983, pp. 18–19).

Now Jennings may well reject empiricism as an epistemological doctrine, but in the absence of an epistemological examination of interpretive social science, and by continuing to equate natural science with positivism, his notion of empirical evidence remains problematical. Jennings's alternative to the synoptic tradition's inability to incorporate values unfortunately results in a conception of policy analysis which, while having gained 'values', has lost the empirical world. Policy decisions in this model are, in the end, based on the analyst's personal characteristics, intuition, and creativity; like the individual subjective preferences or feelings of the synoptic tradition, there is evidently no fact of the matter to be adjudicated here.

In this debate between traditional science and subjectivist interpretation, we have the usual dichotomous treatment of knowledge and values. Traditional science observations are objective and values subjective. For the subjectivist, convinced of the case against science, subjectivity intrudes on data and so-called objectivity looks rather more mind-dependent. But unless additional, coherentist criteria of evidence are used, the case against the objectivity of data becomes the case for 'anything goes'. In practice, interpretivists settle for an uneasy balance, trading a posit of brute data off against the ubiquity of subjectivity their epistemology demands.

As should be clear from our discussion of ethics in the previous chapter, we think that our coherentist resolution of the objectivity/subjectivity dichotomy has consequences for the dispute between synoptic and anti-synoptic theorists in policy studies. Both dichotomies, as we have presented them, cut across each other on several points. On the question of integrating values into policy theory, our coherentism clearly suggests an anti-synoptic approach, at least in methodology, though one which places a premium on attempts at global theorizing. For our semantic holism implies that ethical claims, as part of our whole web of belief, enjoy the same kind of empirical support as other claims in the web. Moreover, they are learnt in much the same way, from infancy onwards, via a process of conjecture and refutation mediated by holistic considerations of theoretical virtue.

Since the most important factor in solving any problem is the presence of good theory, policy advice, in providing solutions to problems (rather than merely misleading or deceiving), will need to preserve in the long term a framework for the growth of knowledge. This is essentially Popper's point about piecemeal social planning, which we will elaborate in the next section. So when it comes to values in policy making and analysis, the values of most fundamental importance will be those concerned with promoting the social relations of inquiry demanded by the epistemic process of conjecture and refutation.

It is arguable that there are worse alternatives in policy than unchecked error. But given the ubiquity of error, and the scope of some policies, the price can be extremely high. Under these conditions, it is reasonable to think that the values of tolerance, freedom of speech and thought, openness of debate and discussion, and a promoting of learning and scholarship would be touchstone values in policy. If so, there will be a congruence between our grounds for incorporating values into policy and our basic approach to the problem of complexity.

Complexity and Policy Choice

In a game of chance, a regular, approximately uniformly dense six-sided die is thrown. It is theoretically possible to calculate the face-up side given the laws of physics and a comprehensive knowledge of the various forces acting on the die; the forces imparted at a toss, the direction and strength of the prevailing wind, the resistance of the substance on which it lands. It would be a prodigious exercise in data gathering and calculation. Several die of nonuniform density would pose more of a challenge. And considered as a physical system amenable to the known laws of nature, human beings in their social life are several orders of magnitude more complex still. Seen against this level of complexity, what needs to be marvelled at is the sheer orderliness of the vast bulk of individual and social human behaviour, and the power of our ordinary conceptual equipment for rendering such a large portion of it predictable and intelligible. It is worth making this point at the beginning of any consideration of why the synoptic approach to policy may not be an achievable ideal, since what we fall short of appears slight in comparison to what we achieve in the normal course of socialization.

The synoptic ideal of policy and planning calls for the identification of all relevant values, a comprehensive survey of all alternative ways of realizing those values as well as the consequences of each alternative, and the selection of a course of action that optimizes the realization of those values. According to Lindblom, the synoptic ideal is not adapted to, among other things, limited human problem-solving capacities, the inadequacy of information, and the cost of analysis (Braybrooke and Lindblom, 1963, pp. 48–51). After defining objective rationality in a clearly synoptic way, Herbert Simon notes, in a discussion of the psychology of administrative decisions, three similar constraints which limit the rationality of decision making: 'knowledge of consequences is always fragmentary . . . values can only be imperfectly anticipated . . . only a few of all these possible alternatives ever come to mind' (Simon 1976, p. 81).

A significant part of the traditional scientific problem of policy analysis is precisely the riskiness of predictions because they are based on inadequate information and computational resources. To help overcome this failing, Lindblom suggested a range of simplifying stratagems in an approach he named 'disjointed incrementalism': for example, limiting analysis to a few familiar alternatives; exploring only some of the (more important) possible consequences of a policy alternative; dividing the work of analysis 'to many (partisan) participants in policy making' (Lindblom 1979, p. 517). Simon would endorse the first two stratagems, with a difference over the third perhaps reflecting a more fundamental disagreement. For Simon sees rational objective choice as a goal which we should approach as closely as is practicable (Simon 1976, p. 241), whereas Lindblom sees striving towards the impossible as mistaken. What seems relevant to this difference is the question of whether risk-free prediction of social phenomena is possible in principle. Popper's anti-synoptic arguments against utopian social planning show that it is not, with the most comprehensive, though not the most decisive, statement of these to be found in *The Poverty of Historicism* (1957).

Looked at as an epistemological problem, the central questions for the policy maker or analyst are: whether the background theories underwriting policy are known to be true, whether proposals will have the social outcomes they purport to have if implemented, and whether we can improve policy through learning from the consequences of our earlier actions. Popper's epistemology implies both a procedure for dealing with analogues in the physical sciences — the familiar framework of learning by conjecture and refutation — and, since this theory of learning is so general, a case for the unity of physical and social science methodology. In particular, the complexity and massive interconnectedness of social life, together with our ignorance, imply for Popper severe constraints on the social relations of social inquiry (Popper 1957, pp. 64–93). The point is that learning in this way requires identifiable potential falsifiers. Systematic social change makes it impossible to connect up the conjectures of large-scale policy with any epistemically useful consequences. Our best hope for rational social improvement therefore lies in planning for small-scale change: piecemeal social engineering.

Can we ever build up our knowledge of social causation, and thus substantially increase the power of our predictive apparatus to make large-scale planning worthwhile? Popper's negative reply is based on two premises: the first is that social change and development is strongly influenced by the growth of knowledge; and the second is that 'We cannot predict by rational or scientific methods, the future growth of our scientific knowledge' (Popper 1957, pp. v–vi). The first premise can pass without comment, but it may be useful to give the essence of Popper's strategy for the second, since it is based on a number of technical arguments discovered after the manuscript for *The Poverty of Historicism* had been finalized. We mention just one argument.

In 1931 Kurt Gödel proved the metamathematical result that for any deductive system, S, of sufficient strength (for example sufficient to include elementary arithmetic) it is always possible to construct a true sentence of elementary number theory, G, that cannot be proven within that system (Quine 1961, pp. 16–18). Gödel also showed that the statement, H, which asserts that G (a Gödel sentence) is undecidable in S, is also undecidable in S. Defining prediction as an instance of deduction from a set of premises (which include the usual rules of deduction), Popper specified a calculating, or predicting machine, C, to correspond to some S (Popper 1950). He then constructed a physical prediction statement, 'one about a [future] physical state of C — that cannot be decided by C' (1950, p. 180). But not only are there some states of C that C cannot predict. If we concatenate all our predictors into some 'society' of predictors, then there will be some future social states that this society cannot predict. Since we also cannot know which states will be unpredictable, Popper concludes that a principled indeterminacy invests all social planning.

We have been suggesting that the way in which a conclusion like this might get translated into consequences for the conduct of rational policy analysis and planning is partly an epistemological issue (a suggestion, incidentally, that Lasswell, Lindblom, Simon and Popper would support). The sort of epistemic holism we have been advocating for the incorporation of values into a broadened science of decision making runs counter to an important point of detail in Popper's analysis. For values, on Popper's (early) view, come out as unfalsifiable and are therefore not a part of a proper scientific theory. (It should be noted, however, that Collingridge 1982 contains a Popperian epistemology and a systematic Popperian methodology for falsifying value claims in policy analysis.) In opposition, what needs to be acknowledged is semantic holism, the complexity of test situations, and the holistic nature of falsification. For example, in identifying so-called crucial falsifying experiments, one must presume as stable, or fixed, a very large amount of background theory.

Just which part of our total theory it is reasonable to count as stable background, immune from the consequences of recalcitrant experience, is controversial, though usually less problematic for very well-structured problems or test situations (see Haig 1987; Lakatos 1970, pp. 91–196). But a corresponding procedure for social experimentation is difficult to specify. This is because the problem of unintended consequences, of ramifying causal chains, blurs the boundary between policies that make for small changes and those whose consequences are more systematic. However, the existence of possibly extravagant unintended consequences follows directly from the anti-synoptic arguments used to underwrite piecemeal change.

The solution everyone adopts in practice is to employ a very old and pervasive theory of social explanation; one that is embedded in the categories of our most familiar commonsense, and which we imbibe when we learn our first language. We are speaking once again of the belief-desire folk-theoretic hypothesis for human conduct. On this hypothesis, people behave the way they do in virtue of a suitable coordination of beliefs and desires; as Aristotle observed, we say of ourselves that we behave rationally.

Since it is a theory that has developed over a very long span of human experience — though until comparatively recently, an experience uninformed by a knowledge of the microphysical causal detail of human life (neuroscience, endocrinology, and the like) — it seems reasonable to expect it to be just about optimal as a predictor of human behaviour under conditions of massive ignorance of causes. And so it appears, even to the point of persuading some theorists of a principled bifurcation between reasons and causes (e.g. Peters 1958; Szasz 1961; Giddens 1982). For these theorists, a causal account is thought necessary only at the edges of reason, where a pathology of the irrational is required (Walker 1984, pp. 93–121).

This is an illusion, of course, since all behaviour is caused, but it makes one wonder how much microphysical detail is required for accurate macrophysical prediction. Popper evidently finds the requirements to be modest, even citing the rationality of social situations as evidence for their being less complicated than corresponding physical situations (Popper 1957, p. 140). A principle more congenial to the less compromising (property monist) materialist is that provided by the physicist Edwin Jaynes:

> If any macrophenomenon is found to be reproducible, then it follows that all microscopic details that were not under the experiment's control must be irrelevant for understanding and predicting it (Jaynes 1985, p. 256).

Reflections on Jaynes's observations are what prompt us to be optimistic about a thorough-going science of administration, at least in the longer term. It is the empirical adequacy of folk theory, its sheer usefulness in getting us around in our social world, which makes it unnecessary for us to focus on the causal detail of human behaviour, at least for most of the time. There are anomalies of course. These exist, as we have mentioned, where reason lapses, or motives seem obscure, or where required beliefs are too strange or implausible to be reasonably posited. But it is precisely the presence of anomalies that drives theory change and development. The challenge is to find a more coherent physicalist account of both anomalies and the empirical success of folk theory. Without such an account in hand it is important to have some reason for treating folk theory instrumentally. Jaynes's observation provides such a reason.

Consider a simple example. Someone throws you a ball and you catch it. The full microphysical causal story for plotting the trajectory of the ball seems formidably complex because of the variety of individual trajectories involved for all the ball's microcomponents. The vital point, however, is that this huge variety cancels out to give a net result able to be characterized approximately (and hence incorrectly) as a homogeneous mass. The folk category 'ball' thus abstracts nicely from all the causal detail that has negligible net empirical effect. Given that we are creatures enmeshed in a comprehensive causal field, it is helpful to see 'inner' explanatory variables like belief, desire, intention, and motive as describing the net result of a myriad of physical interactions. Provided human behaviour is sufficiently regular and predictable to be reproducible under modest conditions, no further queries arise as to the adequacy of these explanatory categories.

We expect the belief-desire hypothesis of our ordinary folk psychology will continue to provide the strategic entering wedge on the problem of complexity in policy analysis for some time to come, since if Jaynes is right only significant failures in prediction will prompt an acknowledgement of important microphysical detail. Still, there are diverse areas where the hypothesis fares badly: for example, learning theory — regrettably still dominated in education by folk psychological sentential processing models — and penology, where the mad/bad distinction has been under attack for some time.

The familiar folk categories of belief, desire, and intention have come to be seen as too parochial for the study of most natural phenomena. If developments in the natural sciences render them likewise for human natural phenomena we may then have the beginnings of a systematic policy science, and a different approach to complexity. In the meantime we prosper by confronting complexity with reliable simple falsehoods (Stich 1983; Churchland 1986).

Summary

The turmoil we have observed as characteristic of current educational administration also appears to reign in the field of policy studies. Like educational administration and organizational theory, the problems encountered in this field also have their roots in an older theoretical debate. Beginning in the early 1950s, this debate concerned the merits of a synoptic, as opposed to a limited, piecemeal approach for the conduct of policy analysis. What fuelled the debate then, and what continues to keep it alive now, is the worry of how values can be made part of the policy process, and how one could go about overcoming a lack of knowledge of the complex human systems which are the objects of policy analysis and decision making. These issues, we argued, are clearly epistemological, and have been recognized as such in the policy literature.

The synoptic tradition's view of the policy sciences, represented most prominently by Harold Lasswell, attempted to acknowledge the complexity of social life by developing sophisticated strategies capable of dealing with it. We pointed out, however, that the tradition was handicapped by its supporting view of knowledge, namely logical empiricism, which denied that values could be empirically supported.

The concern over the alleged value neutrality of policy analysis, already voiced in the early days of the field, has recently been expressed in more systematic ways. Writers such as Aaron Wildavsky, and particularly Bruce Jennings, argue that policy analysis should be seen as a subjective enterprise, appropriately grounded in the interpretive social sciences with their emphasis on human values, intentionality, and intuition. But just as the cultural perspective model came to grief on the rocks of interpretivist assumptions, so Jennings's conception of policy analysis as counsel falters similarly. In addition to the critical comments made regarding interpretivism in Chapter Six, we added here some further concerns regarding the adjudication of 'public interest'. We suggested that the problem of complexity, and hence prediction of social events, was side-stepped in this model.

Given the various answers provided by policy analysts regarding the possibility of prediction in the light of complexity, we examined Popper's argument against large-scale social planning. The argument required some antecedent theory to be used to classify potential falsifiers of policy proposals. We assumed that commonsense folk theory carried much of this burden. We concluded by expressing support for a programme to eliminate folk theory from a comprehensive science of policy.

References

Arrow K.J. (1963). *Social Choice and Individual Values*. (New York: John Wiley and Sons, second edition).

Backoff R.W. and Mitnick B.M. (1986). Reappraising the promise of general systems theory for the policy sciences, in W.N. Dunn (ed.) *Policy Analysis: Perspectives, Concepts, and Methods*. (London: JAI Press Inc.).

Boyd W.L. (1988). Policy analysis, educational policy, and management: through a glass darkly? in N.J. Boyan (ed.) *Handbook of Research on Educational Administration*. (New York and London: Longman).

Braybrooke D. and Lindblom C.E. (1963). *A Strategy of Decision*. (London: Collier-Macmillan).

Callahan D. and Jennings B. (1983) (eds.). *Ethics, the Social Sciences, and Policy Analysis*.

Churchland P.S. (1986). *Neurophilosophy*. (Cambridge, Mass.: M.I.T. Press).

Churchman C.W. (1979). *The Systems Approach and Its Enemies*. (New York: Basic Books).

Collingridge D. (1982). *Critical Decision Making: A New Theory of Social Choice*. (London: Frances Pinter).

Dallmayr F. (1980–81). Values and the methodology of policy studies in *Policy Studies Journal*, 9 (4), pp. 522–534.

Dunn W.N. (1980–81) (ed.). Symposium on social values and public policy – introduction, *Policy Studies Journal*, 9 (4), pp. 518–522.

Dunn W.N. (1983) (ed.). *Values, Ethics, and the Practice of Policy Analysis*. (Lexington, Mass.: D.C. Heath).

Fay B. (1975). *Social Theory and Political Practice*. (London: George Allen and Unwin).

Fischer F. and Forester J. (1987). *Confronting Values in Policy Analysis*. (Beverley Hills, CA: Sage.)

Garson G.D. (1986). From policy science to policy analysis: a quarter century of progress, *Policy Studies Journal* 9 (4), pp. 535–544.

Giddens A. (1982). *Sociology: A Brief but Critical Introduction*. (London: Macmillan).

Habermas J. (1974). *Theory and Practice*. (London: Heinemann, translated by J. Viertel).
Haig B.D. (1987). Scientific problems and the conduct of research, *Educational Philosophy and Theory*, **19** (2), pp. 22–32.
Harsanyi J.C. (1980a). Advances in understanding rational behavior, in J.C. Harsanyi (ed.) *Essays on Ethics, Social Behavior, and Scientific Explanation*. (Dordrecht: D. Reidel).
Hesse M. (1980). *Revolutions and Reconstructions in the Philosophy of Science*. (Boston: Harvester).
Horowitz I. and Katz J. (1975). *Social Science and Public Policy in the United States*. (New York: Praeger).
Jaynes E.T. (1985). Macroscopic prediction, in H. Haken (ed.) *Complex Systems – Operational Approaches*. (New York: Springer-Verlag).
Jennings B. (1983). Interpretive social science and policy analysis, in D. Callahan and B. Jennings (eds.) *Ethics, the Social Sciences, and Policy Analysis*. (New York and London: Plenum).
Jennings B. (1987). Policy analysis: science, advocacy, or counsel, in S. Nagel (ed.) *Research in Public Policy Analysis and Management*. (Greenwich, CT: JAI Press).
Lakatos I. (1970). Falsification and the methodology of scientific research programmes, in I. Lakatos and A. Musgrave (eds.) *Criticism and the Growth of Knowledge*. (London: Cambridge University Press).
Lasswell H.D. (1951). The policy orientation, in D. Lerner and H.D. Lasswell (eds.) *The Policy Sciences*. (Stanford: Stanford University Press).
Lasswell H.D. (1958). Clarifying value judgment: principles of content and procedure, *Inquiry*, **1** (1), pp. 87–98.
Lasswell H.D. (1971). *A Pre-View of Policy Sciences*. (New York: Elsevier).
Lerner D. and Lasswell H.D. (1951) (eds.). *The Policy Sciences*. (Stanford: Stanford University Press).
Lindblom C.E. (1979). Still muddling, not yet through, *Public Administration Review*, **39** November/December.
Lowi T. (1970). Decision making vs. policy making: toward an antidote for technocracy, *Public Administration Review*, **30**.
MacRae D. (1971). Scientific communication, ethical argument, and public policy, *American Political Science Review*, **65**, pp. 38–50.
Mitchell D.E. (1984). Educational policy analysis: the state of the art, *Educational Administration Quarterly*, **20** (3), pp. 129–160.
Nielsen K. (1983). Emancipatory social science and social critique, in D. Callahan and B. Jennings (eds.) *Ethics, The Social Sciences, and Policy Analysis*. (New York and London: Plenum).
Peters R.S. (1958). *The Concept of Motivation*. (London: Routledge and Kegan Paul).
Popper K.R. (1950). Indeterminism in quantum physics and in classical physics: Part II, *British Journal for the Philosophy of Science*, **1** (3), pp. 179–188.
Popper K.R. (1957). *The Poverty of Historicism*. (London: Routledge and Kegan Paul).
Quine W.V. (1961). The ways of paradox, in W.V.O. Quine (1976) *The Ways of Paradox and Other Essays*. (Cambridge, Mass.: Harvard University Press, second edition, enlarged).
Rein M. (1983). Value-critical policy analysis, in D. Callahan and B. Jennings (eds.) *Ethics, the Social Sciences, and Policy Analysis*. (New York and London: Plenum).
Shapiro J.Z. and Berkeley T.R. (1986). Alternative perspectives on policy analysis: a response to Douglas E. Mitchell's 'Educational policy analysis: the state of the art', *Educational Administration Quarterly*, **22** (4), pp. 80–91.
Simon H. (1976). *Administrative Behavior*. (London: Macmillan, third edition, expanded with a new Introduction).
Stich S. (1983). *From Folk Psychology to Cognitive Science* (Cambridge, Mass.: M.I.T. Press).
Szasz T. (1961). *The Myth of Mental Illness*. (St. Albans: Paladin).
Waldo D. (1952). Development of theory of democratic administration, *American Political Science Review*, **46**, pp. 81–103.
Walker, J.C. (1984). Essentialism and dualism in liberal rationalist philosophy of education, in C.W. Evers and J.C. Walker (eds.) *Epistemology, Semantics and Educational Theory*. (Sydney University: Department of Education).
Wildavsky A. (1979). *Speaking Truth to Power: The Art and Craft of Policy Analysis*. (Boston: Little, Brown).

10

Research in Educational Administration: Against Paradigms

With the eclipse of traditional empiricisms as the dominant model for theory and research in the social sciences, largely as a result of influential critiques of empiricist science such as those of Thomas Kuhn and Paul Feyerabend, a more pluralistic approach to educational administration developed in the early 1970s. In the preceding chapters we have considered a range of resulting recent theoretical perspectives on educational administration. Most developments have been in opposition to early and late versions of science of administration. However, while we have been sympathetic to many of the criticisms of traditional science approaches, we have also been critical of the main alternatives offered.

In our view, we do not need alternatives to science: we need better science. Science needs to be expanded to accommodate the many important and valid points made by its critics. The fundamental feature of our programme for such an expansion is the use of a coherentist theory of justification. Foundational justification proceeds typically by identifying an epistemically privileged subset of claims and then attempting to use these to justify other claims. Traditional science of administration characteristically omits from foundations ethical claims and a range of subjective experiences. In response, alternatives have often sought to use other foundations. We believe that the mistake lies with the epistemological enterprise of foundational justification. We have therefore offered a coherentist perspective on a range of theoretical positions in order to show the importance of epistemology, the structure of coherentist critique, and the main outlines of a broadened view of science of administration. Because of the scope of this undertaking, it is best to see it as a series of beginnings, or new directions, rather than as an attempt at a comprehensive statement.

Although we offer no overview of such beginnings, we conclude in this final chapter with a survey of issues in research methodology in educational administration. The paradigms perspective which gave rise to much of the ferment, debate, and resulting pluralism in the field is reflected directly in debates over methodology; debates over whether, for example, different

213

approaches are opposed or complementary. In what follows we offer a coherentist critique of the paradigms debate. Our argument, which draws together a number of earlier results and conclusions, amounts to a defence of the epistemological unity of educational research.

While the thesis of epistemological diversity is advocated by some writers in educational research in particular, the debate between the 'quantitative' and the 'qualitative', the 'scientific' and the 'humanist', or the 'positivist' and the 'interpretive' research traditions has most commonly emphasized the diversity in research methods. In other words, what is considered to be at stake primarily is the suitability of the various available research techniques and methods in the fields of education and educational administration. This is not to say that educational researchers deny that the conduct of inquiry and the development and evaluation of its methods and findings embody a commitment to epistemological assumptions in the final analysis. It is to say, however, that epistemological concerns are often either confused with methodological ones, or they are considered to be settled, since different research methods are believed to be sanctioned by different epistemologies thus neatly carving out distinct 'spheres of influence' of the respective techniques.

In educational research and the social sciences generally, there has long been controversy over these issues as advocates of either research tradition or paradigm have tried to sort out the respective epistemological merits of these approaches and the methodological, practical, and even political relations between them. At present, there are three major views in education and educational administration research which appraise the coexistence of two apparently fundamentally different research paradigms.

The first view, already hinted at above, maintains that there are epistem- ologically different paradigms which partition educational research so that the research traditions turn out to be radically distinct, presenting different ways of knowing or forms of knowledge. In this view, research paradigms are *incommensurable*. This means that neither educational administration research nor any other form of inquiry can provide a rational method for judging between paradigms. As different ways of knowing, they are mutually incompatible, competitive ways of researching the same territory. Let us call this view the *oppositional diversity thesis*.

The second view maintains that we have epistemologically distinct para- digms which, while incommensurable, are nevertheless complementary. They are equally appropriate ways of approaching different, overlapping, or perhaps even the same research problems. We call this the *complementary diversity thesis*. Obviously, these two views agree that there is a fundamental epistemological diversity in educational research, but disagree on how to evaluate this.

The third view, the *unity thesis* (Walker and Evers 1988), denies the epistemological diversity theses of the other two views. It disagrees that

different research methods can be grouped under incommensurable paradigms, and asserts that the very idea of such paradigms is mistaken, even
incoherent. Unlike the former views for whom the question of rationally
integrating, rendering coherent, or even comparing the findings produced
by the different traditions poses a fundamental problem, the unity thesis
is not similarly afflicted. It claims that there are some shared concepts and
standards of justification, meaning, and truth for judging the respective
merits of the traditions so that they can be brought into a productive relation
with one another. This is expressed in the concept of 'touchstone', first
discussed in Chapter Two. It asserts the epistemological unity of educational
administration research, derived from the practical problems addressed.

In this final chapter we argue for the unity thesis. After a discussion of the
term 'paradigm', and of both the oppositional and complementary theses, we
show that the theory that there are research paradigms, or *P-theory*, is largely
responsible for both forms of diversity thesis. We then provide some reasons
for believing that P-theory is incoherent and argue, not unexpectedly, that
our coherentist epistemology sustains the thesis of the epistemological unity
of educational administration research. A central feature of this epistemology
is its account of *touchstone*.

Epistemology and Paradigms in Education and Educational Administration Research

If there is any agreement in the educational administration community, it is
on the field's dependence on developments in other disciplines. Given such
dependence, and in the light of theoretical movements in the social sciences
and education, Boyan recently noted that educational administration, too,
has acquired 'several highly specialized conceptual lenses, through which to
look at a particular slice of the territory . . .' (Boyan 1981, p. 7). Rejecting
for his part the notion of the field's fragmentation, Boyan rather prefers to
describe recent developments as 'new entrants in the restless and continuous
searching to make more and more sense out of the administration, organization, and operation of schools . . .' (1981, p. 8). Joining other writers
such as Sergiovanni and Greenfield, for example, he also notes that the
search for a 'meta-theory or a meta-analytical scheme for all of educational
administration has long passed'; there is no longer the one freeway to travel,
but now there are 'several freeways which run through the territory, with
only a few crossovers and intersections available' (p. 8).

Commenting on new research developments, McCarthy also applauds the
expansion of the number of theoretical frameworks because they 'have laid
the foundation for us to embark on a new era in research in educational
administration' (McCarthy 1986, p. 4). Progress in the field is afoot, she
believes, because many more 'researchers are receptive to emerging research
paradigms and alternative theoretical perspectives' (1986, p. 4). While some-

what more cautious about this new direction of the field, Culbertson never-theless also credits Kuhn's concept of 'paradigm' as having provided the 'most highly influential challenge' to logical positivism (and thus orthodox administration theory):

> In the 1970s this concept became a buzzword in different scholarly com-munities and found its way into the literature of educational administra-tion. While some took comfort in the Theory Movement's paradigmatic qualities and its significant accomplishments, others argued that the movement was passé and needed to be replaced by a new paradigm . . . (Culbertson 1988, p. 18).

Whichever way theorists have assessed the merits of the Theory Movement, it appears that an appropriate and helpful way to conceptualize it and its many challengers is in terms of 'paradigm', the current theoretical diversity in the field as 'paradigm diversity', and the possible takeover of the orthodoxy by a new paradigm as a 'paradigm shift'. Indeed, utilization of the concept, albeit often in imprecise and confused ways as Willower has noted (1988, pp. 743–744), has become widespread in educational administration.

Talk of two fundamental paradigms, as evidenced in the education literature, distinguishes between the 'scientific' and the 'interpretive' or 'humanistic', as already indicated. This distinction is commonly associated with divergent forms of explanation and understanding, an association we have already encountered, *inter alia*, in the writings of cultural perspective and critical theory advocates. Husen characterizes it as follows:

> The twentieth century has seen the conflict between two main para-digms employed in researching educational problems. The one is modeled on the natural sciences with an emphasis on empirical quantifiable observations which lend themselves to analysis by means of mathematical tools. The task of research is to establish causal relationships, to explain (*Erklären*). The other paradigm is derived from the humanities with an emphasis on holistic and qualitative information and to interpretive approaches (*Verstehen*) (Husen 1985, pp. 4335–4336).

In offering a broader, three-way taxonomy of research to account for diversity in inquiry, Popkewitz observes that

> . . . the concept of paradigm provides a way to consider this divergence in vision, custom, and tradition. It enables us to consider science as having different sets of assumptions, commitments, procedures and theories of social affairs (Popkewitz 1984, p. 35).

He assumes that 'in educational sciences, three paradigms have emerged to give definition and structure to the practice of research' (Popkewitz 1984, p. 35). After the fashion of critical theory, he identifies the paradigms as *empirical analytic* (roughly equivalent to quantitative science), *symbolic* (qualitative and interpretive or hermeneutic inquiry), and *critical* (where political criteria relating to human betterment are applied in research). Such a threefold taxonomy is also found in educational administration research in Burlingame's (1985) work. The only difference is that he does not explicitly describe his taxonomy in terms of paradigms but as 'viewpoints' (which, however, match paradigm criteria); he also names the first 'viewpoint' as that constituted by 'behavioural science'. The most developed and best known application of the concept of 'paradigm' to date, however, is Burrell and Morgan's text *Sociological Paradigms and Organizational Analysis* (1982).

Although written in the parent discipline of organizational analysis, this work has become influential enough for Griffiths to commend it as 'the most helpful book written in the past five years' (Griffiths 1985, p. 7). He also provides the reason for his praise. The book

> . . . is so useful because it, in essence, says: Stop arguing about what is *the* method, the *one* way to do research, and use all approaches, because each method allows the researcher to raise questions which could not be resolved by one approach alone (Griffiths 1985, p. 7).

As Burrell and Morgan see it, the four paradigms they identify — the interpretive, functionalist, radical structuralist, and radical humanist — make it possible to examine the world 'in terms of four sets of basic assumptions' (Burrell and Morgan 1985, p. 24) which each identify a separate social scientific reality. Since this is so, the four paradigms are mutually exclusive:

> A synthesis is not possible, since in their pure forms they are contradictory, being based on at least one set of opposing meta-theoretical assumptions. They are alternatives, in the sense that one *can* operate in different paradigms sequentially over time, but mutually exclusive, in the sense that one cannot operate in more than one paradigm at any given point in time . . . (Burrell and Morgan 1982, p. 25).

Clearly, Burrell and Morgan's view is a prime example of the epistemological oppositional diversity thesis. As for Griffiths's generous assessment of their work, it is fair to say that in a later appraisal he is no longer convinced of the fourfold division Burrell and Morgan suggest, believing that to be more a case of arithmetical convenience than of substance (Griffiths 1988, p. 43). Griffiths is also less convinced that we can in fact speak of 'paradigm diversity' in educational administration while conceding that it may have been accomplished in the social sciences. He cites as evidence the paucity of articles dealing with qualitative methods by examining the 230 proposals submitted to the 1985 American Educational Research Association annual meeting in Chicago. He found that only three proposals dealt with qualitative research and only ten employed research paradigms other than functionalism, as defined by Burrell and Morgan (Griffiths 1988, p. 46).

The preponderance of quantitative research is also supported by other studies. Although the paradigm diversity thesis seems to gain prominence in the literature, the reality of research methods is a different one. In fact, Miskel and Sandlin's (1981) examination of articles published in the *Educational Administration Quarterly*, and Lakomski's (1989) parallel study of contributions to the *Journal of Educational Administration* clearly indicate that survey research is still the dominant mode of empirical research as presented in two leading journals in the field. This result is further underlined by Tatsuoka and Silver (1988), as well as Pitner (1988). These writers also point out in addition that survey-descriptive techniques are more often than not used poorly. Among the many pitfalls educational administration researchers fall into, Tatsuoka and Silver mention:

> attributions of practical importance to statistically significant findings . . . unfounded causal inferences based on relational findings, and inappropriate statistics applied to the data at hand (Tatsuoka and Silver 1988, p. 700).

Concerns such as these have, not surprisingly, led quantitatively oriented researchers to demand more competence and rigour in applying these techniques in the hope thus to improve the quality of research carried out.

Summing up, despite the continued overreliance on quantitative methods in practice, there appears to be considerable evidence in both the education and educational administration research literature that theoretical diversity, and in particular two main research traditions embedded in it, can legitimately and properly be described as paradigms. This also applies to the different research programmes of scholars engaged in the study of teaching, as suggested by Shulman (1985, p. 3). Moreover, because these paradigms are supposedly rooted in different epistemologies, they are expected to provide significant gains in that 'different ways of thinking about the world can assist our understanding and lead to the development of new theories' (McCarthy 1986, p. 4).

Before turning to discuss the two versions of the epistemological diversity thesis, we want to draw attention to another issue which is central to the qualitative/quantitative debate, and one we have noted along the way in previous chapters. This has to do with the use of the term 'positivism' in the educational (administration) literature.

Noting the influence of 'positivism' on the formation of research traditions and the paradigms debate, Lincoln and Guba mention another common three-way distinction which they apply to *paradigm eras* — 'periods in which certain sets of basic beliefs have guided inquiry in quite different ways' (Lincoln and Guba 1985, p. 15) — rather than directly to paradigms as such. They identify these paradigm eras as prepositivist, positivist, and postpositivist. The term 'positivist' also has a history of varied usage (see Phillips 1983) but, because of the practice common among educational researchers of defining their perspectives in relation to one or more of the varieties of positivism, it is important to note some of the issues involved in the transition to postpositivism.

Recall that in philosophy of science, views of the nature of science commonly described as positivist have characterized science as value-free, basing its theories and findings on logically simple and epistemically secure observation reports, and using empirical concepts themselves deriving directly from observation. Positivism in this sense, as a form of empiricism, involves a foundational epistemology. Empirical knowledge claims are justified when they are shown to be based on secure foundations, which for logical empiricism is evidence acquired solely through empirical observation. Positivists have maintained that only the sentences of science thus justified (and the 'analytic truths' of logic and mathematics) were objectively meaningful, and that therefore here were to be drawn the limits of genuine knowledge, not simply scientific knowledge. Thus delimited, the domain of knowledge, as we saw, excluded morals, politics, and indeed any field where value judgments were made, including much of educational administration. The movement to postpositivist philosophy of science has occurred because of the undermining of such doctrines.

Now this use of 'positivist' needs to be clearly distinguished from use of the term to describe any view that science, even if conceived nonpositivistically (in the first sense), is the only way to knowledge; and that the task of philosophy, which is not sharply distinguished from but continuous with empirical science, is to find general principles common to all sciences. This means extending the use of such principles even to the regulation of human conduct and the organization of society. The move to a postpositivist (in the first sense) philosophy of science is quite compatible with such a view of the nature of science and its role in human affairs.

Unfortunately, this distinction is rarely clearly observed in epistemological discussions of educational (administration) research. It is one thing to say, with Lincoln and Guba for example, that since it has been recognized that science is more complex than building on theory-free and value-free observations, qualitative inquiry may be recognized as a legitimate approach, that the latest paradigm era sanctions more than one paradigm. It is another thing to identify science with positivism (in the first sense) and on the basis of this identification to attack all views suggesting an epistemological continuity between the natural and the social sciences including educational administration research. Ironically, many of the writers discussed previously, while they reject positivism (in both senses), retain a positivist (in the first sense) view of natural science. In this book we use 'positivist' in the first sense to refer to positivist empiricism, including logical positivism.

In summary, the move from a positivist to a postpositivist philosophy of science has been paralleled by a move from a view of educational (administration) research dominated by the quantitative tradition to a more pluralistic view. The advent of the postpositivist era in education has been characterized by an acceptance of epistemological diversity which, however, insofar as it is formulated in terms of P-theory, leaves educational (administration) research epistemologically divided. The question, then, if there are such divisions as we have noted, is whether the diversity must be oppositional, or can be harmonious.

The Oppositional Diversity Thesis

Quantitative researchers such as Kerlinger, for example, have often seen qualitative research as lacking in objectivity, rigour, and scientific controls (Kerlinger 1973, p. 401). Lacking the resources of quantification, qualitative research cannot produce the requisite generalizations to build up a set of laws of human behaviour, nor can it apply adequate tests for validity and reliability. Moreover, the positivist fact/value distinction is often employed to discredit the claims of qualitative inquiry to produce knowledge, since knowledge is value-free whereas qualitative research is irreducibly value-laden and subjective. In short, qualitative research falls short of the high standards of objectivity and the tight criteria for truth of the quantitative, or 'scientific', paradigm. Given the prestige of science, and a positivist view of science, it is easy to see why quantitative researchers have sometimes even seen qualitative research as opposed to sound scientific method.

In reply, many qualitative researchers, invoking the explanation/understanding distinction, claim that the genuinely and distinctively human dimension of education and educational administration cannot be captured by statistical generalizations and causal laws. Knowledge of human affairs is irreducibly subjective. Greenfield's 'anarchistic' theory is the strongest expression of this view in educational administration. It must grasp the meanings of actions, the uniqueness of events and the individuality of persons. From this perspective, it is easy to see the quantitative tradition as an intrusive, even alien and antihuman, approach to the study of education. 'Science' may be appropriate to the study of nature, but it distorts the study of human affairs. It is little wonder, then, that given a *de facto* domination of educational administration research by the quantitative tradition, qualitative researchers have sometimes seen it in oppositional, even antagonistic, terms.

Thus it is obvious that the debate over whether so-called quantitative research methodology is in conflict with qualitative research methodology does not revolve simply around the use of numbers, of mathematical and statistical procedures. Rather, it concerns the relation of quantification to more basic questions about objectivity, validity, reliability, and criteria for truth. For example, according to Smith and Heshusius, who have recently reasserted the oppositional diversity thesis against the increasing popularity of the other two:

> For quantitative inquiry, a logic of justification that is epistemologically foundational leads to the position that certain sets of techniques are epistemologically privileged in that their correct application is necessary to achieve validity or to discover how things really are out there. . . . From the perspective of qualitative inquiry, this line of reasoning is unacceptable. The assumptions or logic of justification in this case are not foundationalist and, by extension, do not allow that certain sets of procedures are epistemologically privileged (Smith and Heshusius 1986, p. 9).

There are two key epistemological distinctions here. Firstly, 'logic of justification' (our grounds for making claims) is distinguished from research procedures (techniques used to gather, analyse, and interpret data). Secondly, foundational epistemologies, which provide a 'logic of justification' basing our knowledge claims on supposedly secure or certain foundations (such as empirical observations), are distinguished from nonfoundational epistemologies whose 'logic of justification' involves no foundations. Later we shall query the assumption that quantitative inquiry must be foundationalist.

The key epistemological dilemma posed by Smith and Heshusius is that for the quantitative researcher there exists a mind-independent reality 'out there' that is, to some extent, knowable. Disciplined observation of it provides our epistemic foundations. Qualitative researchers, they assert, are committed to denying this. By following certain practices of inquiry that enjoy a cluster of related theoretical advantages — the advantages of internal and external validity, reliability, and objectivity — the quantitative researcher increases the likelihood of discovering something important about that reality. Its properties and the causal structures governing the orderly behaviour of its interrelated parts constitute typical goals of quantitative inquiry. What makes these goals possible, and indeed holds together the theoretical features of such inquiry, is a belief that we can know when a correspondence obtains between the sentences of a theory and the world 'out there'. It is this correspondence that makes our knowledge claims true.

It is precisely this belief that is most often questioned by qualitative researchers. Reality, or at least social reality, they frequently maintain, is something that we construct with our minds as a product of our theorizing. Theorizing shapes reality, rather than the other way around. There is simply no mind-independent or theory-independent reality to match up with or correspond to our sentences, to serve as a check on their acceptability. Under this assumption, the theoretical apparatus we employ to characterize epistemically virtuous inquiry will apparently have little use for familiar quantitative notions. Instead, distinctly alternative networks of theoretical requirements for qualitative research will need to be devised, tied to procedures for getting at subjective, or intersubjective, symbols, intentions, meanings, and understandings.

Critical theorists, as we saw, take this philosophical opposition to the 'intrusion' of the quantitative tradition into the search for knowledge of the 'genuinely human' one step further. In addition to being unable to capture the relation between the human mind and social reality, critical theorists maintain the quantitative (or empirical-analytic) tradition cannot capture the essential role of values in that kind of knowledge we need to improve the human condition. Thus, as we saw earlier, Bates argues that epistemically adequate educational research must be research that makes for *human betterment* (Bates 1980). The 'praxis' tradition in epistemology, well exemplified in recent theory by the writings of Freire (1972) and more particularly in the action research tradition (Carr and Kemmis 1983), provides a rich theoretical context for elaborating further nonquantitative criteria to replace quantitative notions of validity, reliability, and objectivity. In contrast to the usual lines drawn in the quantitative/qualitative debate, the elimination of social injustice, for example, is not merely a matter of constructing alternative realities, or alternative theories. Nor is validity simply a matter of establishing a correspondence between theory and the world, when the goal is social improvement. Rather, what counts as valid inquiry, as epistemically progressive, is limited to what the surrounding epistemology counts as promoting human well-being.

The Complementary Diversity Thesis

Within the epistemologically softer climate of the postpositivist era, many educational and educational administration researchers nowadays believe that the various research traditions, even if incommensurable, are equally legitimate and not necessarily in conflict. The 'scientific' and 'humanistic' approaches are not considered mutually exclusive but complementary to each other. Indeed, Shulman goes so far as to suggest that 'the danger for any field of social science or educational research lies in its potential corruption . . . by a single paradigmatic view' (Shulman 1985, p. 4). This sentiment is echoed clearly by writers in the cultural perspective tradition and is also expressed by Burlingame when he warns professors of educational administration not to pledge 'sole allegiance to a single viewpoint about knowledge and practice . . .' (Burlingame 1985, p. 40). Against what they have regarded as the unwarranted 'positivist', quantitative, domination of educational research, proponents of the qualitative/interpretive paradigm have succeeded in convincing a number of scholars whose work has been within the quantitative tradition, such as D. T. Campbell (1982) and L. J. Cronbach (1975), that the qualitative approach has its own merits.

Writers such as Boyan, McCarthy, and Pitner, for example, have suggested that complementarity must be recognized in view of various distinct desiderata in educational research, not all of which can be met by any one single paradigm. For example, there are pressing educational and social problems requiring policy and practical responses. The information necessary for policy formulation might not be available from controlled laboratory experiments of limited generalizability (or external validity), but might be provided by 'quasi-experiments' (Cook and Campbell, 1979) or qualitative research. This belief was central to the debates between the synoptic and anti-synoptic traditions in policy analysis, and is most pronounced in Bruce Jennings's 'policy analysis as counsel' model which we discussed in the last chapter. Moreover, given the rate of social change, or the constant 'interactive effects' of educational treatments and student aptitudes, generalizations yielded by a quantitative approach might become rapidly out of date. The project of developing a stable set of scientific educational laws may not be viable (Cronbach 1975).

For other writers espousing complementary diversity, the multifactorial complexity of educational problems supports epistemological pluralism. Keeves acknowledges that some approaches are more holistic, embracing greater complexity than others:

> The techniques employed in educational research must be capable of examining many variables at the same time, but not necessarily through the use of complex statistical procedures . . . although these have their place. Anthropologists have evolved procedures for analysing and presenting information from a situation which involves many factors that are very different from those used by psychologists, and different again from those that might be employed by economists and sociologists (Keeves 1986, p. 390).

Nevertheless, according to Campbell (1982), P-theoretical differences are still unavoidable because there remains a need for the kind of research produced by 'the tools of descriptive science and formal logic' (p. 123), which cannot embrace the value judgments characteristic of much nonquantitative educational inquiry. For other writers, fundamental epistemological differences between explanation and interpretation, of course, remain.

In educational research as well as educational administration, acceptance of the epistemological integrity of a nonquantitative paradigm has largely been the result of efforts by qualitative researchers to spell out alternative networks of theoretical requirements for qualitative research. These have tended to run parallel to elements in the received epistemological scheme of quantitative research (validity, reliability, etc.). One influential example, elaborated by Lincoln and Guba (1985), employs the notions of credibility, applicability (or transferability), consistency, and neutrality, as analogues respectively for internal validity, external validity, reliability, and objectivity.

The point here, however, is not so much that there is some loose analogical connection between corresponding terms in these sets. Rather, despite *detente*, the point to note is the persisting apparent epistemological distinctiveness of these theoretically interanimated clusters and their respective embeddings in different epistemologies. Some complementary diversity theorists appear to think that they can have fundamental epistemological diversity without subscribing to something as strong as the P-theory and its incommensurability doctrine. Here, perhaps, epistemological diversity is being confused with methodological diversity, a diversity of techniques of inquiry. Of course the latter is possible but, we maintain, is best underwritten by a touchstone account of epistemic justification, not several incommensurable epistemologies. Such an account does not have to be fixed and absolute; it can change. The point is that at any given time it embraces those epistemological commitments that are shared by researchers. This is the unity thesis. If complementary diversity theorists wish to eschew such epistemological touchstone, then they remain committed to P-theory.

It should be noted that many advocates of equal rights for qualitative research have wished to play down the epistemological differences. Thus Pitner quotes Morey and Luthans as stating that:

> The potential and real disagreements among organizational researchers over these contrasting approaches are unfortunate and can lead to neglect of common interests and interests on both sides (Pitner 1988, p. 118).

Miles and Huberman put the point even more strongly. While they believe in the basic incommensurability of the competing epistemologies, they nevertheless advise researchers to '. . . be open to an ecumenical blend of epistemologies and procedures, and leave the grand debate to those who care most about it' (Miles and Huberman 1984, p. 20). It is more important in their view to develop 'working canons and procedures to judge the validity and usefulness of research in progress' (Miles and Huberman 1984, p. 20; see also LeCompte and Goetz 1982). In addition to ignoring practically what are accepted as basic paradigmatic differences, it may be that exponents of the complementary diversity thesis who persist with the term 'paradigm' do not embrace P-theory's doctrine of incommensurability, although this is rarely made explicit. If they disavow incommensurability, their position would seem to collapse into the unity thesis, with revisionary consequences for the way they have drawn the distinctions between paradigms. These may be more drastic than at first appears. In the case of the explanation/understanding distinction, for instance, Keeves

(1988), in arguing for complementarity, has adopted Giddens's (1984) reworking of this distinction. It can be argued, however, that Giddens leaves the epistemological gap as wide as ever (Walker 1987). But, as we saw, not all complementarists have recognized the seriousness of the problem. As Smith and Heshusius put it, there has been a tendency to 'de-epistemologize' the debate or even ignore paradigmatic differences. Given that paradigms exist, Smith and Heshusius may well be right. But do paradigms exist?

Criticisms of the Paradigms Theory

It is apparent that there is some confusion over both the term 'paradigm' and the problem of identifying unambiguously paradigms of educational research. Some of the confusion comes from the ambiguity of the term 'paradigm' itself. On the one hand, as Husen points out, there would be wide agreement that the most influential use of 'paradigm' stems from the work of Kuhn. However, Masterman (1970) has identified some 22 different uses of the term in Kuhn's book; Kuhn has subsequently published revisions, some substantial, to his original theory (Kuhn 1970a, 1970b, 1974); and finally, not all methodologists embrace Kuhn's ideas uncritically.

Kuhn has also put the principal argument for regarding paradigms as incommensurable, as incapable of being compared or measured against some touchstone standard:

> In learning a paradigm the scientist acquires theory, methods, and standards together, usually in an inextricable mixture. Therefore when paradigms change, there are usually significant shifts in the criteria determining the legitimacy both of problems and of proposed solutions. . . . That observation . . . provides our first explicit indication of why the choice between competing paradigms regularly raises questions that cannot be resolved by the criteria of normal science . . . [scientists] will inevitably talk through each other when debating the relative merits of their respective paradigms. In the partially circular arguments that regularly result, each paradigm will be shown to satisfy more or less the criteria that it dictates for itself and to fall short of a few of those dictated by its opponent (Kuhn 1962, pp. 109–110).

The key claim being made here is that paradigms include both substantive theories and the standards and criteria for evaluating those theories, or *paradigm-specific epistemologies*. As such, it is also claimed, there is no privileged epistemic vantage point from which different paradigms can be assessed; there are only the rival epistemic standards built into each paradigm.

Kuhn's early comments on the task of adjudicating the merits of competing paradigms are instructive: '. . . the proponents of competing paradigms practise their trade in different worlds' (Kuhn 1962, p. 150); 'the transfer of allegiance from paradigm to paradigm is a conversion experience that cannot be forced' (p. 151); such a transition occurs relatively suddenly, like a gestalt switch 'just because it is a transition between incommensurables' (p. 150).

Moreover, the belief that some research traditions are incommensurable can be made to look initially plausible by noting the kind of tradition-specific vocabularies that are used to characterize matters epistemological. As we have seen, methodological reflection on quantitative research commonly trades in such terminology as 'scientific', 'positivist', 'foundational', 'correspondence-truth', 'objective', 'realist', 'validity', 'reliability', 'reductionist', and 'empiricist'. The qualitative network of such terms includes 'nonpositivist', 'antifoundational', 'interpretation', 'understanding', 'subjective', 'idealist', 'relativist', and 'antireductionist'. The fact that key terms of epistemic conduct in one cluster are formed by negating terms in the other cluster readily suggests no common basis for the conduct and assessment of inquiry, and hence the incommensurability of these traditions.

Clearly, for a defence of the epistemological unity of educational research, the most important obstacle is this P-theoretical analysis of research traditions. In beginning our defence of the unity thesis we note that in philosophy, and philosophy of science in particular, P-theory is widely regarded as false. In a major review of the literature following a 1969 symposium on the structure of scientific theories, Suppe remarks: 'Since the symposium Kuhn's views have undergone a sharply declining influence on contemporary work in philosophy of science' (Suppe 1974, p. 647). He goes on to claim that contemporary work in philosophy of science, that is, postpositivist philosophy of science, 'increasingly subscribes to the position that it is a central aim of science to come to know how the world *really is*' (Suppe 1974, p. 649). In social and educational research, on the other hand, especially among qualitative researchers and critical theorists, antirealist belief in paradigms remains strong. In our view, the apparent ubiquity of 'paradigms' in educational research occurs because the epistemological assumptions of the P-theory itself, or its P-epistemology, are largely responsible for structuring differences among research traditions into putative paradigms.

Of course epistemologists in general agree that inquiry structures our knowledge of the objects of inquiry; this is part of what is involved in maintaining that all experience is theory laden. Contrary to Smith and Heshusius, it is not a feature peculiar to qualitative inquiry. The interesting question is whether there is any reason to believe that different research traditions partition into paradigms the way P-theory requires. However, it is rarely noted that whether it is even appropriate to give reasons, to marshall evidence, carefully to analyse research practices and inquiry contexts in order to justify such a belief, will depend on whether P-theory is, by its own lights, a paradigm (or part of a paradigm), or not. If it is, then the relevant standards of reasoning, evidence, and analysis will be peculiar to P-theory, or its encompassing paradigm, and so will have rational epistemic purchase on none but the already committed. To the unbeliever, P-theory would literally have nothing to say for itself. For one to believe that educational research comes in paradigms would require an act of faith; to come to believe it after believing the contrary would require a conversion experience.

There are interesting problems with this view. For example, what happens if we are converted to it? Do we now say that it is *true* that educational and administration research divides into paradigms? Unfortunately the term 'true' is P-theoretical and so we need to determine first whether, for example, the sentences of P-theory correspond to a world of real educational researchers really engaged in incommensurable research practices. If so, then P-theory is not after all a paradigm distinct from those that employ correspondence-truth. If not, then there is a genuine equivocation over the term 'true' which will permit the following claims to be made without contradiction:

(1) it is correspondence-true that the different research traditions are not epistemologically distinct; and
(2) it is P-true that the different research traditions are epistemologically distinct.

But in conceding the equal legitimacy of incommensurable rivals — whether oppositional or complementary — particularly a correspondence-truth rival, the P-theorist seems to be surrendering the capacity to say anything about actual educational research practices and the historical and theoretical context of current research traditions. Worse still, in eschewing any schema for determining the ontological commitments of P-theory, there seems to be no way of knowing what the P-theorist is talking about. As such, P-theory hardly provides a challenge to a realist view of the unity of educational research.

To avoid this dilemma that threatens when P-theory goes self-referential, several options are available. We shall consider two. In the first option, a less parsimonious attitude to rival epistemologies can be adopted by maintaining that correspondence-truth theories, which caused all the trouble, are false, wrong or, as hard-hitting relativists are fond of saying, inadequate. Indeed, getting rid of correspondence truth may be a condition for meaningful P-theoretical claims about theorists living in different worlds; after all, talk of a real world tends to make other worlds pale into nonexistence. A second, opposite, strategy, is to say that P-theory is not a distinct paradigm at all, but rather a set of carefully argued, evidentially supported, correspondence-true claims about the existence of paradigmatic divisions among the major research traditions. It is instructive to note that some methodologists run both these strategies simultaneously. Lincoln and Guba do, as well as Eisner (1979, 1981). For criticism of Eisner, see Phillips (1983).

Arguments for the first option are by now familiar enough. Correspondence-truth is assumed to be located in a network of terms usually associated with the quantitative research tradition. Valid and reliable knowledge about the world is said to be that which is, in some way, derivable from some epistemically secure (or even certain) foundation: in positivist empiricism this foundation is usually observations or first person sensory reports. Objectivity consists in intersubjectively agreed matchings between statements and experience. And, of course, these objectively known statements are correspondence-true just in case the required matching occurs, although sometimes the only reality admitted is sense data.

As we have shown in preceding chapters, there are many objections to foundational empiricist epistemologies, but a version of the earlier argument from self-reference will suffice to illustrate the problems. Although this is not widely recognized in positivist empiricism, epistemology is a task that requires, as Kant saw, a theory of the powers of the mind. What we can know will depend, to some extent, on what sort of creature we are, and, in particular, on what sort of perceptual and cognitive capacities we have. A theory of the mind, however, is something we have to get to know. In the case of empiricist foundationalism what we need to know is that our own sensory experiences will provide us with epistemically secure foundations. Unfortunately for the foundationalist, the theory of mind required to underwrite this claim is not itself an item of sensory experience, nor an observation report. This means that our knowledge of how we know the class of epistemically privileged items is not itself epistemically privileged. Indeed, the sophisticated neurophysiological models of brain functioning now typical of accounts of perception and cognition are quite ill-suited to serving the regress pattern of foundational justification. For they so far outrun the purported resources of any proposed foundation that the whole point of foundational justification here collapses. More generally, our knowledge of our perceptual powers, or possible foundations, like our knowledge of everything, is theory laden. The result is that there is no epistemically privileged, theory-free, way of viewing the world. There is thus no reality that can be seen independent of competing theoretical perspectives. This applies as much to the empirical sciences, and the quantitative tradition in educational administration research, as to other areas (Walker and Evers 1982, 1986).

However, from the fact that all experience is theory laden, that what we believe exists depends on what theory we adopt, it does not follow that all theories are evidentially equivalent, or equally reasonable. There is more to evidence than observation, or as Churchland argues: 'observational excellence or "empirical adequacy" is only one epistemic virtue among others of equal or comparable importance' (Churchland 1985, p. 35). The point is that some theories organize their interpretations of experience better than others. An earlier example employing subjectivist scruples on evidence will illustrate this point. A theory which says that I can leave what I interpret to be my office by walking through what I interpret to be the wall will cohere less well with my interpreted desire to leave my office than a theory which counsels departure via what I take to be the door. It is all interpretive, of course, but some organized sets of interpretations, or theories, are better than others. The theory that enables a person to experience the desired success of departing the perceived enclosure of an office enjoys certain epistemic advantages over one that does not. With all experience interpreted, though, the correct conclusion to draw is not that we have no adequate objective standard of reality, but that objectivity involves more than empirical adequacy. Success in getting in and out of rooms is something of a benchmark for objectivity. There are superempirical, theoretical tests which can be couched in a *coherence epistemology*. One advocate of coherence epistemology, the postpositivist philosopher Quine, sums up this standard of reality:

> Having noted that man has no evidence for the existence of bodies beyond the fact that their assumption helps him organize experience, we should have done well, instead of disclaiming evidence for the existence of bodies, to conclude: such, then, at bottom, is what evidence is, both for ordinary bodies and molecules (Quine 1960a, p. 251).

Quine's point here foreshadows a significant epistemological consequence of this attack on foundationalism. According to Quine, and many coherence theorists, we need to distinguish sharply between the theory of evidence and the theory of truth, as we argued in some detail in Chapter Two (see Williams 1980). Theory of evidence is concerned with the global excellence of theory, and involves both empirical adequacy inasmuch as this can be achieved, and the superempirical virtues of simplicity, consistency, comprehensiveness, fecundity, familiarity of principle, and explanatory power. Once we have our best theory according to these coherence criteria, it is the resulting theory itself that we use to tell us what exists and how the theory's sentences match up with that posited reality. What corresponds to true sentences is therefore something that is determined after the theory of evidence has done its work. It is not something that figures *a priori*, or in some privileged foundational way in the determination of the best theory.

This conclusion suggests that P-theory critiques of foundationalism draw too radical a conclusion. In terms of the quantitative/qualitative debate, for example, the coherence epistemology sanctioned by the most powerful criticisms of empiricist foundationalism, cuts across the familiar methodological, putatively paradigmatic bifurcation. In acknowledging the theory ladenness of all experience it is nonpositivist and nonfoundational. It agrees that our window on the world is mind-dependent and subject to the interpretations of theorists. On the other hand, it can be realist, scientific, objective, reductionist, and embrace correspondence-truth. This possibility raises serious doubts about P-theorists' claims concerning the diversity of educational administration research, whether oppositional or complementary.

A more systematic objection to P-theory can be raised, however, by examining the epistemological warrant for incommensurability. The belief that research methodologies comprising incommensurable networks of theoretical terms are epistemically autonomous is sustained in large measure by a particular theory of meaning, notably that terms gain what meaning they possess in virtue of their role in some network or conceptual scheme. Where conceptual schemes or theories are said to be systematically different, no basis exists for matching the terms of one theory with those of another. So expressions such as 'validity' or 'truth', which appear as orthographically equivalent across different schemes, are really equivocal, with systematic differences emerging as differences in conceptual role. Both Kuhn and Feyerbend maintain versions of the conceptual role theory of meaning. The trouble, however, is that they maintain implausibly strong versions of it, for if meaning is determined entirely by conceptual role then incommensurable theories become unlearnable.

This all turns on the modest empirical fact that as finite learners we need some point of entry into an elaborate systematically interconnected vocabulary like a theory. But in order to learn some small part of a theory, say a handful of expressions, P-epistemology requires us to have mastered the whole theory in order to appreciate the conceptual role played by these expressions. It is at this point that the theory of meaning begins to outrun its own epistemological resources: it posits learned antecedents of learning that cannot themselves be learned. We cannot understand the parts unless we have mastered the whole, and we lack the resources to master the whole without first scaling the parts. An implicit feature of the epistemology driving P-theory's account of meaning as conceptual role is thus an implausibly strong theory of the powers of the mind. (We should note in passing that a P-theoretical attack on correspondence-truth appears to depend on a correspondence-true theory of mind.)

Once again we have observed P-theory getting into difficulty over self-reference. In this case an epistemology should come out knowable on its own account of knowledge. The chief advantage of arguments from self-reference is that they focus directly on the superempirical virtues or weaknesses of a theory.

Inasmuch as we are impressed by such theoretical shortcomings as inconsistency, lack of explanatory power in relation to rivals, use of ad hoc hypotheses, and so on, we are allowing these criteria to function as touchstone in the evaluation of epistemologies and research methodologies. Of course we can ignore these vices in theory construction: they are not extratheoretical privileged foundations by which all theorizing can be assessed. But methodologists in the main research traditions who expect their inquiries to command attention, serve as a sound basis for action, or constitute a particular or definite set of knowledge claims have, as a matter of fact, been unwilling to play fast and loose with such virtues as consistency. This is usually on the formal ground that a contradiction will sanction any conclusion whatever — or simplicity and comprehensiveness — on the ground that the ad hoc, or arbitrary addition of hypotheses, can be used to explain anything whatsoever, and hence nothing at all. Indeed, a theory cannot be empirically significant unless it is consistent. With P-theory's theory of meaning exhibiting the superempirical weakness of lack of explanatory power in relation to what it sets itself to explain, and with that weakness being traceable to a theory of mind, we should observe that whether epistemologies or methodologies are incommensurable turns on such things as empirical theories of mind or brain functioning, theories of learning and cognition. Epistemology itself is therefore continuous with, and relies upon, empirical science. In Quine's words, epistemology is 'naturalized' (Quine 1969). One consequence is that interpretive theorists, for example, must, incoherently, rely on the 'scientific' paradigm in order to show the incommensurability of their own paradigm with the 'scientific'.

The Unity Thesis

Although the paradigms perspective is seriously flawed, some account of the kind of unity educational administration research actually enjoys still needs to be given. In arguing against P-theory, we have already drawn on coherence epistemology. To conclude this chapter, we shall briefly outline a particular version of coherentism, or epistemological holism, which has achieved considerable prominence in postpositivist philosophy and has more recently been applied to educational philosophy (Walker and Evers 1982). In particular, it has been argued that there is no logically consistent way to partition the domain of knowledge into radically distinct forms of knowledge (Evers and Walker 1983).

We note that a more productive epistemological agenda for educational administration research can be provided by responding to the second strategy a P-theorist can adopt in defending diversity. Recall that this strategy involved denying that P-theory was a distinct paradigm, conceding correspondence-truth, but arguing that fundamental epistemological diversity still occurred in educational research. In replying to this claim we can note that the strategy will need to employ superempirical epistemic virtues to be persuasive. To be effective against a wide range of theoretical perspectives these virtues (consistency, simplicity, fecundity, etc.) will need to be recognized as such by rival epistemologies and hence function as touchstone. As a result, the P-theorists' strategy is already compromised. To complete the job, however, we need a coherence epistemology that yields a touchstone coherent account of itself and its own epistemic virtues, that is unproblematically self-referential in scope, and that can account for the touchstone-recognized successes of alternative epistemologies and their research extensions.

In our view, the epistemology that best accounts for knowledge, its growth, and evaluation is a form of holistic scientific naturalism (in Quine's 'epistemology naturalized' sense of 'naturalism'), a theory that makes ready use of our best or most coherent theories of perception and cognition. On this view, we are acquiring our theory of the world from infancy onward. Indeed, as Quine (1960b) has shown, theory precedes all learning and hence commences with our innate complement of dispositions to respond selectively to the environment. Human knowledge is dependent on the kind of creature we are and, as human beings, we are all one kind of creature. We share genetically derived, though culturally expressed, refined and modified touchstone standards and procedures. Added to these is further culturally produced touchstone we acquire as social beings sharing material problems in concrete social contexts. Our knowledge is made up of our theories, whose existence is to be explained causally, as problem-solving devices. There are numerous philosophical accounts of how theories can be analysed as problem-solving devices (e.g. Lakatos 1970; Laudan 1977). In the case of epistemological theories, the problems arise from theoretical practice, including empirical (e.g. educational) research. Clearly, there are certain issues concerning whether a theory is addressing the right problem, and we will need a theory of how to distinguish between real problems and pseudoproblems, and between better and worse formulations of problems. Here our epistemology would lean on a theory of evidence and experiment, on the pragmatic relations between 'theory' and 'practice' (Walker 1985b).

One real problem, shared by all educational researchers, is how best to conduct inquiry into human learning itself. Without this problem there could be no debate about whether educational research is epistemologically diverse. For there to be an issue at all presupposes at least some sharing of language, including general epistemological terminology such as 'truth', 'meaning', 'adequacy', 'interpretation', 'paradigm', and so on.

Competition remains, of course, but it is competition between theories, including theories of educational research methodology, not paradigms. Competition arises because, in addition to touchstone, there are unshared — which is not to say incommensurable — concepts, hypotheses, and rules of method. Indeed, this is part and parcel of our being able to distinguish one theory from another in a competitive situation. There can be genuine competition between theories, however, only when they have an issue over which to compete, some shared problem(s). Theory A is in competition with theory B when one or more of its sentences is contrary to sentences in theory B. For this situation to obtain, theories A and B must be attempts at solving at least one common problem. To identify a shared problem involves some conceptual common ground and, if only implicitly at first, some shared method: the concepts have to be deployed. Thus we begin to discover and negotiate touchstone theory which, unlike the privileged epistemic units of foundational epistemologies, is merely the shifting and historically explicable amount of theory that is shared by rival theories and theorists. Beginning with identification of common problems, we can proceed to identify further touchstone and elaborate the touchstone frameworks within which theories compete.

Having identified common ground between theories, we next rigorously set out their differences and test them against the touchstone by empirical research and theoretical analysis, seeking to identify the strengths and weaknesses of each, and reach a decision on the theory which is strongest under present circumstances, taking into account past achievements and likely future problems.

Other features of this epistemology include its capacity to survive its own test of self-reference, its unified account of validity and reliability, its denial that all science consists of sets of laws, and of any fundamental epistemological distinction between explanation and understanding (Walker 1985a), or between fact and value judgments (Evers 1987).

Finally, although we have maintained that such a coherentist epistemology is a sound way of underwriting the epistemological unity of educational administration research, achieved through touchstone analysis, it should be stressed that it is as much a competing theory as any other, and subject to touchstone testing. Granted that it shares touchstone with other epistemologies, arguments can of course be mounted against it. But to engage in such arguments, all participants would be implicitly conceding the epistemological unity of research.

Summary

Contemporary research in education and educational administration seems to have settled for the notion that different research methods are underwritten by their respective epistemologies, and that educational research is guided by paradigms. Where disagreements occur, they concern the relationship between the paradigms, namely, between the 'quantitative/positivist' on the one hand, and the 'qualitative/hermeneutic' on the other. We identified three views of this relationship. The first maintains that paradigms, as different ways of knowing, are incommensurable, and thus in opposition to each other (the oppositional diversity thesis). The second view holds that, despite their incommensurability, paradigms are complementary and can be employed fruitfully to study the many objects of educational research (the complementary diversity thesis). The third, preferred, alternative argues that the epistemological diversity presumed in the other two is mistaken (the unity thesis). Since the thesis of epistemological diversity is premised on the existence and validity of paradigms, we examined this originally Kuhnian theory (P-theory, as we called it) and found it to be wanting. In particular, P-theory fails, we argued, because the case for incommensurability requires an exceptionally strong version of the conceptual role theory of meaning. The result is that P-theory cannot be learned. We concluded that P-theory is incoherent.

Finally, we applied the framework of our coherentist epistemology to argue for the unity of research in educational administration which, unlike its competitors, does not posit foundations but employs coherence criteria, both in the defence of its own assumptions and as critical weapons against other theories' knowledge claims. Since even rival epistemologies do not advocate lack of consistency as a virtue, consistency and other coherence criteria can function as touchstone when arbitrating between competing claims or theories. Because our coherentist conception of educational administration research methodology is in principle open, believing in theory competition which builds on initial touchstone, however modest, we argued that it facilitates the growth of knowledge. A research methodology which possesses this quality, we submitted, is truly educative, in education and educational administration alike.

References

Bates R. J. (1980). New developments in the new sociology of education, *British Journal of Sociology of Education*, **1** (1), pp. 67–79.

Boyan N. J. (1981). Follow the leader: commentary on research in educational administration, *Educational Researcher*, **10** (2), pp. 6–13.

Burlingame, M. (1985). Pity the poor professor of educational administration: the puzzlements of knowledge and of practice, *The Journal of Educational Administration*, **23** (1), pp. 39–52.

Burrell G. and Morgan G. (1982). *Sociological Paradigms and Organizational Analysis*. (London: Heinemann, reprinted).

Campbell D. T. (1982). Experiments as arguments, in E. House (ed.) *Evaluation Studies Review Annual*. (Beverly Hills: Sage).

Carr W. and Kemmis S. (1983). *Becoming Critical: Knowing Through Action Research*. (Victoria, Australia: Deakin University Press).

Churchland P. M. (1985). The ontological status of observables: in praise of the superempirical virtues, in P. M. Churchland and C. A. Hooker (eds.) *Images of Science*. (Chicago: University of Chicago Press).

Cook T. D. and Campbell D. T. (1979). *Quasi-Experimentation. Design and Analysis Issues for Field Settings*. (Chicago: Rand McNally).

Cronbach L. J. (1975). Beyond the two disciplines of scientific psychology, *American Psychologist*, **30** (2), pp. 116–126.

Culbertson J. A. (1988). A century's quest for a knowledge base, in N. J. Boyan (ed.) *Handbook of Research on Educational Administration*. (New York and London: Longman).

Eisner E. (1979). *The Educational Imagination*. (New York: Macmillan).

Eisner E. (1981). A rejoinder, *Educational Researcher*, **10** (10), pp. 25–26.

Evers C. W. (1987). Epistemology and the structure of educational theory: some reflections on the O'Connor–Hirst debate, *Journal of Philosophy of Education*, **21** (1), pp. 3–13.

Ever C. W. and Walker J. C. (1983). Knowledge, partitioned sets, and extensionality, *Journal of Philosophy of Education*, **17** (2), pp. 155–170.

Freire P. (1972). *Cultural Action for Freedom*. (Harmondsworth: Penguin).

Giddens A. (1984). *The Constitution of Society*. (Cambridge and Oxford: Polity Press and Blackwell).

Griffiths D. E. (1985). Administrative theory in transition, in D. E. Griffiths *Administrative Theory in Transition*. (Victoria, Australia: Deakin University Press).

Griffiths D. E. (1988). Administrative theory, in N. J. Boyan (ed.) *Handbook of Research on Educational Administration*. (New York and London: Longman).

Husen T. (1985). Research paradigms in education, in T. Husen and T. N. Postlethwaite (eds.) *International Encyclopedia of Education*. (Oxford: Pergamon).

Keeves J. P. (1986). Theory, politics and experiment in educational research methodology: a response, *International Review of Education*, 32 (4), p. 390.

Keeves J. P. (1988). Social theory and educational research, in J. P. Keeves (ed.) *Educational Research, Methodology, and Measurement. An International Handbook*. (Oxford: Pergamon).

Kerlinger F. N. (1973). *Foundations of Behavioral Research. Educational and Psychological Inquiry*. (New York: Holt, Rinehart and Winston, second edition).

Kuhn T. S. (1962). *The Structure of Scientific Revolutions*. (Chicago: University of Chicago Press).

Kuhn T. S. (1970a). Postscript — 1969, in T. S. Kuhn *The Structure of Scientific Revolutions*. (Chicago: University of Chicago Press, second edition, enlarged).

Kuhn T. S. (1970b). Reflections on my critics, in I. Lakatos and A. Musgrave (eds.) *Criticism and the Growth of Knowledge*. (London: Cambridge University Press).

Kuhn T. S. (1974). Second thoughts about paradigms, in F. Suppe (ed.) *The Structure of Scientific Theories*. (Chicago: University of Illinois Press).

Lakatos I. (1970). Falsification and the methodology of scientific research programmes, in I. Lakatos and A. Musgrave (eds.) *Criticism and the Growth of Knowledge*. (London: Cambridge University Press).

Lakomski G. (1989). The journal of educational administration: mainstream, tributory, or billabong? in G. Harman (ed.) *Review of Australian Research in Education: No 1*. (Armidale: Australian Association for Research in Education).

Laudan L. (1977). *Progress and its Problems. Towards a Theory of Scientific Growth*. (London: Routledge and Kegan Paul).

LeCompte M. and Goetz J. (1982). Problems of reliability and validity in educational research, *Review of Educational Research*, 52 (1), pp. 31–60.

Lincoln Y. S. and Guba E. G. (1985). *Naturalistic Inquiry*. (Beverly Hills: Sage).

Masterman M. (1970). The nature of a paradigm, in I. Lakatos and A. Musgrave (eds.) *Criticism and the Growth of Knowledge*. (London: Cambridge University Press).

McCarthy M. (1986). Research in educational administration: promising signs for the future, *Educational Administration Quarterly*, 22 (1), pp. 3–20.

Miles M. and Huberman M. (1984). Drawing valid meaning from qualitative data. Towards a shared craft, *Educational Researcher*, 13 (5), pp. 20–30.

Miskel C. and Sandlin T. (1981). Survey research in educational administration, *Educational Administration Quarterly*, 17 (4), pp. 1–20.

Phillips D. C. (1983). After the wake: postpositivistic educational thought, *Educational Researcher*, 12 (5), pp. 4–12.

Pitner N. J. (1988). The study of administrator effects and effectiveness, in N. J. Boyan (ed.) *Handbook of Research on Educational Administration*. (New York and London: Longman).

Popkewitz T. (1984). *Paradigm and Ideology in Educational Research*. (London: Falmer Press).

Quine W. V. (1960a). Posits and reality, in S. Uyeda (ed.) *Bases of Contemporary Philosophy*, *Vol. 5*. (Tokyo: Waseda University Press).

Quine W. V. (1960b). *Word and Object*. (Cambridge, Mass.: M.I.T. Press).

Quine W. V. (1969). Epistemology naturalized, in W. V. Quine *Ontological Relativity and Other Essays*. (New York: Columbia University Press).

Shulman L. (1985). Paradigms and research programs in the study of teaching. A contemporary perspective, in M. C. Wittrock (ed.) *Handbook of Research on Teaching*. (New York: Macmillan, third edition).

Smith J. K. and Heshusius L. (1986). Closing down the conversation. The end of the qualitative/quantitative debate among educational inquirers, *Educational Researcher*, 15 (1), pp. 4–12.

Suppe F. (1974) (ed.) *The Structure of Scientific Theories*. (Chicago: University of Illinois Press).

Tatsuoka M. and Silver P. (1988). Quantitative research methods in educational administration, in N. J. Boyan (ed.) *Handbook of Research on Educational Administration*. (New York and London: Longman).

Walker J. C. (1985a). Materialist pragmatism and sociology of education, *British Journal of Sociology of Education*, **6** (1), pp. 55–74.

Walker J. C. (1985b). The philosopher's touchstone. Towards pragmatic unity in educational studies, *Journal of Philosophy of Education*, **19** (2), pp. 181–198.

Walker J. C. (1987). Giddens on structure and agency. Unpublished. (University of Sydney, Australia: Department of Social and Policy Studies in Education).

Walker J. C. and Evers C. W. (1982). Epistemology and justifying the curriculum of educational studies, *British Journal of Educational Studies*, **30** (2), pp. 312–329.

Walker J. C. and Evers C. W. (1986). Theory, politics, and experiment in Educational Research Methodology, *International Review of Education*, **32** (4), pp. 373–387.

Walker J. C. and Evers C. W. (1988). The epistemological unity of educational research, in J. P. Keeves (ed.) *Educational Research, Methodology and Measurement: An International Handbook*. (Oxford: Pergamon).

Williams M. (1980). Coherence justification and truth, *Review of Metaphysics*, **34** (2), pp. 243–272.

Willower D. J. (1988). Synthesis and projection, in N. J. Boyan (ed.) *Handbook of Research on Educational Administration*. (New York and London: Longman).

Author Index

Achinstein, P.   3
Adorno, T.   151
Aldrich, H.E.   61
Alexander, H.A.   98
Apple, M.W.   138, 149
Argyris, C.   117, 188–9
Armstrong, D.M.   22
Arrow, K.   108–9, 196
Athos, A.G.   115
Austin, J.L.   22, 25
Ayer, A.J.   22, 49, 51

Barker, F.   3
Barnard, C.   46, 50
Bates, R.   12, 13, 139, 148, 222
Beauchamp, T.   177
Begum, H.   172
Benn, S.I.   132
Benson, J.K.   137–47, 150, 163
Bentham, J.   174
Berger, P.   117
Berkeley, T.R.   192
Bernstein, R.J.   123, 150-1
Bidwell, C.E.   61, 66
Blair, D.H.   109
Blumberg, A.E.   51, 52
BonJour, L.   ix, 37, 42, 43
Bowles, S.   138, 149
Boyan, N.J.   223
Boyd, W.L.   192
Brandt, R.B.   173
Braybrooke, D.   192, 196–7, 206
Bredo, E.   123, 148
Bridgman, P.W.   49, 57
Burlingame, M.   217, 222
Burrell, G.   61, 217–18
Burris, B.   138

Callahan, D.   199
Campbell, D.T.   223
Carnap, R.   49, 52, 54

Carr, W.   149, 222
Childress, J.F.   177
Churchland, Patricia   ix, 25, 37, 95, 210
Churchland, Paul   ix, 13, 25, 27, 37, 41–2, 90, 95–6, 228–9
Churchman, C.W.   196
Cicourel, A.V.   123
Coladarci, A.P.   50
Collingridge, D.   208
Cook, T.D.   223
Corbally, J.E.   123–4
Cronbach, L.J.   223
Culbertson, J.A.   47, 216

Dallmayr, F.   156, 199, 204
Davidson, D.   179
Davies, J.L.   99
Deal, T.   115
Denhardt, K.G.   139, 163
Denhardt, R.B.   139, 163
Descartes, R.   21, 22
Dewey, J.   ix, 84–6, 185–6
Dews, P.   138, 150–1
Dickson, W.J.   46
Dilthey, W.   118, 120
Duhring, E.   145
Duignan, P.   185
Dunn, W.N.   199

Eisner, E.   228
Engels, F.   142, 145–6
Evers, C.W.   172, 187, 214, 228, 231, 233

Fay, B.   123, 203
Feigl, H.   3, 7, 33, 50, 52–7, 84
Feinberg, W.   123, 148
Feyerabend, P.   1, 3, 13, 41, 42, 79–81, 83, 96, 98, 101, 213, 230
Fischer, F.   199
Follett, M.P.   46

Forester, J.   199
Foster, W.P.   139, 148, 160
Frankena, W.K.   167, 174
Freeman, J.H.   61
Freire, P.   222

Gadamer, H-G.   118–23, 134
Gallie, W.B.   171
Garfinkel, H.   117
Garson, G.D.   1, 192, 194, 198
Geertz, C.   112, 116–17
Getzels, J.W.   50, 66
Giddens, A.   1, 94, 112, 118, 145, 151,
    209, 225
Gintis, H.   138, 149
Giroux, H.   139
Glaucon   99
Godel, K.   208
Goetz, J.   224
Goffman, E.   117, 123
Goldman, P.   137
Goodman, N.   35
Gouldner, A.W.   145, 159
Greenfield, T.   x, 2, 76–96, 98, 124, 129,
    166, 215, 220
Gregory, K.L.   123
Griffiths, D.   1, 10, 50, 51, 55–7, 60–1, 66,
    76, 80–2, 217–18
Gronn, P.C.   78, 83
Gross, B.M.   46
Grossberg, S.   95
Guba, E.G.   66, 218–19, 224, 228
Gulick, L.   46

Habermas, J.   12, 13, 123, 138, 140, 144,
    149–63, 203
Hacking, I.   27
Haig, B.D.   208
Halpin, A.   10, 50, 51, 57, 59, 60
Hamlyn, D.W.   23–4
Hannan, M.   61
Hanson, N.R.   28
Hare, R.M.   172
Harris, K.   29
Harsanyi, J.   177–82, 195–6
Heidegger, M.   151
Hempel, C.G.   7, 32, 57
Heshusius, L.   221, 225–6
Hesse, M.   7, 13, 161, 203–4
Heydebrand, W.   137–8, 142–4, 150, 163
Hills, J.   76, 80–1
Hirst, P.H.   129
Hodgkinson, C.   x, 98–110, 166, 176
Hooker, C.A.   5, 13
Horowitz, I.   198
Hoy, W.K.   46, 60-2, 64–73

Huberman, M.   224
Hudson, W.D.   167
Hume, D.   31, 167
Husen, T.   216, 225
Husserl, E.   83

Jackson, P.   123
James, W.   78
Jaynes, E.T.   209
Jelinek, M.   114
Jennings, B.   193, 199–205, 223
Jermier, J.M.   137

Kahn, R.L.   62–4
Kahneman, D.   179
Kant, I.   77–8, 180
Katz, D.   62–4, 198
Keat, R.   123, 145
Keeves, J.P.   47, 223–4
Kemmis, S.   148–9, 222
Kennedy, A.   115
Kerlinger, F.   65–6, 220
Kuhn, T.   1, 3, 13, 81, 83, 96, 213, 216,
    225, 230
Kurtzman, D.R.   169

Lakatos, I.   208, 232
Lakomski, G.   117
Lasswell, H.   193–6, 208
Laudan, L.   232
Lawrence, P.R.   61
LeCompte, M.   224
Lerner, D.   193
Levi-Strauss, C.   116
Lincoln, Y.S.   218–19, 224, 228
Lindblom, C.E.   192, 196–8, 206–8
Litterer, J.A.   62, 66
Lorsch, J.W.   61
Lowi, T.   198
Luckman, T.   117
Lycan, W.   38

Mabbott, J.D.   175
McCarthy, T.A.   159, 215, 223
McCloskey, H.J.   176
MacPherson, R.J.S.   185
MacRae, D.   199
Marx, K.   153–4
Masterman, M.   225
Mayo, E.   46
Mead, G.H.   117
Metcalf, H.C.   46
Meyer, M.W.   61
Miles, M.   224

Mill, J.S.   98, 101, 174
Mills, C.W.   146–7
Miskel, C.G.   46, 60–2, 64–73, 218
Mitchell, D.E.   192
Mitnick, B.M.   194
Mitroff, I.I.   114
Moore, G.E.   169–72
Morgan, G.   61, 217–18
Morris, C.   49

Nadler, D.A.   66–7, 69
Negt, O.   138
Newton, I.   58
Nielsen, K.   199, 204
Nisbett, R.E.   179

O'Hear, A.   162
Ollman, B.   142
Ouchi, W.G.   115

Pascale, R.T.   115
Peirce, C.S.   156
Perrow, C.   61
Peters, R.S.   132, 209
Peters, Th.J.   115
Petrie, H.G.   128
Pettigrew, A.M.   124
Peukert, H.   151
Pfeffer, J.   61
Phillips, D.C.   x, 1–2, 129–30, 132, 219, 228
Pitner, N.J.   218, 223–4
Plato   98, 100–1, 109
Pollak, R.A.   109
Pondy, L.R.   114
Popkewitz, T.   216–7
Popper, K.   7, 35–7, 52–3, 101, 155–6, 183, 186, 205, 207–9
Price, H.H.   25
Prior, A.N.   168
Putnam, H.   60

Quine, W.V.   ix, 13, 24, 59, 83, 86–7, 130–2, 168, 171, 183–5, 208, 229, 232

Rabinow, P.   113
Rawls, J.   172–5, 180–2
Rein, M.   199
Ricoeur, P.   122
Roche, M.   123
Roethlisberger, F.   46
Ruse, M.   185
Russell, B.   26, 32

Salancik, G.R.   61
Sandlin, T.   218
Schon, D.   117, 188
Scott, W.R.   61, 63
Sergiovanni, T.J.   92, 123–6, 128, 131, 134, 215
Shapiro, J.Z.   149, 192
Shils, E.A.   125
Shulman, L.   218, 222
Silver, P.   218
Simon, H.A.   14–16, 46, 48–51, 55, 57, 100, 102–4, 166, 178, 188, 198, 206–8
Singer, P.   38
Skinner, B.F.   172–3, 176
Smart, J.J.C.   173, 175
Smircich, L.   114–17, 126
Smith, J.K.   221, 225–6
Stich, S.   96, 179, 210
Strike, K.A.   133
Sullivan, W.M.   113
Suppe, F.   32, 34, 226

Tatsuoka, M.   218
Taylor, C.   91–3, 118–19, 121–3, 125–6, 128–9, 131, 134
Taylor, F.   46
Thompson, J.D.   51
Tushman, M.L.   66–7, 69
Tversky, A.   179

Unger, P.   23
Urry, J.   123, 145
Urwick, L.   46

Van Manen, M.   149
Vaughan, D.J.   99

Waldo, D.   198
Walker, J.C.   134, 187, 209, 214, 225, 228, 231–3
Waterman, R.H.   115
Watkins, P.   139
Weber, M.   83, 118, 126–7, 149
Weick, K.E.   61, 117
White, A.R.   129
Whitehead, A.N.   32
Whitty, G.   149
Wildavsky, A.   199

Williams, M.   ix, 25, 172, 229
Willis, P.   123
Willower, D.   x, 2, 47, 61, 76, 80–1, 83–5,
  216
Wilson, E.O.   185

Wittgenstein, L.   121,132
Wolcott, H.   124

Young, M.   149

Subject Index

Act utilitarianism and rule utilitarianism
  commonsense morality 176
  Hodgkinson's moral theory 176
Action, problems of 141
Action research tradition 222
Administration
  as a humanism 100
  as a moral and philosophical activity 100
  as philosophy in action 100
Administration, science of, traditional 11
Administrative Behaviour 14–16, 48, 166
Administrative decision making 14
  and bounded rationality 15
  and feedback loop structures 15
  efficiency 15
  optimal decisions 15
  organizational values and goals 15
  'principles of administration' 15
Administrative problems, everyday
  Greenfield's theory and advice on 92
Administrative Science Quarterly 114
Administrative theory 56
Administrative theory
  and theory/practice problem 10
  and value question 10
  in education 19
Administrative theory and practice
  the reality of organizations 82
Alternative accounts of educational
    administration
  and human emancipation 137
  critical theory 137
  Neo-Marxist views of organizations 137
Alternative subjectivist epistemologies
  soundness of 84
Anti-Dühring 146
Anti-synoptic objections
  fact/value distinction 197
  multiplicity of values 197
  value neutrality of policy analysis 198
Arrow's Impossibility Theorem 109, 197
  and Hodgkinson's theory of organizational
    decision making 109

Autonomy of ethics thesis 104
  is/ought dichotomy 167
    as an instance of the deductive
      fallacy 168
  naturalistic fallacy 167, 169–70
  vocabulary criterion 168

Behavioural science approach 46, 84
Belief-desire folk-theoretic hypothesis for
    human conduct
  and its empirical adequacy 209
  as an optimal predictor 209
  coherent physicalist account of 209–10
Benson and crisis in organizational
    theory 140
  Kuhnian puzzles:problems of action,
    power, levels and process 141–2
Broad foundationalism
  and induction 34
  and phenomenalistic ontology 33
  background theory of evidence 33
  correspondence rules 33–4
  educational administration 33
  epistemically privileged knowledge
    claims 32
  falsificationism 32
  foundational observation reports 34
  induction and limits of confirmation 35
  limits of confirmation 34
  logic of confirmation 32
  Logic of Scientific Discovery 35
  logical empiricism 32
  logical positivism 32
  logical positivists of the Vienna Circle 33
  operational definitions 33–4
  Popper's attack on problem of
    induction 35–6
  Received View 32
  Received view's theories of evidence and
    meaning 34

Central claims of hermeneutics
  Ch. Taylor's view 119
  Gadamer's specific version of 120
  H-G Gadamer and Ch. Taylor 118
  hermeneutic procedure 120
Classical confirmation theory, failure of 83
Classical empiricism 112
  methodological weaknesses 8
  self-reference 8
Closed systems approach 179
  organizations as teleological systems 64
Coherence as a touchstone theoretical
    virtue 42
Coherence epistemology
  and attack on foundationalism 229
  and correspondence truth 230
  and the quantitative/qualitative
    debate 229
  as realist, scientific, objective,
    reductionist 230
  theory of evidence and theory of
    truth 229
Coherence justification, and theories of
    educational administration 9
Coherence theory of evidence, as distinct
    from coherence theory of truth 42
Coherentism
  and adjudication of theories 40
  and empirical adequacy as sole criterion of
    epistemological adequacy 41
  and explanatory simplicity 41
  and extra-empirical virtues 37
  and growth of scientific knowledge
    through falsification 37
  and scientific realist perspective on
    administrative theory 44
  as alternative to foundational
    justification 162
  BonJour's argument of 'observation
    requirement' 43
  comprehensiveness 41
  five rules for guiding comparison of two
    theories 38-9
  new science of administration 40
  superempirical virtues 42
Coherentist account of value 110
Coherentist attack on substance dualism
  appeal to intentions in explanation of
    human behaviour 130-1
  case of teaching as intentional act
    129-30
  Quine and indeterminacy of radical
    translation 131
Coherentist epistemic criteria 77
Coherentist epistemological critique 76
Coherentist epistemology 19
  and problem of error correction 15
  and simplicity 15

Coherentist naturalistic scientific view of
    social science 90-1
Coherentist resolution of synoptic/
    antisynoptic debate 205
  promoting social relations of inquiry 206
Commonsense folk theories
  and question of values 70
  knowledge, belief, desire, meaning, truth
    as terms of 42
  organizational effectiveness 70
Communicative action 149
Communicative competence and Ideal
    Speech situation
  and discourse and its relation to
    interaction 156-8
  and Peirce's model of empirical
    science 156
  conception of Ideal Speech situation 156
  consensus theory of truth 156-8
  'founded' consensus 157
  ideal speech situation 157
Complementary diversity thesis 214
  and alternative networks of theoretical
    requirements for qualitative
    research 223
  and epistemological pluralism 223
  and explanation/understanding
    distinction 224
  epistemological diversity as confused with
    methodological diversity 224
  equally legitimate research traditions 222
  P-theory and its incommensurability
    doctrine 224
  'quasi-experiments' 223
  synoptic and antisynoptic traditions in
    policy analysis 223
  touchstone account of epistemic
    justification 224
Complexity and policy choice
  'disjointed incrementalism' 207
  riskiness of predictions 207
  synoptic ideal of policy and planning 206
Complexity of all test situations 39
  and epistemic holism 40
Conception of culture in organizational
    theory 114
  and organizational analysis 116
  as 'critical variable' 115
  as 'root metaphor' 115-16
  as tool for managerial influence and
    control 116
  cognitive perspective 117
  'culture-as-root' metaphor 117
  'culture-as-variable' 117
  myths, rituals, legends and
    ceremonies 115
  organizations as subjective
    experience 116

Confirmation theory, classical, failure of   83
Consensus theory of truth   161
Contradictions   144
'Corporate Culture'   115
Critical theory   150, 155
  and administration   12
  and epistemological justification   150
  and positivistic science   12
  as developed by Jürgen Habermas   138
  and public administration   139
  as superior to orthodox administration
    theory   148–9
  cognitive or knowledge-constitutive
    interests   153–4
  communicative action   149
  emancipatory interest   153
  Habermas's rejection of
    epistemology   151
  human emancipation   14
  in social and educational studies   148
  instrumentalist connection between
    knowledge and social action   152
  Knowledge and Human Interests   12
  knowledge constitutive interests   12
  positivist self-understanding of
    science   152
  practical interest   153
  purposive-rational action   149
  'technological rationality'   152–3
  theory of cognitive interests   150
  theory of communicative competence   151
Criticisms of the paradigms theory   225–9
  see also Paradigms theory, criticisms of
Criticism of policy analysis as
    counsel   203–5
  see also Policy analysis as counsel,
    criticisms of
Criticisms of 'understanding'
    explanation   128–9
  see also 'Understanding' explanation,
    criticisms of
Critiques of logical empiricism   4
  see also Logical empiricism, critiques of
Cultural knowledge
  and epistemic privilege of 'inner'
    phenomena   113
  and foundational pattern of
    justification   113
Cultural perspective
  and human subjectivity and meaning   113
  and naturalism   114
  and rational choice   113
  and the problem of knowledge   112
  as an alternative to science   112
  as successor to open systems models   114
  coherence of interpretations   114
  foundational theories of justification   112
  in educational administration   123, 126

  as opposed to educational administration
    as applied science   124
  Greenfield's 'anarchistic' model   124
  Sergiovanni's distinction between
    behaviour and action   125
  Sergiovanni's view as recommending a
    multiple-perspective position   124
Cultural perspective tradition   222

Deductive fallacy   168
  vocabulary criterion   168
Descartes' deceitful demon
  and realist causal accounts of belief
    acquisition   43
Dewey's theory of value   186
Dialectical analysis
  and coherence criteria for theory
    choice   147
  and organizational studies
    and praxis   144
    and traditional 'organization-boundary'
      problem   143
    Benson's four principles: social
      construction/production, totality,
      contradiction and praxis   143
    'morphology' and 'substructure'   143
  as being replaced by an empirical theory
    of power   147
  criticisms of   147
Dialectical method   146
Dialectics   144
Dispute between Greenfield and Willower
  role of subjectivity in theory choice   84
Distorted communication   161
Dualism between natural science and social
    science
  and substance dualism   129
  property dualism   129

Educational administration
  and hermeneutical science
    criticisms of   91–2
    problems with interpretations of
      behaviour   93
  and theory of knowledge   1
  alternative accounts of   137
    see also Alternative accounts of
      educational administration
  as technology of control   13
  empirical research in   79
  human subjectivity   1
  organizations   1
  quantitative research in   218
  subjectivist turn   4
  theories of
    and coherence criteria   9

244   SUBJECT INDEX

and coherence justification 9
as learnable 9
Theory Movement 9
values 1
Educational Administration: theory, research and practice 47
Feigl's account of scientific theory 47
logical empiricism 47
omission of ethics 47
operational definition 47
pragmatism 47
Educational Administration Quarterly 218
Educative administration
and organizational learning 188
Effectiveness 71
Eichmann in Jerusalem 176
Emancipatory potential of policy analysis 204
Empirical democratic conceptions of policy studies
'public interest' 196
social welfare function 196
Empirical research in educational administration 79
Empirical testing, holistic nature of 83
Empiricism, classical 8, 112
see also Classical empiricism
Empiricism, traditional 83
Empiricism's theory of language 10
Empiricist accounts of evidence, traditional 72
Environment and culture as explanatory features of organizations
open systems approach 48
philosophical influences of 48
Epistemic holism and values in a science of decision making 206
Epistemological diversity thesis 214
complementary diversity thesis 214
oppositional diversity thesis 214
Epistemological holism
as sanctioning a new science of administration 59
web of beliefs 59
Epistemological reflections on Hoy and Miskel's theory of educational administration 67–71
capacity for feedback 68
coherentist suggestions for theory development and elimination of explanatory dualisms 70
distinction between ontology and epistemology 68
explanatory status of systems theory 68
open systems models 68
problems of discovering goals in terms of intentions 71
systems theory 70

Epistemologies, alternative subjectivist, soundness of 84
Epistemology and paradigms in education and educational administration research 215
Kuhn's concept of 'paradigm' 216
Popkewitz's three paradigms 217
Equifinality 63
Ethical theory and educational administration 166
and holistic epistemology 166
and a substantive ethics 166
Experience and nature
and intersubjective agreement 85
positivistic science 85
Extra-empirical virtues 86
Extra-empirical virtues of system 8

Failure of classical confirmation theory and falsificationism 83
Falsification 81
Falsificationism, failure of 83
Feigl's definition of theory 65
Feigl's view of theory 51–5
his turn to empirical realism 53
logical empiricism 54–5
Feyerband's anarchistic theory of knowledge 80
Five rules for theory comparison 43
Folk intentionalist idiom 92
Folk psychology 94
and ordinary language 95
Folk theories 172
Folk theory of the world 90
Foundational epistemologies
and coherence justification 5
as incoherent 6
scepticism 6
scientific laws 6
universal generalizations 6
Foundational epistemology
method of doubt 20
radical strict foundationalism 21
regress of reasons 20
scepticism 19–20
Foundational justification schemata
critique of empiricism 79
ubiquity of interpretation 79
Foundationalism, broad 32–5
see also Broad foundationalism
Foundationalism, modest strict 25–30
see also Modest strict foundationalism
Foundations
empirical 86
subjective 86

General and open systems, key features of 62–3
Getzels and Guba's social system model 66
Greenfield and Willower, dispute between role of subjectivity in theory choice 84
Greenfield revolution 76–7
  criticism of behavioural science approach to educational administration 76
  importance of human subjectivity 76
  nature of social science, truth and reality 76
  social reality as a human invention 76
Greenfield's anarchistic theory of organization
  as collapsing traditional standards of objectivity 80
  human choice, will, subjectivity 80
Greenfield's epistemological critics
  Willower on Greenfield's critique of administrative science 84
  Willower on phenomenology 83
Greenfield's epistemology
  and Dewey's early criticism of empiricism 85
  and epistemological critics 80–1
  and objectivity 77
  and social theory 80
  and subjectivism 77
  and Willower's Deweyan philosophical stance 85–6
  as alternative to traditional conceptions of scientific knowledge 77
  coherentist criticisms of 87
  complexity of test situations 78, 80
  empirical theory as underdetermined by the data 78
  his views on our knowledge of the natural world 77
  observation is theory laden 78
  standard of truth 79
  subjectivist 'alternative' view 83
  theory ladenness 82
  underdetermination of physical theory by observational evidence 80
  world as mediated by interpretation 77
Greenfield's theory and advice on everyday administrative problems 92
Greenfield's view of interpreted social reality 95
Griffith's administrative theory
  and operational definitions 57
  as based on Feigl's account 56
  as eschewing values 57
  coherentist objections to 57–9
  'decision making', 'organization', 'power' and 'authority' as key terms of 57
  theory of meaning 57

values as propositional claims and as variables 57
Growth of knowledge, through conjecture and refutation 15

Habermas and the construction of empirical reality 161
  and causal sources for learning 162
  meaning and truth of empirical propositions 161
Habermasian interests and their epistemological status 152
  and transcendental justification 155
  as quasi-transcendental 155
Habermas's theory of knowledge 140
Handbook of research on educational administration 2
'Handmaiden' role of policy analysis 198
Harsanyi's decision theory
  attractiveness of to systematic administrative theory 178
Harsanyi's general theory of rationality and Bayesian rationality 179
  and theory of social causation 179
Harsanyi's preference utilitarian model the maximin rule as guiding action 182
Harsanyi's utilitarian theory 196
Heidegger's hermeneutic circle 120
  hermeneutic procedure 121–2
Hermeneutic circle 91–2
Hermeneutical science and educational administration 91–3
Hermeneutics 117
  central claims of
    Ch. Taylor's view 119
    Gadamer's specific version of 120
    H-G Gadamer and Ch. Taylor 118
    hermeneutic procedure 120
Hodgkinson on humanism in administration 98–101
  and the politics of administration 99
  Arrow's theorem 98
  Plato's Republic 99
Hodgkinson's analytical model for classifying values 105
  problems for adjudication of values 106–7
  transrational values 105
  values hierarchy 107
Holistic nature of empirical testing 83
Hoy and Miskel's theory of educational administration
  and congruence 67
  as serving organizational problem analysis 67
  behavioural science approach 66
  definition of theory 65

Human relations approach   46
Hume's attack on induction   36

Ideal Speech situation
  and communicative competence   156–8
  and demand for equality   159
  and regress of doubtful evidence   160
  and social change   160
  as model of rationality   160
  as procedural model of negotiation   158
  communicative and linguistic
      competence   159
  membership in   159
In defence of objectivity
  deriving from Dewey and Quine   86
Incommensurability and the conceptual role
      theory of meaning
  and its theory of the powers of the
      mind   230
Induction
  Hume's attack on   36
  problem of
    nature is uniform   31
    Popper's attack on   36–7
    principle of induction   31
Interpretation   78
The Interpretation of cultures   112
Interpreted experience   86
Interpretive administration and decision
      making   126
Interpretive leader   125–6
  and conflicting values   125
Interpretive policy analysis as
      rhetorical   203
Interpretive social science
  and causal assumptions in folk
      explanations   91
'Interpretive turn' in the social sciences   117
  and its 'anti-positivist' stance   118
  central claims of   118
  concept of understanding or
      verstehen   118
  Weber's notion of social science   118
Interpretivist views of 'inner' episodes
  and coherentist view of evidence for
      interpretations   133
  and scientific physicalist theories of
      human behaviour   133
  coherence of an interpretation   133
Is/ought dichotomy   168
  vocabulary criterion   168

Jennings's policy analysis as
      counsel   199–200
  and criticisms of positivistic policy
      analysis   200

and cultural perspective model in
    educational administration   200
and hermeneutic tradition's theory of
    meaning   200
and intention   202
and notion of coherence   202
and practical reason   202
and scientific objectivity   201
as depending on insight and
    creativity   202
its justification   201
Journal of Educational Administration   218
Justified True Belief
  circularity problem   5
  derived and immediate knowledge   5
  regress problem   5

Key features of General and open
    systems   62–3
Knowledge and Human Interests   12–13,
    150–1
  and foundational justification   162
Knowledge constitutive interests
  and threatening major incoherence   13
Kuhn-Feyerabend critique of logical
    empiricism   3
Kuhn's argument for paradigms as
    incommensurable
  and antirealist belief in paradigms   226
  and postpositivist philosophy of
    science   226
  and Unity thesis   226
  paradigm-specific epistemologies   225

Language as embodying commonsense or
    'folk theories'   24
Lasswell's synoptic approach to policy
    science and empiricism   194
  and fact/value distinction   195
  and moral beliefs   195
  and value clarification   196
Law of contradiction, criticisms of   145–6
Law of limited variety   63
Leadership
  and democracy   101
  as based on a meritocracy of the will   100
  Plato's elitist politics of   100
Levels, problem of   141
Logic of Scientific Discovery   52
Logical empiricism
  falsification   7
  Griffith's administrative theory   55
  hypothetico-deductive method   7

Logical empiricism, critiques of
    Kuhn-Feyerabend 3
    theory ladenness of observation 4
    underdetermination of theory 4
Logik der Forschung 52

Marxist education theory 149
Method of understanding 83
Modern materialism and intentions 131
    intentions as promissory notes for electro-
        chemical mechanisms 132
Modest strict foundationalism 25
    and distinction between foundational and
        derived knowledge 28
    and foundational observation reports 30
    and intrusion of theory 28
    and observable/unobservable
        distinction 30
    and theory-free experiences 30
    and theory laden observation
        statements 28
    as epistemological strategy for
        justification 28
    foundational evidence 26
    instrumentalism 26, 30
    knowledge of observables 26–7
    problem of induction 30
    problems with perception 27
    theoreticity in ordinary perception 29
Moral knowledge and non-foundational
        epistemology
    and the web of belief 183
    innate dispositions 183
    standards of similarity 184
The Morality of Leadership in Education 106

Naturalistic fallacy
    as unwarranted dogma of classical
        empiricism 171
Naturalistic science of administration 94
Nature, content, and structure of
        administrative theories
    as shaped by foundational varieties of
        empiricism 84
Nature of knowledge
    Kuhn-Feyerabend critique of logical
        empiricism 3
    logical empiricism 3
    Vienna circle 3
Negative entropy 63
Neo-Marxist and critical theory accounts of
        administration
    communicative competence 140
    contradiction 140
    dialectic 140

ideal speech situation 140
    ideology 140
    interests 140
Neo-Marxist explanation of organizations
    as superior to orthodox organizational
        theory
    as grounded in dialectical analysis of social
        phenomena 145
Neo-Marxist views of organizations
    and traditional theory 138
    dialectical analysis 138
Neuroscience
    human learning and memory 95
    introspection 95
    naturalistic account of human
        subjectivity 95
    plasticity of mind 95
New orthodoxy
    as comprising open systems and
        contingency theory 60
1964 NSSE Yearbook 10
Normative framework for administrative
        practice
    and conjecture and refutation 185
    and connection between values and
        feedback models of knowledge
        growth 187
    and revisions to folk moral
        judgments 186
    as a form of rule consequentialism 186
    decision and action as educative 185
    ethical claims and empirical claims 186
    touchstone conditions for adjudicating
        moral theories 185–6

Objectivity
    as determined by coherence
        considerations 87
    causal source of experience 87
Objectivity, in defence of deriving from
        Dewey and Quine 86
Observational evidence 78
Old orthodoxy
    as comprising the closed systems view 60
    as assuming structural-functionalist
        framework 60
On Liberty 98
The Open Society and its Enemies 101
Open systems approach 179
Operational definition 72
Oppositional diversity thesis 214, 220–1
    and Greenfield's 'anarchistic' theory 220
Ordinary language philosophy
    and modest foundations 23
    as challenging the demand for radical
        foundations 23
    as countering the Cartesian sceptic 22

classic attack on epistemic privilege in
    ordinary language   24
  its central difficulty   24
Organizational double loop learning
    structures   189
Organizational effectiveness   72
Organizational reality
  and differences in interpretations   89
  and interpretations of interpretations (the
    double hermeneutic)   89
  and knowledge   88
  and ontological reality   88
  and science   90
  and subjectivity   90
  and theory   90
  as defined by nonbrute data, meanings,
    human intentions, actions, and
    experiences   88
  as invented social reality   88
  as meaningful and rule-governed
    action   89
  as socially constructed reality   88
Organizational theory, recent shifts in   61
  see also Recent shifts in organizational
    theory
Orthodoxy, New   60
Orthodoxy, Old   60

P-theory   215
  and self-reference   230
Paradigms and promises   160
Paradigms approach
  and empirical evidence   3
  as attack on objectivity in social
    sciences   3
  incommensurable   3
  relativism   3
  subjectivism   3
Paradigms perspective   213
  and epistemological unity of educational
    research (unity thesis)   214
Paradigms theory, criticisms of
  confusion over the term 'paradigm'   225
  correspondence truth   227–8
  experience is theory laden   228–9
  foundational empiricist
    epistemologies   228
  neurophysiological models of brain
    functioning   228
  objectivity   229
  ontological commitments of P-theory   227
  realist view of the unity of educational
    research   227
  theory of the powers of the mind   228
Peters, R.S. and the dualist explanation of
    human action   132–3

Philosophy and administration   101
  and distinction between administration
    and management   102
  and subjective, affective, noncognitive
    preferences   103
  and value analysis   103
  ethical reasoning and behaviour   103
Philosophy and educational
    administration   80
The Philosophy of Leadership   106–7
Philosophy of mind   90
Phronesis   203
Policy analysis
  and the synoptic tradition   192
  emancipatory potential of   204
  'handmaiden' role of   198
  interpretive, as rhetorical   203
  recent developments in   198–9
    see also Recent developments in policy
      analysis
  values and complexity   192
Policy analysis as counsel, criticisms of
  and knowledge of intersubjective
    meanings   204
  decision making   204
  dichotomous treatment of knowledge and
    values   205
  folk-theoretic account of human
    behaviour   204
  its instrumentalist conception of natural
    science   203
  systematic indeterminacy of
    interpretation   204
Policy science, policy analysis, and
    values   193–7
Policy studies, empirical democratic
    conceptions of   196
  see also Empirical democratic conceptions
    of policy studies
Popper's antisynoptic arguments against
    utopian social planning   207
  knowledge of social causation   207
  to underwrite piecemeal change   208
Popper's attack on the problem of
    induction   36–7
  hypothetico-deductive method   53
Popper's social and political theory   186
  and policy analysis   187
Positivism
  identification of science with   219
  use of the term in educational
    (administration) literature   218–19
POSDCORB   46
The Poverty of Historicism   207
Power, problem of   141
'Praxis' tradition in epistemology   222
Preference utilitarianism   177, 179, 195
  and Harsanyi's decision theory   177–8

Preponderance of quantitative research in educational administration   218
Problem of induction
  nature is uniform   31
  principle of induction   31
Process, problem of   141
Property dualism   129
Public Administration Review   198
Purposive-rational action   149

Quantitative research in educational administration, preponderance of   218
Quine's naturalistic and holistic account of learning
  and the revision of values   185
  coherence considerations   184

R.S. Peters and the dualist explanation of human action objection to substance dualism   132–3
Radical and modest foundations fail to blunt the sceptical challenge   24–5
Radical strict foundationalism   23
  Cartesian method of doubt   22
Rawl's theory of justice   173
  and the maximin rule   180–1
  as applied to administrative contexts in education   181
  as deontological   180
  categorical imperative   180
Reality
  mind-dependent   4
  multiple realities   4
Recent developments in policy analysis   198
  advocacy model of   199
  and interpretive social science   199
  and theory building   199
Recent shifts in organisational theory
  contingency theory   61
  from studying structure to studying process   64
  modern human ecology   61
  natural selection model   61
  organizations as open systems   61
  racial minorities in administration   61
  resource-dependence model   61
  role of women in   61
  unions   61
Reducing the mental to the physical   133
Reduction, coherence and varieties of utilitarianism   172–7
  behaviouristic causal analyses of moral judgments   173
  folk moral theory   173

Republic   98
Research in educational administration
  against paradigms   213
  and coherentist theory of justification   213
  quantitative, preponderance of   218

Schools as open social systems   65
Science of administration, traditional and operational definitions   11
Science, meaning, and values   203–6
Science, traditional views of
  logical empiricism   14
  positivism   14
Scientific explanation   144
Second law of thermodynamics   63
Simon's distinction between facts and values   48–50
  administration as decision making under conditions of bounded rationality   49
  distinction between policy and administration   49
  ethics and subjective human values   49
Simon's model of scientific administrative theory   55
Simon's philosophy   103
Social science, interpretive   91
Sociological paradigms and organizational analysis   217
  Burrell and Morgan's four paradigms   217
Speaking truth to power: the art and craft of policy analysis   199
Subjectivist epistemologies, alternative soundness of   84
Subjectivist explanation and causal mechanisms in human behaviour   93–4
Subjectivist methodology
  and explanation   90
  understanding and sense-making   90
Substance dualism   129
  coherentist attack on   129–31
Superempirical virtues   231
Symbolic view of culture   116–17
Synoptic/anti-synoptic debate
  and the theory of knowledge   193
  coherentist resolution of   205–6
The Systems approach and its enemies   196
Systems theory
  ontology of unobservables   81

Theories of educational administration   *see* Educational administration, theories of
Theory comparison, five rules for   43
The Theory of Communicative Action   150

Theory Movement 2, 50, 53, 62, 65
 and logical empiricist account of scientific
  theory 9
 and theories of educational
  administration 9
 dominant orthodoxy of behavioural science
  approach 47
 educational organizations as complex
  systems 47
 in educational administration 46
 new orthodoxy 59
  in educational administration 47
 organizations as closed systems 48
 philosophical influences of 51
 scientific management 46
Theory/observation distinction 71
Theory of mind
 empirical psychology of learning 6
Theory ladenness of interpretation
 management by objectives, cost benefit
  analysis, and behavioural objectives 71
Thesis of epistemological diversity 214
Touchstone theory 172
 and the growth of reasoning 183
Towards a philosophy of administration 106
Traditional empiricism 83
Traditional empiricist accounts of
 evidence 72
Traditional science of administration
 and operational definitions 11
Traditional views of science
 logical empiricism 14
 positivism 14
Truth making
 as a matter of will, desire and
  intention 101
Truth-as-consensus 160

Understanding a text correctly
 Gadamer and 'perfect coherence' 122–3
 Taylor and 'insight' 123
'Understanding' explanation, criticisms
  of 128
 and foundational conception of evidence in
  natural science 129
Unity thesis 214
 and holistic scientific naturalism 232
 and theories as problem-solving
  devices 232
 as unproblematically self-referential 232
 culturally produced touchstone 232

 epistemological unity of educational
  research 233
 Quine's 'epistemology naturalized' sense of
  naturalism 232
 self-reference 233
 superempirical virtues as touchstone 231
 touchstone 233
 unified account of validity and
  reliability 233
Utilitarianism, different strands of 177
 act utilitarianism and rule
  utilitarianism 175
 Bentham-Mill tradition 174
 naturalistic fallacy 174
 teleological or consequentialist
  theories 174
 utilitarian reduction of folk morality 175

Value, coherentist account of 110
Value choice and rationality in
  administration
 and Arrow's Impossibility Theorem 108
 rational theory choice 108
 subjective knowledge 108
 utilitarian ethics 108
Values and administration 103–6
 naturalistic fallacy 104
 Simon's view of facts and values 104
 values as distinct from facts 104
Vienna Circle 3
Virtues of system
 coherence 4
 coherence considerations 4
 comprehensiveness 4
 conservativeness 4
 consistency 4
 extra-empirical 4
 fecundity 4
 simplicity 4

Weber's means-end scheme 149
Weber's notion of verstehen 126–7
 and decision criteria based on 'inner'
  phenomena 128
Willower and Greenfield, dispute between
  role of subjectivity, in theory
  choice 84
Word and Object 83